WITHDRAWN

From *A Visit to William Blake's Inn* by Nancy Willard, illustration © 1981 by Alice Provenson and Martin Provenson. Reproduced by permission of Harcourt Brace Jovanovich, Inc.

Introducing
Children
to the Arts

A Practical Guide for Librarians and Educators

Introducing
Children
to the Arts

A Practical Guide for Librarians and Educators

Lea Burroughs

G. K. Hall & Co. • Boston

Library of Congress Cataloging-in-Publication Data

Burroughs, Lea.
     Introducing children to the arts: a practical guide
for librarians and educators / Lea Burroughs.
       p. cm.
     Bibliography: p.
     ISBN 0-8161-8818-1
     1. Arts--Study and teaching (Elementary)--United States--
Bibliography. I. Title.
Z5940.5.U6B87 1988
[NX503]
016.7--dc19   88-14770
                      CIP

This publication is printed on permanent/durable acid-free paper
MANUFACTURED IN THE UNITED STATES OF AMERICA

*This book is dedicated
with respect and affection
to my mentor and friend,
Betty Bacon*

Contents

Contents

Foreword

When we involve children in a program of crafts or storytelling in the classroom or the library, we tend to concern ourselves with the nuts and bolts of our work. Get out the publicity, set up the room, prepare the materials, and hope for the best. And if we do a proper job, the best result will be an enthusiastic response from the children. Fortunately for us, there are a number of excellent books that guide us in the practical planning and carrying out of successful programs.

This book is something more. To be sure, it does help us with suggested workshops, bibliographies, and the like, but it also makes us look at what we are doing in a larger context. For the children's program in the school or library is not an isolated event, but part of a continuing process. This process has a history and a meaning that embrace our program, however small it may be.

For the most part, we do not think about this background (which is rather like the glimpse of Mozart playing the piano in one of Sendak's illustrations for *Outside over There*), but it's there all the same. In storytelling we are most aware of it; and although we may not consciously see ourselves as inheritors of the old grandmother by the fire or the minstrel before the high table, the tradition hovers at the back of our minds and influences what stories we tell and how we tell them. But we probably do not think about the commedia del l'arte when we put on a puppet show or the development of the stringed instrument when we work on a music program.

Yet, as we know from our experience with storytelling, this understanding of history and theory, emotional meaning and technical development, really does influence the quality of our programs. And that is the contribution of Lea Burroughs's book. For each type of program, she discusses the scope of the art in question--its history, its development, its essential nature, its social and personal impact. We may very well ask what this has to do with a Saturday morning program for a dozen or so children in the United States. Yet this kind of background knowledge and feeling influences our choice of recordings for a music program, our way of involving the young audience in theatricals, the tone of our voice as we read a poem.

Theory and practice are a unified whole, and *why* is as important as *how* in reaching children with the meaning and pleasure of artistic creation. Hence this book that brings the two together.

--Betty Bacon
Former lecturer, School of Library and
Information Studies, University of
California, Berkeley; former coordinator of
children's services, Solano County Library,
California

Acknowledgments

In the several years it took to research and write this book, many people and the collective contribution of many institutions contributed to its final form. I would like to thank them all and, in particular, those who follow.

To Betty Bacon, who helped me with unfailing generosity in the chapters' shaping, and Meghan Robinson Wander, my wise and insightful editor, all my thanks. I'm grateful as well to the staff at G.K. Hall, and especially Cecile Watters, whose immaculate copy editing taught me something, and Michael Sims, development editor extraordinaire, thanks.

To Katie Dodd, whose gay, subtle illustrations give each art a special flavor and integrate so richly, I am most grateful.

To Audrey Wood, Linda Geistlinger, and all the children's librarians at San Francisco Public Library; to Martha Shogren and the Berkeley Public Library and to the librarians and staff of the San Francisco State Library; to Virginia Pratt of the Library School Library at the University of California at Berkeley; to Linda Artel of the University Museum Film Library, and Leigh Hartz, film director of the Richmond Public Library, thanks.

Special people played a significant role in the gestation of each chapter as it came along. In the art chapter, the artist Leigh Hyams read and commented, as did my artist friend John Jehu; Debra Disman's book illustration class for children at the De Young Museum was a model for a successful series of classes in the Bay Area libraries; Judy Shannon's work with children in the Arts Factory in San Francisco and Joan Bryan's program at the Children's Center for the Creative Arts were bold and imaginative and their ideas and style were an inspiration to me.

In the formation of the architecture chapter I must thank my father for the consistent beauty of his work and the depth of his teaching; the architects George Howe and Iver Lofving, whose understanding I have absorbed; the librarians of the Environmental Design Department at the University of California at Berkeley; and the contractors Dick Brown and Arthur Earle, whose comments on the construction and workshop aspects were invaluable.

In the dance chapter I should really thank the dancers of the New York City Ballet, who engendered my first great love for dance, as well as my teachers at the Graham School in New York, and, more particularly, the dancers Barbara Kohn and Cheryl Yonker, for their help in the movement workshop. Also, thanks to Blanche Maulet for research assistance at the San Francisco Public Library Art and Music Department.

My years of studying and writing music formed the basis of that chapter, but I must especially acknowledge Constant Vauclaine, my first composition teacher, and Martha Massena, my teacher of piano, then at the Curtis Institute of Music; Peter Danner, fine musician, who read and made suggestions for my manuscript; and Tom Walther, to whom I owe the instrument-making workshop.

For the poetry chapter I particularly want to thank Robert Hass, the poet, whose teaching and criticism have both been inspiring to me; the Poetry Center staff at San Francisco State University, who were very helpful; and, above all, the children I have read to and worked with over the years.

Dotty Myers kindly contributed ideas for the workshops in theater, and Gina Hyams's suggestions and book ideas were very helpful in the theater chapter.

The story chapter owes a debt a number of people; a special thanks to Margaret Wyatt for her insightful criticism, to Kate Farrell for her encouragement and example, and, above all, to my students at the University of California at Berkeley, whose interest and creative response gave storytelling a new strength and meaning for me.

For help in typing, layout, and copyreading of the manuscript I want to thank both Beth Miller and Suzanne Wheat.

I need to give thanks also to Ruth Amernick, special children's librarian at the San Francisco Public Library, for her generous contribution of ideas for special children, and to Sonya Kaufman at the School of Education and

Acknowledgments

Psychology Library at the University of California at Berkeley, for her expert teaching and monitoring of my computer research.

Last, I must thank Mae Durham Rodger, whose rich example and fine teaching provided the basis for my years as a children's librarian.

San Francisco

Introduction

Over the past twenty-five years a quiet revolution has been underway in the children's room of America. From a nearly silent passive environment where children came to hunt for information and enjoy stories, it has evolved little by little into a setting for much more active experiences.

Films, records, tapes, television, and videos have made their way through the door, lending color and richness to the collections; above all, the "live" program, or introduction to ideas and concepts as diverse as robots and circuses, has become a common practice.

It is this last that interests me in particular. Especially in the arts, a *live* sense of a poem, a painting, or a building, cannot come from words on the printed page alone, or even from a film or a record; but with the direct involvement of teacher, performer, or guide, the arts can gaily spring to life in the imagination of a child. The arts are a gold mine for children; we need to mine our collections for that gold and share it with them, whether performing mime, reading poems out loud, telling stories, leading a neighborhood walk to look at buildings, or even helping children build instruments.

Live workshops in the arts are a vital tool for children, especially in the children's library, where sections of books on the fine arts often seem pallid, limited in scope, underused, or out-of-date. Architecture, for instance, is rarely presented to children, and the few books on it are usually restricted to a few sedate black-and-white histories holding down the shelves. Lately, David Macaulay's wonderful descriptions of cathedrals, pyramids, and cities, and Harvey Weiss's sophisticated craft and model books have enlivened the scene. But there is still very little for young readers (and that hardly exciting) about landscape architecture, about interaction of landscape and house, or about the fascinating world of city planning.

In the visual arts, painting and sculpture, there have always been lots of books, especially craft and how-to books. But the beautiful volumes on history and painting, and the great artists along with them; the new compelling photography books; the unusual works like the old *Going for a Walk with a Line* and the Metropolitan Museum's *The Christmas Story* must be introduced to children if they are to use them. Pietro Ventura's beautiful book *Great Painters,* and M. B. Goffstein's tiny, sensitive introduction could shine at an art appreciation workshop. And films that suggest a strong connection between child and painting like *Liang and the Magic Paintbrush* could give a strong backup to fine art books in abundant display.

The dance section, after years of neglect, is filling up; ballet in America, as well as ethnic dance and many forms of modern, have become popular art forms. Now the two or three little out-of-date works on ballet that were once the only choice are being replaced by new, lively ones and they are circulating! Books and films on popular dance trends and folk traditions are plentiful, too, and there is great dance music available on records and tapes. But the biographies of famous dancers like Martha Graham and Katherine Dunham, and works on alternate forms of serious contemporary dance like jazz and modern--these need exposure and introduction. A sure way to get them moving into circulation is by bringing in a live dancer or dance group to interest and inspire the children.

Music, the nonverbal art, has in the past largely been the subject of books on the classical orchestra and on how to play instruments (except drums, sax, guitar, and electronic instruments--what children want). Biographies of classical composers, although rather colorless and censored, exist, as do a few good folk song collections. Quite lately a few needed works on theory and jazz have crept in that are useful. But music itself is the important thing, and now that most libraries have record and tape collections and many have special listening rooms, music can and should come off the shelves and be heard. This puts the emphasis where it should be, on experiencing music. Instrument-making classes could be held, which would give children a chance to get right into music making, fashioning instruments they can use for performance and composition. Books and records to be checked out could be displayed. This is also a good chance for children to get to know the adult section, picking out records and tapes to serve as examples.

Poetry, like dance, is thriving: Kenneth Koch, in his ground-breaking book *Wishes, Lies and Dreams,* started a renaissance in the teaching of poetry to children some years ago, and teachers come in frequently now looking for material on how to do it. Children ask for poetry, too, especially funny poetry, or they go looking for poems to read on their own; here the current emphasis on sharing and understanding poetry is encouraging them to speak up. In short, poetry has regained respectability in the work of the child, and that is exciting. Teachers are using contemporary poetry far more than in the past, and much can be done in the children's room to take advantage of this. An increasing number of valuable and original anthologies has appeared, which can help children start writing as well as reading the great poets of many countries.

Then there is the traditional library art, storytelling, which has recently undergone a revival, as did poetry ten or twenty years ago. Storytellers are in the schools, on radio, television, and tape, and there are storytelling workshops and classes everywhere; children are seemingly bombarded with stories of all kinds. But the children's librarian with good training in storytelling and access to strong folk and fairy-tale collections is in an excellent position to introduce enduring world literature to children living in an increasingly trendy age. Children need to hear stories told "just plain," as well as dressed up and fancy. In addition, they need exposure to stories from all cultures and a chance to read and speak as well as hear them. This presents a unique opportunity for library programming: professionals, children's librarians, or guests can teach children how to tell stories themselves and can support use of the literature resources as well. Storytelling is a natural in the children's room.

Then the theater. Recently it has received more attention in the children's room because of the popularity of puppetry. Clear, well-written books on how to make puppets, build stages for them, and produce shows are now an attractive feature of most children's libraries. The output of plays, however, is slim. Vital, well-written puppet plays and well-made, sensitive folktale adaptations that are exciting and treat children with dignity, like Ted Hughes's *Tiger Bones and Other Plays for Children,* are still in short supply. The need certainly exists for books and films on improvisation, too, an art especially suited to children and to their development. In the meantime creative programming can enliven and illustrate what books we do have, in puppetry, live theater, mime, and improvisation.

In my book I have devoted the chapters to introducing each of seven arts, either by history or by internal structure, whichever seemed appropriate. I have then explored how children experience that art and what it means for them. At the close of each chapter, I included a few sample workshops to be used as live introduction to the various arts, and at the end of each section I offer a guide to films, records, tapes, videos, and books to help with selection of materials.

The center of the design, the workshop, is a form ideally suited to the secure, comfortable, open quality of the children's room. Educators and librarians are in the fortunate position of being able to become entrepreneurs in their production, introducing the arts in the intimate, lively, engaging way children respond to.

I have designed the workshops most often as a sequence, but they are meant to be employed in an accordionlike fashion, using just one section for a single day's introduction, for instance, or stretching out another that seems to be going well and attracting an eager audience to several more sessions. In every case follow-ups and related programs could enrich school, library, or community after the main workshop is over. They are directed at a broad spectrum of ages, which reflects my experience as a public library children's librarian, but they can be used successfully with two-year groupings or single classes. The age span is less important than a sense of familiarity with children and their interests.

The workshops are somewhat more centered on subject than child because, once again, that reflects my experience as a librarian, but they can be used in a more child-centered way by educators or adapted to the more populated and changing world of the day-care center. Here, cutting and revising to suit large groups, adding films or videos, and inviting outside artists should be helpful in gearing the workshop to the center's needs. Artists in the field chosen are frequently available, so I have often suggested asking their cooperation as an alternative. Especially in urban and suburban situations, universities, art schools, theaters, conservatories, churches, and free-lance organizations such as storyteller pools and puppeteers exist that can be called on to contribute help. Frequently, for a small sum or none at all, these groups are delighted to give their time and skill.

Children's response to all this is warm and enthusiastic. They bring to the experience all their own secret, special knowledge and wakening curiosity. Although we never know whom we may have touched deeply with a quickening of interest or a sudden understanding of an art, the possibility is there, so the work is rewarding. Children's enthusiasm for the library or the classroom often depends on their active participation, and the workshops can provide an engaging design.

The sets of bibliographies, filmographies, video suggestions, and discographies can back up these workshop activities where appropriate. These lists were designed for children's use, the basis of my criteria for their choice. In nonfiction I looked for clarity, simplicity, authenticity, and depth of research, a thorough knowledge of the discipline, an interest and excitement in it, a crystal-clear structural organization, and sympathy, even empathy, for children's needs and their point of view. Less obvious but interesting to me was an original perspective that would engage the child.

A large portion of the books, films, records, and tapes is to be found currently in most public and school libraries. Many are in print, but some are not. Out-of-print materials that are of classic stature are apt to be reprinted from time to time, and some, of course, are simply to be mourned. If a certain volume or nonprint material seems vital, interlibrary loan can be helpful.

New and wonderful books for children are published every year, and sizable bibliographies could be created from new releases alone. But I have chosen many older books, books that live, in my opinion. One notable plus of a bibliography well peppered with lasting favorites is that small-budget libraries unable to purchase liberally from the publishers' current lists may find their own fairly small collections already contain many treasures. Rediscovery of these books, a reconception of their pedagogical value in introducing children to the arts, may stimulate the librarian's own creativity with these materials already at hand.

Most important is what is done with the lists of reflective research tools available. Here I hope that the workshops will suggest to the children's specialist some concrete ways of adapting books, records, and films for creative use. In the library children doing research projects in many areas--special countries, anthropology, children's literature, costume design, history, and so on--can enrich their study with books and media on the arts, as can the beginning adult, and, of course, the child who is just plain interested. The books, films, records, and pictures I recall here gave me intense pleasure, and I hope their use will excite others through the imagination and expression of the world's artists.

The deeper purpose of this book is to show how the children's library can act as a catalyst for children's discovery of the fine arts.

Good luck!

Architecture

I look through the top loop of the gate to a little bronze frog glinting in the sun, reflecting himself in the tiny dark pool by the fence of green vines.

This is the garden.

I open the gate, walk down the path of flat story stones to an old thick tree with wooden slats nailed up the trunk, and start my climb. Soon I'm balanced on the aerie floor where no one can see me; I am alone, but I am safe; the walls are wooden, the pine needles smell of sun and incense, I can hear my neighbors' hummingbirds visiting their fuchsias.

I look through the secret opening in the wall between the branches and I can see the river, the big boats making their way, huge cranes balanced on the estuary side. I walk home this way, seeing the piers and the warehouses, hearing the boat horns, turning up our street by the big market and the bowling alley.

This is the town.

Thus does the child see his environment; it surrounds and envelops him, as the water and plants envelop their fish. To introduce architecture to children is to show them what they already know: their outdoor room, their house, their town--not just buildings, but spaces and how people fit in them.

A house is a shelter, starting with the intimate ecstasy of the space directly underneath the enormous mahogany dining room table in a grandmother's house. In a home space of safety, the carved wooden feet of the table marking the boundary, is where the house starts. Later, as the child grows older, the shelter changes shape in proportion to chronology, and the design becomes more sophisticated. A dining room table for a three-year-old, a dollhouse at five, the sprawl of upside-down furniture in the living room and summer forts; at nine the high greenness of the treehouse; and the intricate disaster of the fifteen-year-old's sanctuary where, defending against the neatness so destructive to the creative dreamer, everyone, for a few years, sings the Beach Boys' song "In My Room."

In each of these shelters the basic elements of design are consistent: a door to get in and out of, a window to frame the world outside; a place to sleep and dream; a wall, an arch and here is the interior problem.

Around these, the child's most intimate home spaces, lie a spectrum of shelters. First, in one's own house, each room has its own function that frames the question of design: the kitchen must serve for preparing food, it must be warm and well lit, able to house grains, hang garlic strings, and store root vegetables; it must be inviting and practical, as befits the heart of the house. The basement may serve as work or storage space, roller-skating rink or study, but it must in every case be waterproof, well lit, and clearly thought out. The family room or living room is everyone's space and everyone's problem (that is part of the design problem of living rooms), and it must serve for a variety of activities: conversation, repose, reading, listening to music, watching television.

Then, out of doors, there are other shelters: a garage to serve as car shelter or to house a woodworking or hobby center, a potting shed or greenhouse, a doghouse or rabbit hutch. A plant shelter needs space for potting, compost, storage, and tools; animal shelters must provide warmth, comfort, and protection from the elements. Even the little fish tank has its intimate environmental problems that require speculation and solution.

Function raises the questions; for instance, a library must house books safely and in imaginative ways; a school must be sturdy, ready to be of service to children with bright, quiet, ample spaces; a garage must be utilitarian, capacious, and resistant to all weathers. Out of the process of answering these questions of function the practical design vocabulary of the architect will emerge. Each room's design problems become working questions: what do we need for the activity expressed by the space we're working with, how will it take shape according to these needs, and how will we fashion that shape?

For the child, many examples of these shelters are available for design study, for questioning: if not at home, there are neighbors to visit nearby, the people upstairs, the example of grandparents with a different life-style, a varied set of needs. Each one will reveal the considerations an architect deals with in designing and building structures: function, materials, construction, interior design, and, very important, landscape.

Once function has been determined, the question of materials assumes importance and the elements that shape the kind of materials used: climate, cost, and topography, the character of the region. The strength and endurance of materials is critically important, too, not only to keep the wolf out as in "The Three Little Pigs" (an excellent introduction to structural functioning for children), but in real life as well. In rainy climates, insulation and weatherproofed materials must be used; very cold climates require materials strong enough to keep out snow and harsh winds, to keep people warm for months at a time, yet flexibly arranged so that during hot summers increased air and light can be introduced for coolness. Children need to look at their own dwellings and those of their neighbors, and notice what's been used to build them, and to think about why.

The topography of an area brings its own set of requirements: for instance, in an earthquake region, it is unsafe to use rigid, nonflexible materials, as they tend to crack and splinter under earthquake pressure. In hurricane country, the foundations and building materials must withstand strong winds. They must be solid, yet not rigid. Conditions of the soil and whether the terrain is flat or hilly are other factors. Each has unique demands that can be satisfied only by certain materials.

Then these requirements must be balanced by a series of other considerations: budget, ease of acquisition and transport, aesthetics, and function of structure. For reasons both of budget and ease of transport, local materials are favored by architects and construction people; they are cheap, easy to find, and frequently beautiful and appropriate to the countryside. But not all will fit the requirements of topography and climate, so a process of elimination is set in motion.

Of course, every part of a house is not built of the same material: we need to look at the particular function to consider the best kind of material to use, and we have to think how it will work aesthetically. A resonance of textures must be sought, and their solution will give a subtle firmness to the design.

Children can observe architectural distinctions, they can think out the problems, and they can be very imaginative in their solutions; no one has told them that things have to be a certain way, so their imaginations have an edge of freshness. And for the craft of architecture, the construction, they have an instinctive feeling. At the age of one, they are building with blocks and playing with clay; they like to make things; they construct castles from sand at the beach and medieval towers from Legos at preschool. At home they mastermind houses from furniture and outside jury-rig tree houses in the yard and at the park. It seems to come more naturally to build shelters than to think about them, and among girls and boys, for a span of a decade or so, it is a source of creative delight. So in introducing the basic elements of construction, the wall, the arch, the cantilever, and the space flowing around them, we are introducing to them once again something they already know, putting a name to an activity.

But how do you construct an aerie? How do you really build a house? Beneath the poetry lies a concrete, matter-of-fact set of building principles, processes, and materials. Or as Mies van der Rohe said, "The art of architecture begins where two bricks are carefully laid together."

At the library, children can look at a wall, right there, and get an idea of how "two bricks are carefully laid together" to form it; walking over to the doorway, they can observe the construction of an arch. Outside the door, they can pinpoint numerous examples of materials and construction methods: the retaining walls nearby, the arch over the gate to the stone church across the street, the wood frame house next to it, and the concrete garage at the corner.

Each is a different example of building construction and each can be explored and explained. Children can experience the alchemical, powerful feeling of grasping the facts, of walking the architectural bridge to reality that construction represents. Once acquainted with methods, they can appreciate the craftsmen and women who meticulously render a design into action: the carpenters, builders, plumbers, and electricians, and the contractor who will interpret the design and supervise the work.

So as a study example, let's take a wood frame house as a basic construction unit, and see how it's done, step by step. As the children soon will see, if this is the house that Jack built, he has built it to resemble himself: skeleton, interior functions, face facade, and decoration.

First, comes the foundation: a hole, dug to a depth well below ground level, as large as the blueprints specify, and then filled with poured concrete in an inverted T-shape. The wall is eight inches thick.

Upon this will be erected the frame of the house, like a skeleton, later to be covered and painted. First, a wooden plate, the mudsill, is fastened down over the foundation by bolts, and upon these are nailed the basic elements of floor construction, the joists. These are short wooden units and they are placed horizontally on edge; upon them a diagonal sheathing of boards is laid.

The walls are made of vertically placed wooden units called studs, placed a short distance apart. Upon them will rest the weight of successive stories as they are erected. This is done by repeating the simple pattern of laying joists, superimposing a diagonal sheathing of boards, and then adding more studs.

When the roof is reached, whether pitched or flat, roof joists are laid together running straight across from wall to wall. Then plywood sheathing is laid across the joists, and, for a pitched roof, further boarding is laid on a slant; then shingles are attached, thus affording water drainage, and tar and gravel are applied as a sealer. This last step is repeated in layers to keep the tar from being broken down by the sun, thus protecting the house from leakage in rainy weather. Adding insulation to regulate heat may be part of the weatherproofing at this stage or soon after.

Within the open wood frame, in hollows provided for them, the major installations of rough plumbing and heating and wiring are done. The studs are bored through to attach pipes and secure wires, so the completed frame looks like a complex physiognomy of wood, pipe, and wire: the skeleton acquires a functioning inner system.

These facts of internal house construction, transmitted to children, can come as quite a surprise; they normally take their light and water supply for granted. They find it is a conscious, complex matter to harness energy sources and make them functional, and they learn that wiring and plumbing are separate, demanding skills.

When these steps are completed, walls are made to look as we normally see them: a siding, either wood, metal, or masonry, is attached to the frame like a skin, either horizontally or vertically, and upon this can be decoratively laid any number of exterior materials, such as stucco, brick, or shingles. Then it can be painted, stained, or left to weather.

In addition, the details of the house, its face of windows and doors, are being attended to. Windows now are prefabricated and are laid as a total unit into openings prepared for them; doors are erected in joist-and-strut-constructed openings; stairs are built of metal or wood, treads and risers resting on stringers; and a chimney, usually stainless steel piping insulated with layers of vermiculite to absorb heat, is put into place.

Now, the construction complete, a new element emerges, the element most familiar to children: the house is ready for an interior design. Choosing chairs, beds, posters, and desks is great fun--and yet there is another approach: an architect, responsible for organic form, working for beauty, must begin again at the beginning. Every planner, sitting in the middle of the room, must ask the basic questions of formative design: How could I best use that wall? Shall I build a platform by a window, by the bed? What will I be doing here? What does the room need to fulfill that function? Thus form will follow function, and the art someone called "undecoration" can emerge. It may be more at the heart of the calm, uncluttered beauty of certain contemporary structures than the superimposition of dozens of department store items. With the media's emphasis on purchasing power instead of building imagination, this value can too easily be forgotten. Then, of course, each room must be painted and lit, hung with mobiles, banners, curtains, and plants. Collections are installed and all the fun of imprinting private patterns upon living space enjoyed.

Outside is another aspect to study--that of exterior decoration. Through history, especially in Europe and the Orient, the art of architectural design has traditionally included an interest in sculpture and art used outside the house: a drain in the shape of a fantastic animal face, a door handle carved like a flower, a mural painted on a screen in the entranceway, a weathervane made to fly in the wind like a bird. The gentle use of imaginative artistic design as an adjunct to shelter building gives a light touch that can enhance its meaning.

Thus, first in the construction, then in the artistic play, the richness and complexity of the architect's work shows itself; it develops in this interplay among the theoretical, the practical, the manual, and the artist's leap to the unknown through a process of inspiration. No art has so firm a hold on the business and workaday world, on the one hand, and the world of the imagination, on the other. An architect seeks to find the solution that lies at the center of the problem, and his work flowers at exactly the point where the solution becomes clear, inside and then outside.

In the twentieth century this interplay has more and more become the meaning of "architect": a designer of environment, in harmony with people, expressive of landscape, aware of community. So the natural next step in the job of shelter design is outside--to see what kind of garden to give to a house, what will express it most effectively. The art of landscaping, without which a structure is naked and harsh, lies in devising a harmony of planting and shelter that will create an environment that suggests completion, rest and beauty: the gate, the path, the frog, and the tree. In the imaginary garden described as a child would encounter it, all these elements show themselves.

Every little garden was once a patch of land, shapeless, and playing host to native plants and shrubs. At some time, perhaps when the house was built, a gardener, with knowledge of plants and a sense of design, decided to make something of the space, to arrange colors and textures and shapes within it to satisfy himself and to give pleasure to others. In our day a landscape architect, a specialist in garden design and plant selection, is often put in charge of this phase of planning.

However it is done, in the garden each gate top frames a view, no matter how small, of one special arrangement in nature. The child opens the gate, enters the garden, and moves to a new experience of the day. Pathways, short or long, divide the garden space for practical use, and lead the way to a place for sitting outside, to a work area further along, or to a place to play with a tree swing or a construction. In the country or large yard some wilderness may be left for children to invent their own play. Whatever the goal, each path presents a choice, organizes the space, and invites the eye to follow its line, routing footsteps away from ground cover and plants. The flat story stones of the imaginary garden are local stones chosen carefully and brought in free of charge from the surrounding countryside.

The little pond, tucked into a corner, offers immediate spiritual refreshment; it casts a water spell and gives a home to water plants. Plants loving to be near water grow thickly around it. The frog glinting in the sun is man-made, the magic addition of sculpture to the garden that is funny, that is friendly, that enchants children. It is a bridge between the austerity of the natural world and the human understanding of it.

7

And the tree? It was perhaps there when the gardener went to work designing the space. How much shade it cast, how big it was, what kind of light would filter through its branches and leaves, its habits, whether it was deciduous or not--all these characteristics affected the positioning of the pond, the kinds of plants used around it, the sort of grass planted. Even the shape of the path had to interact gracefully with the scale of the tree.

For a place to sit, a bench might be installed, or a little group of furniture to frame the garden. Precisely as a window frame delimits a view, the outdoor furniture becomes a formal limitation that gives a sense of significance and, curiously, of privacy--furniture low enough for friendliness, extending the meaning of the house so that house and garden become closely related, integrated structures.

This has become quite a fancy garden, but the ecology that is basic to its design can take a million forms, from a miniature rendering in a tray setting to a vegetable tub on a back porch or the arrangement of hanging plants in an apartment window. Here are intention, design, and plants; combined they come alive as a garden, conventional or not. In the sparest of spaces the language of texture, raked earth, expressive use of interesting stones, and pots of tiny bonsai trees creates the garden art of Zen. In the country the wild field and woods nearby, casually cut back and trimmed a few times during the year, provide another sort of garden altogether.

Leaving the home environment, house and garden, for the neighborhood opens up a whole new world of shelter to explore and examine: the warehouse to store things, boats or trains to haul them, a supermarket to display and sell them, and the houses nearby that make up the neighborhood with their intimate mysteries of domesticity. Children have probably taken this network for granted as their given territory for exploring, but now as they begin to achieve architectural awareness, they may question the pattern of planning and movement in the town. They may leap forward to grasp the secret at its heart--that of relationship--the relationship of trade to neighborhood, of traffic network to public buildings, of park to port, the equipoise of a living area, of nature with production, the rhythms that join people together in the process of living.

Imagine a walk with children out the garden path into this town, a river town; they are immediately aware of many elements. Closing their eyes they smell fish, hear the boats' hooting on their way in and out of the town ports, the trucks' noisy rumbling through the streets. They feel the sea wind, often harsh in winter, but soft now in early autumn.

A day in this world starts quietly in a neighborhood of small houses, rather old and established. The first work rush and heavy traffic pass. Here and there a mother pushes a baby along in her stroller, some older people from the convalescent home take their morning walks, the delivery trucks make their rounds. Some children have skipped school and are hanging out, whispering, planning mischief. The neighborhood mom-and-pop store is stocking up, serving a few early customers, but business is pretty quiet; later in the day it will fill up with kids and householders, and later still, with after-work supper shoppers and last-minute purchasers. People like to meet and chat here, compare notes. The owners know everyone and act as a neighborhood newspaper.

Later in the morning the quiet gives old and young a chance to get out and take some air; householders do errands, shop, stroll, go to the library, and exchange news with the neighbors. The neighborhood is residential, with a few shops. People feel safe. The harbor sounds are faint, the waterfront a way off.

At noon some nearby workers return for lunch, the postman delivers mail, some students bike back along the paths to eat at home. Now it is the sleepy early afternoon time--time to nap, think, rest. A little later the rhythm quickens again. Children come home from school shouting to one another, playing games, complaining about homework; the parents of the young ones will be up and out, greeting older children, taking care of errands. The neighborhood begins to move outside, leaving privacy, feeling the congenial mid-afternoon hubbub. Now the little stores fill up, more deliveries are made, children's games are in full sway. The street is for people, the beat is lively. Householders come out on their stoops to chat and get some late summer sun. The timid, the very old and young, seem to fade off a little; it is a robust busy time.

As the sun moves away, the traffic quickens and the big rush home is on. Householders and children move off the street to prepare dinner and do homework or chores, leaving the street for workers coming by foot or car. After-work runners come out, heading for park and river walks. The children play hard and the neighborhood is a complex weave of traffic, children, returning workers.

Slowly the rush eases off. Evening is a quiet time on the street; most people stay home, visit with their families, perhaps go to sleep early. The traffic quiets, some people walk their dogs, and the rhythm slows. During the night only a few airplanes and an occasional starting car disturb the silence.

The rhythms are clear, the relationships straightforward. The patterns of interaction may have developed spontaneously or through the accumulation of multiple small-scale plans, but to endure they ultimately require a wide-angled view of people, conditions, and needs--city planning. Distance from homes and apartments to a park, a school or a hospital, offices, shops, service stations; density, setbacks, height restrictions; the balance of residential, commercial, and industrial use; garbage collection, public transportation, traffic flow, air and water quality and noise control, beautification--all enter into city planning and design.

The problem of access must also be explored. Merchants want maximum access to bolster trade, and thus they encourage the use of private cars; the patronage of suburban shoppers may depend upon the availability of parking spaces or a garage. But townspeople and planners, fearing that noise, air pollution, and crowding will damage the fabric of city living, may argue for fuller development of public transportation. Town or city planning is typically full of such seemingly insoluble problems, arising from diametrically opposing views. The issues of town planning have high visibility these days and high intensity in the local political process. Master plans receive the input of a battery of technical experts, but people in neighborhoods and towns are beginning to want some say and are moving to take more active roles in decisions that affect the land use, tax base, and ambience of their communities.

Children, too, can become very concerned with neighborhood decisions: whether a roller-skating rink or a park should be built, whether elevators should be manned in a development, whether bicycle paths should take precedent over parking space. City planning has aspects of living theater. Its theoretical aspect can become a game plan for children, and they can be encouraged to explore their neighborhood this way, to ask questions and get to the environmental heart. Pondering the problems found there is the beginning of a deep understanding of town.

The house, the garden, the town--three major elements of environmental design, of architecture. This walk has introduced us to how children perceive and experience each one and what they can do to become aware of the aspects and problems presented by the discipline and thus make architecture a living thing for themselves.

BIBLIOGRAPHY

Note: Picture-story books are indicated with the symbol PS.

House

Arkin, Alan. *Tony's Hard Work Day.* Pictures by James Stevenson. New York: Harper & Row, 1972. PS

Ardley, Neil. *Tomorrow's Home.* New York: Franklin Watts, 1981.

Barton, Byron. *Building a House.* New York: Greenwillow Books, 1981. PS

Cartner, W. C. *Fun with Architecture.* London: Kaye & Ward, 1968.

Ceserani, Gian Pable. *Grand Constructions.* Illustrated by Piero Ventura. New York: G. P. Putnam's Sons, 1983.

Clark, Evelyn Vallentin. *A Guide to Architecture for Young People: Exploring Old Buildings.* New York: Roy Publishers, 1955.

Devlin, Harry. *What Kind of a House Is That?* New York: Parent's Magazine Press, 1969. PS

Fairhurst, P. *Making a Model Village.* London: Transworld, n.d.

Fenton, D. X. *Ms.--Architect.* Philadelphia: Westminster Press, 1977.

Gay, Kathlyn. *Junkyards.* Hillside, N.J.: Enslow Publishers, 1982.

Giblin, James Cross. *The Skyscraper Book.* New York: Thomas Y. Crowell, 1981.

Haldane, Suzanne. *Faces on Places.* New York: Viking Press, 1980.

Heide, Florence Parry. *My Castle.* New York: McGraw-Hill, 1972. PS

Hiller, Carl E. *From Teepees to Towers: A Photographic History of American Architecture.* Boston: Little, Brown, 1967.

_____. *Caves to Cathedrals: Architecture of the World's Great Religions.* Boston: Little, Brown, 1974.

Hoag, Edwin. *American Houses: Colonial, Classic and Contemporary.* Philadelphia: J. B. Lippincott, 1964.

Hoberman, Mary Ann. *A House Is a House for Me.* New York: Viking, 1982.

Iger, Martin, and Eve Marie Iger. *Building a Skyscraper.* New York: Young Scott Books, 1967.

Macaulay, David. *Castle.* Boston: Houghton Mifflin, 1977.

_____. *Cathedral: The Story of Its Construction.* Boston: Houghton Mifflin, 1973.

_____. *Mill.* Boston: Houghton Mifflin, 1983.

_____. *Pyramid.* Boston: Houghton Mifflin, 1975.

_____. *Unbuilding.* Boston: Houghton Mifflin, 1977.

McGrath, Molly, and Norman McGrath. *Children's Spaces: Fifty Designers Create Environments for the Young.* New York: Morrow, 1978.

Madian, Jon. *Beautiful Junk: A Story of the Watts Tower.* Photographs by Barbara Jacobs and Lou Jacobs, Jr. Boston: Little, Brown, 1968.

Mayer, Jerome S. *The First Book of Mechanical Drawing.* Illustrated by the author. New York: Franklin Watts, 1963.

Michelson, David Reuben. *Housing in Tomorrow's World.* New York: Messner, 1973.

Moore, Lamont. *The First Book of Architecture.* New York: Franklin Watts, 1961.

Robbins, Ken. *Building a House.* New York: Four Winds Press, 1984.

Scher, Paula. *The Brownstone.* Pictures by Stan Mack. New York: Pantheon, 1973.

Schertle, Alice. *In My Treehouse.* New York: Lothrop, 1983. PS

Schlein, Miriam. *My House.* Illustrated by Joe Lasker. Chicago: Albert Whitman, 1971. PS

Shay, Arthur. *What Happens When You Build a House.* Chicago: Reilly & Lee, 1970.

Spier, Peter. *O, Were They Ever Happy!* New York: Doubleday, 1978. PS

Turley, W. E. *Designing and Making Toy Buildings.* New Rochelle, N.Y.: Soccer, 1964.

Watanabe, Shigeo. *I Can Build a House!* New York: Philomel Books, 1983. PS

Weiss, Harvey. *Model Buildings and How to Make Them.* New York: Thomas Y. Crowell, 1979.

Wilson, Forrest. *Architecture and Interior Environment: A Book of Projects for Young Adults.* New York: Van Nostrand, Reinhold, 1972.

Wondriska, William. *Mr. Brown and Mr. Gray.* New York: Holt, Rinehart & Winston, 1968. PS

Garden

Baker, Sam S. *The Indoor and Outdoor Grow-It Book.* New York: Random House, 1966.

Bush-Brown, Louise. *Young America's Garden Book.* New York: Charles Scribner's Sons, 1962.

Dowden, Anne Ophelia. *This Noble Harvest: A Chronicle of Herbs.* New York: Collins, 1979.

Fenton, D. X. *Gardening . . . Naturally.* New York: Franklin Watts, 1973.

_____. *Plants for Pots: Projects for Indoor Gardeners.* Philadelphia: J. B. Lippincott, 1969.

Johnson, Hannah Lyons. *From Seed to Jack-o-Lantern.* Photographs by Daniel Dorn. New York: Lothrop, Lee & Shepard, 1974.

Kirkus, Virginia. *The First Book of Gardening.* New York: Franklin Watts, 1956.

Mintz, Lorelie Miller. *Vegetables in Patches & Pots: A Child's Guide to Organic Vegetable Gardening.* New York: Farrar, Straus & Giroux, 1976.

Munari, Bruno. *A Flower with Love.* Translated by Patricia Tracy Lowe. New York: Thomas Y. Crowell, 1974.

Paul, Aileen. *Kids' Gardening: A First Indoor Gardening Book for Children.* New York: Doubleday, 1974.

Selsam, Millicent. *Eat the Fruit, Plant the Seed.* New York: William Morrow, 1980.

_____. *Play with Plants.* New York: William Morrow, 1978.

Wickers, David, and John Tuey. *How to Make Things Grow.* New York: Van Nostrand, Reinhold Co., 1972.

Town

Hiller, Carl E. *Babylon to Brasilia: The Challenge of City Planning.* Boston: Little Brown, 1972.

Hirsch, S. Carl. *Cities Are People.* New York: Viking Press, 1968.

Macaulay, David. *City.* Boston: Houghton Mifflin, 1974.

_____. *Underground.* Boston: Houghton Mifflin, 1976.

Munzer, Martha. *Planning Our Town.* New York: Alfred Knopf, 1964.

Pinkwater, Daniel Manus. *The Big Orange Spot.* New York: Hastings House, 1977.

Schwartz, Alvin. *Old Cities and New Towns: The Changing Face of the Nation.* New York: Dutton, 1968.

From *Castle* by David Macaulay.   © 1977 by David Macaulay.   Reprinted by permission of Houghton Mifflin Company.

FILMOGRAPHY

Skyscraper. 15 min. Color. Branden.

This is an excellent introduction to contemporary high-rise building. Wisecracking construction workers tell this story, which is fun, fast-paced, and thorough in its detailed coverage of each step: designing the building, digging the hole, laying the foundation, erecting the skeleton and walls, installing plumbing, and decorating the offices. Children will like the tough-funny dialogue, the jaunty score, and practical work accomplished while finding out quite a lot in passing about city life, city seasons, and city people.

Tuktu and the Snow Palace. 14 min. Color. Films, Inc.

In this tale within a tale of Eskimo igloo building, we watch the tribe building as we hear a tale narrated of a starving boy who finds shelter and survival within the magical, nurturing igloo structure. Although the film is not exciting, there is a practical, immediate appeal to children as they see how to render concrete the abstract materials; and, too, they can identify with the children in the film, enjoying the warm tone and cheerful quality.

WORKSHOP

A Workshop in Architecture: House, Garden, Town

Note for Special Children:
For some special children the architecture workshop will be quite accessible. Deaf children should have no trouble with it. Blind children are adept with their hands, their sense of space, and their inner vision, and can play with blocks and build models. Any child who can use his or her hands can experiment in modeling with materials such as metal, clay, or glue, and can work through city planning. All children, including those in wheelchairs, can journey around the neighborhood, experiencing it in new ways.
Introduction: This is a workshop consisting of six gatherings designed to bridge the theoretical and practical architectural worlds for children. It is planned for a small group of older boys and girls to introduce them to the areas discussed within the chapter: house, garden, and city planning.

Ages: 10-13.

Time: Ninety minutes.

Structure: A goal will be set for each person to design and construct a model shelter, with accompanying garden plan and town map. Materials specified for each meeting should be assembled ahead of time in the space allocated for the workshops. If possible, arrange for an architect to come in; a landscape architect would be welcome at the garden session (no. 4).

Environment: A quiet space with a work table or tables and chairs; although a separate room is helpful, it is not essential. Changing exhibits of various kinds can be stimulating and enrich the workshops. Try statements of famous architects that please you, blow-ups of architectural photos, pictures of houses, gardens, and towns designed to synchronize with each workshop; appropriate books and periodical reviews on the topic of the week (including folk and fairy tales that might relate to it); and, finally, the grand exhibit of their own models to be displayed in the children's room at the close of the series.

1. House

Materials: Paper, pencils, and crayons.

Introduction: When children are assembled, introduce to them the notion of a shelter. This could be a dog house, dance studio, fish tank, fort, church, or space ship. Then ask questions about their vision of a shelter and let this be the lead toward a general definition of architecture. Tell the children about the workshops to come, the models they will construct, and any visitors you plan on having. Now suggest an interior trip to get started.

Playing with Space: Ask children to sit down anywhere and, closing their eyes, to go into themselves and find a specific place where they want to be. What is it? What function does it serve? What is the location? What sort of climate surrounds it? Then, with these questions in mind and starting on the ground, shape a foundation, walls, a window, a skylight perhaps, and a door; finish with the ceiling. Now ask how it feels, how it smells. How does the light come in? What can they hear? Ask them to walk around in their imaginary space, experiencing their room in whatever form it has taken.

When the trip is over, ask volunteers to share with the group how it felt to design and build a place of their own and what exactly it was like--a verbal rough draft, so to speak. Its location should be decided upon.

Then to build a model of such a space, ask them to consider what construction materials will be necessary. Pass out paper and pencils and ask each one to make a list, starting with the stuff they have at home and adding what they don't. Perhaps others can supply these items; have an exchange. Be sure they include such tools as scissors and glue. Ask them to make rough drafts of their models at home and bring them in the next week. For this, great drawing is not important, specificity is.

After a stretch, take a short neighborhood walk, letting them see and talk about the kinds of shelters to be found, and ending with the library. Ask them to bring their sketch, their "junk" materials, and their tools for the model-making sessions the next week.

2. House: Model-making

Materials: Set out the viable junk you and the children have been collecting for the workshops: old crates, cartons, bits of fabric, interlocking pieces, Erector sets, towel rolls, cardboard boxes, balsa wood bits, lumberyard scraps, and anything else useful for building a model shelter. Tools should be assembled. In addition, for this workshop, you may want to invite a handy friend to help supervise the work if this is not your strong point.

Introduction: Ask to see some rough drafts of projected models. Tell what some are and ask one or two to say what their models are for, to describe them; ask them to mention some of the design problems inherent in it and their ideas toward a solution. Make recommendations about scale of the models, if appropriate. Discuss actual construction problems in terms of the function and location decided upon. Other children can contribute and suggest the actual uses of materials to solve any problems.

Playing with Space: Now, closing their eyes, the children should focus on their shelter, allowing it to take shape in terms of constructing a model. What are the problems? What are the solutions? How will it look exactly?

The rest of the time for this session will be spent in actual construction of each child's model shelter. Ten minutes or so before it is time to stop (although some will not be done) ask them to sit in their own places again. Introduce the idea of their exploring their neighborhoods, being aware of houses and gardens. Within your town or city there are undoubtedly a few rather imposing buildings distinguished frequently by more or less classical facades. Suggest they look at some of these solid landmarks: the library, school, museum, auditorium, church, or city hall. Public buildings are good sources for inspiration and possible subjects for home model work time. Ask them to go on with their model at home. Suggest they contact one another if they want to work on any problems with their models or to get together.

3. House: Interior

Materials: Their model, scraps of felt and balsa wood, pencils, crayons, felt-tip pens, watercolors, charcoal, or tempera.

Playing with Space: When the children come in, have them sit in their own place and imagine the next step. What colors would they like to use on the walls, ceiling, and trim of their shelter? How would they like the light to come in? What texture would be attractive to use in this space? Then, if the space is to be humanly useful, how is it to serve its purpose? What would they need to make it workable? Have them share with others their ideas about the interior.

Have them sketch their interior solutions, then complete a transfer of sketch ideas to the structure itself, if practical. If it is not feasible to decorate the actual model, outline solutions or sketch them. Add whatever exterior details emerged in their imagination. Suggest that they complete whatever is left at home.

4. Garden

Introduction: Invite an architect to come and talk to the children. If possible, try to find a landscape architect or one who is enthusiastic and knowledgeable about landscape, too. Have this be a time for a talk about the profession, as introduction to the real thing. Ask the architect to look at models volunteered by members of the group and comment. Now introduce the idea of the garden and have the visitors talk about what this means, and specifically perhaps in terms of one or two of the models. This will be half the workshop. After the visitors have gone, continue with the second half.

Materials: Crayons, pencils, and paper.

Playing with Space: Have the children sit down, close their eyes and take an imaginary walk outside their model shelter. What is there? How would they like the land around them to look? Would they have a path? A small pool? What sort of gate or fence would they need? What kind of vines, walls, ground cover and trees would they like? Have them set forth some ideas they've had for their landscaping and talk about these, discussing any problems that have emerged.

Suggest they work on their garden at home, combining it with their models. Also at home they can inspect their own gardens. Hanging pots, window boxes, containers, vines, street trees all qualify and can be utilized for their projects as well as more conventional garden spaces. This is a good place to introduce some of the concepts of good gardening practice: the cultivation and enrichment of soil, weeding, pruning, repotting or replanting, and so on. Eliciting their observations of their own and neighboring gardens and plants can be useful in understanding these concepts.

5. Town

Materials: Crayons, pencils, and paper.

Playing with Space: When children have occupied their places, ask them to imagine walking from their furnished model shelter and garden to do something they like. How would they get there? Where is it? What neighbors would they pass on the way? What other shelters would they see? What are they used for? Ask them to open their eyes and suggest that they choose roles they have envisioned for themselves, perhaps related to their shelter models, and act out for a few moments their part in the town.

Now have the children draw a simple map of a town with streets and houses, parks, public buildings, and shops. Suggest they think of this as part of a large collaborative project for the last week: the cooperative town.

At home they can spend the week integrating in their minds their house, garden, and town. They should take note of the way their own town is organized. What are its problems and how would they like to see them solved? Suggest that they have their own models and gardens finished and ready to bring in for the last workshop.

6. Town: Collaborative Project

Materials: A large work table covered with paper sheets or bound-together newsprint; crayons, pencils, charcoal, glue, and felt tip pens.

Introduction: Explain the idea of putting together their models, gardens and town maps as part of a large town to be mapped out on the table.

Start with volunteers who will draw in streets, park areas, public buildings, and so on. Then invite all to come together with their own models, deciding where they want them and putting them in place. Then they can draw or paint in the other sections and structures of the town not represented by models. Now the town is done: have a party! Put the town up for a long exhibit in the children's room.

Art

"Tick-tack! Tick-tock!" said the clock loudly.

"Oh, be quiet!" cried Jane furiously, and picking up her box she hurled it across the room.

It crashed against the glass face of the clock and, glancing off, clattered down upon the Royal Doulton Bowl.

Crrrrrrrrack! The bowl toppled sideways against the clock . . .

"I say, that hurt!"

"Here silly!" said the voice. "Up here!"

"But--" began Jane, half to herself and half to the voice, "I don't understand."

. . . And suddenly, she was no longer in the cool Day Nursery but out in a wide, sunlit meadow, and, instead of the ragged Nursery carpet, a springing turf of grass and daisies was spread beneath her feet.

--Mary Poppins Comes Back

Jane is alone, being punished for punching her brother, Michael, when she is catapulted into the picture in the Royal Doulton bowl. So begins a new story, her own with the triplets, William, Everard, and Valentine, their frightening old grandfather, and the great, dark, ancient house in which they live. Leaving behind her everyday world, she merges with the mysterious, beautiful world of the picture and when she comes back she is changed, older, wiser.

From *Mary Poppins Comes Back* by P. L. Travers, illustrated by Mary Shepard. Copyright 1935, © 1963 by P. L. Travers. Reproduced by permission of Harcourt Brace Jovanovich, Inc.

Art's role for children is just this: the immediate, powerful evocation of another world into which they can go at any time. Pictures require no speech, they are free, they are not in an acquired language; they are quiet, patient, and available at any age for experience and pleasure. Beginning in the very early years, children can appreciate art in this way of living in pictures, and they will come back changed, seeing their lives differently, subtle though this may be. The growth is nonverbal, mostly under the surface, but it is real: children who grow up with pictures (only a few are enough), with a "Royal Doulton bowl," are fortunate, learning to transport themselves to other places, to enrich their inner life, and to give sustenance to their emotional world.

All the visual arts--sculpture, painting, weaving and crafts, collage, and film--are available to children in the world outside. But in the library, it is books that bring the artist's message. Picture books and, later, illustrations in books for older children play an essential role in children's learning process, appealing as they do to the direct interests of the child, and concerning their own world or the world of imagination. This gentle, nonpedagogical way is the language of artists who in writing and designing their work for children make art completely accessible to them.

At the same time, in a style sympathetic to children, illustrators are passing on their own interpretive view of the world, the vision of the artists who have influenced them, the ideas they have developed in the sculpture, painting, or filmmaking they do apart from illustration, and the richness of the culture from which they come. When Beni Montresor shows us the palace and throne room in *May I Bring a Friend?* he shows also the intricate, opulent world of Uccello and the masters of the Italian Renaissance. And we get a sense of his skill as a set and costume designer in the theater. In *Tikta-liktak* James Houston's powerful primitive woodcuts reflect his years with Eskimos, studying their culture and their art, and children inherit his understanding of that world as well as the exciting account of Tikta's heroic journey. Leo Politi's broad-faced, generous people, his calm, colorful style, and strong-lined drawing bring children the tradition of Diego Rivera of the great Mexican artistic renaissance of the 1930s and 1940s as well as the color and smells of Mexico itself.

Used with the permission of Charles Scribner's Sons, an imprint of Macmillan Publishing Company. From *Rosa* by Leo Politi. © 1963 by Leo Politi.

Illustration by Beni Montresor from *May I Bring a Friend?* by Beatrice Schenk de Regniers. Text © 1964 Beatrice Schenk de Regniers. Pictures © 1964 Beni Montresor. Reproduced with the permission of Atheneum Publishers, an imprint of Macmillan Publishing Company.

In picture books far-away environs are presented in ways easily accessible to children. Remy Charlip in *Four Fur Feet* pulls the child into his beautiful world of strange yet familiar landscapes, the real world made somehow simpler, clearer, a place to rest and wander. Children are excited by the pictures, so unusual and yet so safe at the same time. Later they ask to see the book again, and years later still they remember: this world has become a place to visit, the deeper influences not consciously understood, yet giving a rich texture to the memory. But this vivid and primitive world apparently created with such ease has within it a complex of technical components: space, rhythm, design, and texture; detail, story, line, and color, all the elements of art. The artist devotes years of practice and effort to achieve command of them, and then can make seemingly trivial lines or shapes assume powerful expressiveness.

For artists, some of these aspects of craft are more natural than others and stand out for us. Gustave Doré's sense of vast space in his illustrations for *Perrault's Fairy Tales* creates strange worlds; the people at the foot of the castle in *Puss and Boots* seem so tiny compared to the height of the Gothic castle, and the scale gives a brooding quality; the light shining off the castle stones doubles the distance in the unreal night, and the child reading the story enters into the adventure. In contrast, the powerful, spare lines of Randolph Caldicott project (apparently so carelessly) such a robust sense of life, fun, and gentle irony that children enjoy it immediately. Each line is essential; nothing is wasted; Mr. Frog's crook-bent legs express passion and absurdity in equal amounts. So line alone can be a potent tool.

From *Perrault's Fairy Tales,* illustrated by Gustav Doré. New York: Dover Publications, 1969.

And color--for children it is vital, accessible the moment they open their eyes to life, and at its most intense in childhood. Picture books assume great importance because of this mirror to their inner vision, and many illustrators have shared their feel for color with them. Kate Greenaway's delicate, nostalgic colors, like late summer fruit and country vines, seem to pull a child into the page, the eye resting on the quiet blue chair, reveling in the apricot satin and immaculate white toeshoes of the girl, while the lonely cat, scruffy-colored, gives a homely feeling and balances the design. In contrast, Garth Williams in *Little Fur Family* uses cold, dominant, almost harsh greens and blacks to give a sense of the woods' largeness, of possible danger, it is a lonely coloration. Only the Fur Child is a warm brown, exploring his world, safe and secure in its immensities.

For rhythm you cannot beat Leslie Brooke, whose large and wicked pig dances across the page, one paw up and the other akimbo, to the beat of an unheard but powerful music, pleasing the hippos and rustling the tree leaves. This rhythmic sense carries through the whole book as well, marching with delicious foolishness from giraffe to bird to lion to monkeys. The animals curve and balance across the pages and the words are set in just right so as to pull one on through the garden. The whole book is a dance. When Johnny Crow's party is over, the child has been entertained and exercised, renewed and fed.

And the Pig
Danced a Jig
In Johnny Crow's Garden.

From *Johnny Crow's Garden.* New York: Frederick Warne & Co., 1986.

spring
spring

primavera
pree-mah-veh'-rah

printemps
pran-tawng

primavera
pree-mah-veh'-rah

From *See Again, Say Again: A Picture Book in Four Languages.* Woodcuts by Antonio Frasconi. © 1964 by Antonio Frasconi. Reproduced by permission of Harcourt, Brace, Jovanovich, Inc.

The more subtle question of texture, the exact feel of color, mass, and contrast, is given beautiful attention by Antonio Frasconi. Here is "Spring" from *See Again, Say Again: A Picture Book in Four Languages:* the hot, tussled feeling of field grass, the airy heat of the sun, the cold, strip-mined texture of the black hills, the mottled sun and shade of the field to the left, darkened by birds, the sturdy whitewashed stone of the little houses under the hill. Here the child learns to play with the feelings close by in his world, to define a variety of moods and subtle meanings in his life.

And deeply, subtly also, he is absorbing a point of view. In I. B. Singer's *Zlateh the Goat,* Maurice Sendak designs a poignant portrait of the value of nurturing, of listening and loving patience. Zlateh's milk saves Aaron's life in the frozen, snow-bound hut where they are trapped, and how kind, how plain and yet questioning she is, as she stands sturdily, ready to help. So values are transmitted continually to children in books. The fact that pictures don't talk but state their meaning wordlessly adds greatly to their impact on children. They don't get it mixed up with authority, and they have time to absorb it, privacy to sort it out.

From *The Kate Greenaway Treasury,* edited by Edward Ernest, illustrated by Kate Greenaway. © 1967 by The World Publishing Company.

Then, around the subject, the artist builds a framework, constructing a sort of architecture, a formal design that draws all the elements together, giving structure that holds them. *Baboushka* of Sidjakoff is a small book with a strong overall architectural design that illustrates this: here, from the tree-lined inner cover, one is led through Baboushka's story in a series of pictures, each one of which is essential in telling the tale. From the immaculate kitchen, cornerstone of the design, one moves with the king's train from safety to wild storm and then out again to the bare loneliness of Baboushka on her front porch in the quiet snow, determined now to begin her eternal wanderings in search of the child. The line of the royal train moving across the page balances the white starkness of one page with the violent blue of the next. Each succeeding page answers a visual question raised by the page before and in turn raises a question resolved by the architecture and action of the page that follows.

In contrast, some artists concentrate with delight on the details inside a picture, letting the building of a design take care of itself through the arrangement that emerges. Ellen Raskin does this in *Nothing Ever Happens on My Block*. As Chester sits glumly on his sidewalk (because he has nothing to do and his neighborhood is so dull), he completely fails to notice that directly behind him are a lost parachutist, a forlorn but steadfast witch in a window, two little girls reaching 1,405 with a jump rope, a gardener, a window cleaner, a blue roofer, a disdainful and pregnant orange cat and a postman distributing mail to the lady-who-plays-the-flute.

Poor Chester.

Children are in their element with this picture, sharing equally in delight of detail with the artist, poring over each new manifestation of Chester's folly. Children are enriched by all this detail, too: life moves by so fast, but here they have a chance to sit quietly and pore over each special person or color or thing, time to absorb and get things straight.

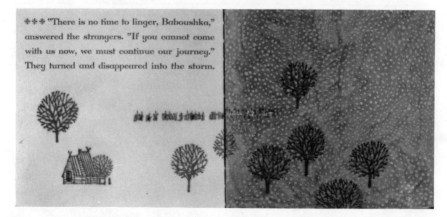

Illustration by Nicholas Sidjakov from *Baboushka and the Three Kings* by Ruth Robbins. © 1960 by Ruth Robbins for the story and Nicholas Sidjakov for the illustrations. A Parnassus Press Book. Reprinted by permission of Houghton Mifflin Company.

Illustration from *Nothing Ever Happens on My Block* by Ellen Raskin. © 1966 by Ellen Raskin. Reproduced with the permission of Atheneum Publishers, an imprint of Macmillan Publishing Company.

Indians on the warpath,

Storytelling is another very important aspect in children's books; although it is common to all forms of literature, it is especially valuable to children as they can follow and enjoy life's adventures where more adult features of mood and style seem less important to them. In picture books, where the illustrations tell the story, the artist must have a strong narrative sense that clearly and dynamically unfolds the tale. In *Tim All Alone* by Edward Ardizzone, one almost need not read the text. As we follow Tim in his adventures, from first to last, the pictures act out each happening clearly, accompanied by conversational balloons and unified by watercolors whose sensitive shades repeat and identify the characters as they appear.

Last, and subtly important, is a way of showing what it is to be an artist, a sharing of the nature of creativity that some artists convey especially well. Bruno Munari in his work is always at play, playing with images, playing with ideas, punning around. If "the birds are infinite" why not let them go right off their pages, infinitely into infinite space? If there is an exit sign from the zoo, why not have it lead the reader right out of the book? Children love this lighthearted and playful approach, which serves to connect the picture directly with their own world. And, more subtly, the suggestion is being made: how can I look at my world differently, more creatively and immediately?

Illustration from *Tim All Alone* by Edward Ardizzone. First American edition © 1957 by Henry Z. Walck, Inc. Reproduced by permission of Oxford University Press.

At the same time on another level, the child is absorbing some sense of history. Doré's world is that of a France still in the Dark Ages; there is a different perspective in the vast mysteriousness, bizarre faces, and strange effects of his pictures than there is in the late twentieth-century commercially oriented America that surrounds the child. Caldicott's folk are landed gentry of late eighteenth-century England, and they show a robust humor and physicality quite foreign to us.

Yet with all this difference the lesson is that feelings, easily expressed in art, are universal through all times and diverse settings, thus clarifying and expanding a child's understanding of himself, his family and his friends. In his neighborhood he will find a Chester (though perhaps not the parachutist) and the jump ropers, look for the witch, and spruce up his own territory with a new insight and imagination. And when he looks up, the sun will have taken on that particular benevolence and penetration of Frasconi's country.

From *Bruno Munari's Zoo* by Bruno Munari. Reproduced by permission of Philomel Books. © 1963 by Bruno Munari.

Opposite to this experience, the appreciative experience, is the child at work on her own. For a child to express art herself is to integrate and mirror her receptivity in a delicate interplay, taking in and giving out. A child feels all the excitement of color, the sensual stimulation of texture, the power of thrust in a line she draws that makes a picture come alive. Rhythm, architecture, and detail are all a young artist's to strive for, play with, and explore. Now the child gathers together all the information of color and texture and line in the neighborhood, the weather, her mother's nose, a chair-back, the family car. The chance to express herself becomes a chance to understand her own world. Doing it herself, finger painting, drawing, building, making a collage, she expands her interior world with an ease that is the signal characteristic of the graphic arts for children.

Within the experience lies a rich core of life: for children art is fun, a form of play that turns into a trip, an adventure of discovery that unfolds with the colors. In creating their own world, in sensual exploration, they free up their inner selves for growth and new ideas. In what children choose to draw, they find relationships with objects, experiences, and dreams that are personal and special to them, not imposed from the outside.

In this unfolding through the making of art, as the years go by, the child is actively building a road to adulthood through stages of work: the exploratory scribbles of the preschooler develop by seven into a broader understanding, a personal mapping of his reality, and his skills expand. In the nine- and ten-year-old, relationships with friends are explored in art, technique is sharpened, and media becomes a form of experiment and play. Then, if art is pursued into the intense, problematic world of the adolescent, technique becomes paramount, all phases of the self are examined and explored intently, and self-consciousness begins to be absorbed, soon to be transmitted as the mature view.

In these years, the natural process of making art is having a deep effect on the child, which is apart from the actual artwork he produces and apart from his sense of the experience of making it. He is developing empathy with the world and setting vital life habits of self-instruction and self-reliance. Rather than responding to regulation set from without, the accommodation to the power of others, he is becoming familiar with his own flow of creative power and developing the experimental, exploring side of his nature. In creating art, a child learns to listen to his impulses, to experience flexibility, to free his inner self. Art is magic to practice and over the years bestows ineradicable gifts.

In the children's room a rich opportunity exists to give children a space for these activities, both passive and active: a free feeling, quietness, a nonjudgmental, warm atmosphere are the characteristics of the library, and access to the pictures of others are part of its natural resource. Art workshops of all kinds can be conducted here for all ages, encompassing a range from art history to work in finger painting, sculpture, watercolor, drawing, and book illustration. Engaged in these, children will not only develop their psychological selves but enrich their sense of form, rhythm, and visual perception. Out of this, a new understanding of art and of books can be born.

Being the teacher is a demanding and very special role. Elementary-level fine art teachers are usually artists themselves, with a special gift for teaching and a real interest in each child. Their experience gives them a sense of developmental timing, and their noncritical attitude and characteristic genuine friendliness create an atmosphere of self-trust and free up self-expression. They encourage children to respond to each other's work and lead them on with questions to explore further and further.

Side by side with the art teacher, the children's librarian has a vital role as demonstrator of what has been and is being done in art. By showing picture books in story hour she is opening up new works for children, many of whom get their first taste of fine art at this time. For older children, noticing the exhibits and changing pictures in the library as well as reading books with illustrations builds a foundation of taste and appreciation of excellence, year after year.

Children's librarians who love art and picture books may be interested in giving workshops in art appreciation, illustration for children's books, or the elements of design as shown in picture books. For the actively creative workshops many children's librarians may want to call upon art teachers in the community, but others, for whom art is a principal interest, may feel comfortable and professionally prepared to lead it themselves. In either case, whether or not the children's librarian is interested in teaching them herself, she can supply the workshops: the teacher, opportunity, materials, space, and time. By providing the entrepreneurial work she will be giving to children the chance to explore life behind life, life within life, that spirit which is the meaning of art. In Mondrian's words, "the surface of things gives enjoyment, their inwardness gives life."

Illustration from *Tikta'liktak: An Eskimo Legend.* © 1965 by John Houston. Reproduced by permission of Harcourt Brace Jovanovich, Inc.

BIBLIOGRAPHY

History

Discovering Art (series). Books on periods of great art through the ages published in New York by Pantheon Books during the 1960s and 1970s.

Gardner, Helen. *Gardner's Art through the Ages.* Revised by Horst de la Croix and Richard G. Tansey. 5th ed. New York: Harcourt Brace, 1970.

Glubock, Shirley. *The Art of Africa* and other books in series, covering a wide geohistorical area, published in New York by Atheneum during the 1960s and 1970s.

Price, Christine. *Made in the Middle Ages.* New York: E. P. Dutton, 1961.

Ruskin, Ariane. *The Pantheon Story of Art for Young People.* New York: Pantheon, 1964.

Ventura, Piero. *Great Painters.* New York: G. P. Putnam's Sons, 1984.

Appreciation

Campbell, Ana. *Paintings: How to Look at Great Art.* New York: Franklin Watts, [1970].

Chase, Alice. *An Introduction to Art.* New York: Platt & Monk, 1962.

Conner, Patrick. *Looking at Art: People at Work.* New York: Wayland Publishing, 1982.

Cummings, Robert. *Just Imagine.* New York: Charles Scribner's Sons, 1982.

Downer, Marion. *Children in the World's Art.* New York: Lothrop, Lee & Shepard, 1970.

_____. *Discovering Design.* New York: Lothrop, Lee & Shepard, 1966.

_____. *The Story of Design.* New York: Lothrop, Lee & Shepard, 1963.

Grigson, Geoffrey, and Jane Grigson. *More Shapes and Stories: A Book about Pictures.* New York: Vanguard Press, [1967].

MacAgy, Douglas, and Elizabeth MacAgy. *Going for a Walk with a Line: A Step into the World of Modern Art.* Garden City, N.Y.: Doubleday, 1959.

Payne, Roberta M. *Looking at Sculpture.* New York: Lothrop, Lee & Shepard, 1968.

Raboff, Ernest. Art for Children (series). Includes Chagall, Klee, Picasso, Velasquez, Rousseau, Toulouse-Lautrec, Renoir, and others. Published in Garden City, N.Y., by Doubleday from 1970 to 1980.

Biography

Armstrong, William. *The Story of Grandma Moses: Barefoot in the Grass.* Garden City, N.Y.: Doubleday, 1970.

Braider, Donald. *George Bellows and the Ashcan School of Painting.* Garden City, N.Y.: Doubleday, 1971.

Feelings, Tom. *Black Pilgrimage.* New York: Lothrop, Lee & Shepard, [1972].

Flexner, Thomas. *The Double Adventure of John Singleton Copley.* Boston: Little Brown [1969].

Greenfeld, Howard. *Marc Chagall.* Chicago: Follett Publishing, 1967.

Hollman, Clyde. *Five Painters of the Old West.* New York: Hastings House, 1965.

Honour, Alan. *Tormented Genius: The Struggle of Vincent van Gogh.* New York: William Morrow, 1967.

Horwitz, Sylvia. *Francisco Goya: Painter of Kings and Demons.* New York: Harper & Row, 1973.

Hyman, Linda. *Winslow Homer: America's Old Master.* New York: Doubleday, 1973.

Redman, Selden, and Carole Cleaver. *Horace Pippin: The Artist as a Black American.* Garden City, N.Y.: Doubleday, [1972].

Rockwell, Anne F. *The Boy Who Drew Sheep.* New York: Atheneum, 1973. Biography of Giotto.

Turk, Midge. *Gordon Parks.* New York: Thomas Y. Crowell, 1971.

Ventura, Pierre. *Great Painters.* New York: G. P. Putnam's Sons; Milan: Arnoldo Montafiore & Sons, 1984.

Williams, Jay. *Leonardo da Vinci.* Illustrated with the paintings, drawings and diagrams of Leonardo da Vinci. New York: Harper & Row, 1965.

Wilson, Ellen Janet [Cameron]. *American Painter in Paris: A Life of Mary Cassatt.* New York: Farrar, Straus and Giroux, 1971.

Autobiography

O'Kelley, Mattie Lou. *From the Hills of Georgia: An Autobiography in Paintings.* Boston: Little, Brown, 1983.

Wong, Jade Snow. *Fifth Chinese Daughter.* New York: Harper & Row, 1950.

Picture Books

Bjork, Christina. *Linnea in Monet's Garden.* New York: Farrar, Straus, Giroux, 1987.

Chorao, Kay. *Ida Makes a Movie.* New York: Viking Press, 1959.

Freeman, Don. *Norman the Doorman.* New York: Viking Press, 1959.

Goffstein, M. B. *Lives of the Artists.* New York: Harper & Row, 1980.

_____. *Goldie, the Dollmaker.* New York: Farrar, Straus, & Giroux, 1969.

Isadora, Rachel. *Willaby.* New York: Macmillan, 1977.

Johnson, Crockett. *Harold and the Purple Crayon.* New York: Harper & Row, 1959.

_____. *A Picture for Harold's Room.* New York: Harper & Row, 1960.

Kesselman, Wendy. *Emma.* Garden City, N.Y.: Doubleday, 1980.

Lionni, Leo. *Little Blue and Little Yellow.* New York: Aster Honor, 1959.

McPhail, David. *Magical Drawings of Moony B. Finch.* Garden City, N.Y.: Doubleday, 1978.

Myers, Florence Cassen. *ABC: Museum of Fine Arts, Boston.* New York: Abrams, 1986.

_____. *ABC: Museum of Modern Art, New York.* New York: Abrams, 1986.

Rossetti, Christina. *What Is Pink?* Illustrated by José Aruego. New York: Macmillan, 1971.

Veluthijs, Max. *The Painter and the Bird.* Reading, Mass.: Addison-Wesley, 1975.

Zolotov, Charlotte. *Mr. Rabbit and the Lovely Present.* Illustrated by Maurice Sendak. New York: Harper & Row, 1962.

Reader

Bang, Holly Garrett. *Tye May and the Magic Brush.* New York: Greenwillow Books, 1981.

Bulla, Clyde. *Daniel's Duck.* New York: Harper & Row, 1979.

Coerr, Eleanor. *The Josefina Story Quilt.* New York: Harper & Row, 1988.

Drawing, Painting, and Printing

Bolognese, Don. *Drawing Spaceships and Other Spacecraft.* New York: Franklin Watts, 1982.

Bolognese, Don, and Elaine Raphael. *Pen and Ink.* New York: Franklin Watts, 1986.

_____. *Pencil.* New York: Franklin Watts, 1986.

Borja, Corinne, and Robert Borja. *Making Collage.* Chicago: Albert Whitman, 1972.

Cummings, Richard, pseud. *Make Your Own Comics for Fun and Profit.* New York: H. Z. Walck, [1975].

Hawkinson, John. *Paint a Rainbow.* Chicago: Albert Whitman: [1970].

_____. *Collect, Print, and Paint from Nature.* Chicago: Albert Whitman, 1964.

Marks, Mickey Koar. *Painting Free: Lines, Colors and Shapes.* New York: Dial Press, 1965.

_____. *Op-tricks: Creating Kinetic Art.* Philadelphia: J. B. Lippincott, 1972.

Rauch, Hans-George. *The Lines Are Coming: A Book about Drawing.* New York: Charles Scribner's Sons, [1978].

Seidelman, James E., and Grace Mintonyz. *Creating with Paint.* New York: Crowell-Collier Press, 1967.

Spilka, Arnold. *Paint All Kinds of Pictures.* New York: Henry Z. Walck, 1963.

Sculpture

Fine, Joan. *I Carve Stone.* New York: Thomas Y. Crowell, 1979.

Haldane, Suzanne. *Faces on Places: About Gargoyles and Other Stone Creatures.* New York: Viking Press, 1980.

Leyh, Elizabeth. *Children Make Sculpture.* New York: Van Nostrand Reinhold, [1972].

Naylor, Penelope. *Sculpture.* New York: Franklin Watts, 1970.

Paine, Roberta M. *Looking at Sculpture.* New York: Lothrop, Lee & Shepard, 1968.

Rieger, Shay. *The Stone Menagerie.* New York: Charles Scribner's Sons, 1970.

Weiss, Harvey. *Clay, Wood and Wire.* Reading, Mass.: Young Scott Books, 1956.

_____. *Collage and Construction.* New York: Young Scott Books, [1970].

Photography

Bourgeois, Jacques. *Animating Film without a Camera.* New York: Sterling Publishing Co., 1974.

Coe, Brian. *George Eastman and the Early Photographers.* London: Priory Press, 1973.

Davis, Edward. *Into the Dark: A Beginner's Guide to Developing and Printing Black and White Negatives.* New York: Atheneum, 1979.

Dolan, Edward F., Jr. *The Camera.* New York: Julian Messner, 1965.

Glubock, Shirley. *The Art of Photography.* New York: Macmillan, 1977.

Hobson, Andrew, and Mark Hobson. *Film Animation as a Hobby.* New York: Sterling Pub. Co., 1975.

Hood, Robert E. *Twelve at War.* New York: G. P. Putnam's Sons, 1967.

Leen, Nina. *Taking Pictures.* New York: Holt, Rinehart & Winston, 1977.

Manes, Stephen. *Pictures of Motion and Pictures that Move: Muybridge and the Photograph of Motion.* New York: Coward, McCann & Geoghegan, 1982.

Owens-Knudsen, Vick. *Photography Basics.* Englewood Cliffs, N.J.: Prentice-Hall, 1983.

Siegel, Beatrice. *An Eye on the World: Margaret Bourke-White, Photographer.* New York: Frederick Warne, 1980.

Simon, Seymour. *Hidden Worlds: Pictures of the Invisible.* New York: William Morrow, 1983.

Turk, Midge. *Gordon Parks.* New York: Thomas Y. Crowell, 1972.

Book Illustration

Blegvad, Eric. *Self-Portrait: Eric Blegvad.* New York: Addison-Wesley, 1979.

Cross, Jeanne. *Simple Printing Methods.* New York: S. G. Phillips, 1972.

Daniels, Harvey, and Sylvie Turner. *Exploring Printmaking for Young People.* New York: Van Nostrand, Reinhold, [1972].

Hirsch, S. Carl. *Printing from a Stone: The Story of Lithography.* New York: Viking Press, 1967.

Painting, Printing, and Modeling. Color Crafts Service, vol. 5. New York: Franklin Watts, 1972. Includes sculpture, printmaking, and painting introductions.

Rockwell, Harlow. *Printmaking.* New York: Doubleday, 1973.

Weiss, Peter. *Simple Printmaking.* New York: Lothrop, Lee & Shepard, 1976.

Witty, Ken. *A Day in the Life of an Illustrator.* Mahwah, N.J.: Troll Associates, 1981.

Book Design and Book Making

Bartlett, Susan. *Books: A Book to Begin On.* New York: Holt, Rinehart & Winston, 1968.

Greenfeld, Howard. *Books: From Writer to Reader.* New York: Crown, 1976.

Simon, Irving. *The Story of Printing: From Wood Blocks to Electronics.* New York: Harvey House, 1965.

FILMOGRAPHY-VIDEOGRAPHY

Films

Clay. 10 min. b/w. Phoenix.

Out of clay came the powerful, primeval forms that compose and shape our world and people in it, too: one after another we see them created and then dissolved in this animated fantasy of creativity. Children will enjoy the fresh, witty look at form as well as the expert score.

Ezra Jack Keats. 17 min. Color. Weston Woods.

Although it is marred by a stiff, somewhat sentimental narration, this interview with the artist/illustrator is worthwhile for the glimpses it gives us of his childhood influences, his way of working, his enthusiasm and love of neighborhood, color, and sound. Keats's books *Peters's Chair* and *A Letter to Amy* are emphasized.

Glass. 10 min. Color. McGraw-Hill/Contemp.

A documentary that tells how glass is made. Contrasting ancient and modern methods, Glass is told with a jazzy score entirely by filmed action, and is an absorbing study of the craft.

Hailstones and Halibut Bones. 6 min. Color. Sterling.

This film takes an animated trip through colors in a warm, well-narrated rendering of the popular poetry book by Mary O'Neil. Despite a tendency to the cute and sentimental, the feeling for color and childhood is conveyed successfully.

Harold and the Purple Crayon. 8 min. Color. Weston Woods.

In a most original rendering of spontaneous artistic creativity, Harold journeys around his world, unfolding it for us as he draws his way through a magic night. Moving from his room to building his town and then back home, the film shows Harold's efforts with a color and feeling that are interesting and sensitive.

Lapis. 10 min. Color. Pyramid.

Accompanied by a warm, beautiful Indian score, *Lapis* explores optics, op-art, and the abstraction of form in a sensitive parade of shifting colors and light. The film shows how colors, all by themselves, can express both mood and ideas.

Liang and the Magic Paintbrush. 29 min. Color. Reading Rainbows.

Liang is a small boy who longs to paint and is bequeathed a magic paintbrush by an old man who appears before him. From then on everything he paints leaps to life. Liang shrewdly decides only to benefit others with his new gift, but the greedy emperor, hearing of it, insists on taking his brush away from him. At last Liang gives in, but he paints everything so large that a great storm sweeps the emperor and all he owns into the sea forever. As is typical of the Reading Rainbow productions, the story itself is richly designed and told with clear bright frames and a resonant style. But the long, heavy introduction and poststatement are ponderous and dull. Consider showing only the story section.

Little Blue and Little Yellow. 9 min. Color. Contemporary.

A pleasant adaptation of Leo Lionni's unusual picture book, representing each color as a spot with a personality and then telling a little story about their goings-on that illustrates the qualities of color. A bit slow, but nice.

Maurice Sendak. 14 min. Color. Weston Woods.

In a rather formal, yet compelling film, Maurice Sendak introduces us to his world, his apartment in New York City, the music and literature he loves, giving us some of the quality of his childhood. Urbane and elegant, Sendak leaves a strong impression of his personal integrity as an artist, as well as sharing with us some of the enduring beauty of his work.

Mole as Painter. 11 min. Color. Phoenix.

A jewel of a film: mole refuses to be intimidated by fox, and then scares fox to death by adorning first himself and then a delighted group of small animal friends with alarming mask-faces from cans of paint. *Mole* manages to be extremely funny in just the way children love, while showing spontaneously the value of community as well as the fun and beauty of art.

What Is a Painting? 24 min. Color. Metropolitan Museum of Art Seminar.

This rather formal teaching film from the Metropolitan Museum of Art in New York features John Cannaday narrating a series of explanations of paintings that clarify the formal aspects of art. The film is a serious exploration of the art of painting, suitable for use with older children in an introduction to art.

Video

David Macaulay in His Studio.

Specifically directed toward older children or young adults particularly interested in art as a career, this interview with David Macaulay emphasizes his education, his travel research (that is, Cairo, for *Pyramid)* and the important little things that have inspired him along the way in his multifaceted career as architect, artist, and book writer. Although somewhat self-conscious and dry, the film suggests a sense of detail in art that could be very useful to the selected audience.

The Incredible San Francisco Artists' Soap Box Derby. 24 min. Color. Phoenix.

A very lively piano ragtime score accompanies this wonderful, whimsical festival of Krazy Kars built by San Francisco artists simply for the fun of it in this show to support the San Francisco Museum of Modern Art. James Suzuki, Fletcher Benton, Don Potts, and others show a string of banana-shoe-enormous pencil-hands and breadloaf soapboxes taking off before an ecstatic audience of children who watch these wonders come racing down the hill. Art is shown as reachable and fun but also as a matter of great professional skill. Highly recommended.

WORKSHOPS

Introduction: These workshops can be conducted by those who would like to lead their own or by an instructor from outside. Museum schools, art schools, free-lance artist-teachers, and local college and university art departments are all good sources for teachers. For these workshops six weeks should be allowed. A few books chosen to illustrate the content of each workshop can be set up ahead of time.

An Introduction to Art

Ages: 9-12.

Number of Children: 8-10.

Time: Ninety minutes.

Space: A fairly large room with tables available, if possible. If not, floor space and newspapers will do. There should be a sink with running water available.

Materials: Basically, a roll of newsprint, paper towels, scissors, pencils, and a trash can will be needed in addition to the materials listed under individual sessions. Have children bring in smocks or old clothes to wear.

Arrangement of Time: Loosening up; structured time; criticism and idea exchange; clean up.

1. Drawing: Portraiture

Materials: Charcoal, pencils, felt-tip pens, crayons, newspaper, a stapler.

Introduction: The first few minutes are important to children. They quickly find a mood or feeling that can identify and flow into the workshop time. Each time plan a few minutes of imaginative play that will lead into the workshop. Ideas include playing statues, dancing in a circle and freezing into a group statue, assuming a few animal-yoga poses, playing at being trees in a forest.

Live Portraits: Begin by asking the children to do some yoga poses and then ask one child to stay in an easy pose such as frog, child, tree. Ask the children to choose a drawing tool and newsprint and draw the portrait. Have them do two or three "portraits" of the yoga poses and see what their pencils do.

Growing Portrait: Tell the children to sit down with a new drawing tool and paper. Draw a cat in profile and ask who is following it, what it is coming to in its walk, if it is on a leash, and other questions that occur to you. Have the children answer and suggest one idea after another until they have drawn a story--a "growing" portrait.

Lifesized Portraits: Have the children pair off: one child lies down and the other draws around him or her. Use two thicknesses of paper and when the portrait is complete, cut through them. Have the nonposing child draw in the features with charcoal or crayon. If desired, the portrait can be stuffed with torn newspaper, stapled together, and go home to visit the child's family.

Idea Exchange: What do the children think of what they've done? Have they any ideas for each other or for things to do at home? Suggest that they get a sketch pad and draw around the house/neighborhood during the week.

2. Painting: Mood Imagery

Materials: Watercolors, tempera in muffin tins, brushes, newsprint, fresh water and jars for cleaning brushes, record player, tape recorder.

Music: Choose from your collection, or that of the library, simple, tuneful instrumental pieces such as guitar music, ragtime piano, music for percussion (Béla Bartók's *Music for Strings, Percussion, and Celesta*), piano solo (Ravel's *Pavane for a Dead Child*), electronic music, or a piece of current popular music familiar to the children.

Introduction: Have the piece you've chosen playing as the children enter. Ask them to sit down quietly and give each one a set of clean papers to work with.

Have them close their eyes for a moment and take a look at the pictures being created by the music inside their minds. What do they see? What scene takes shape? Perhaps only colors or shapes or lines, even words, will appear. Instead of their telling it in words, have them dip into the tempera colors with a brush or their fingers and let the scene or impressions take

48

shape on the paper. Repeat this pattern with new pieces of music, playing each one briefly. When several have been worked up, ask them to pick their favorite. Put these on the wall for display.

Idea Exchange: What pieces do they reflect/express? Ask the group to guess and to suggest appropriate titles.

3. Painting: Still Life

Materials: Same as above, plus odd objects and some fruit for still-life arrangements.

Possible Book Display: Books that show still lives from various periods.

Introduction: Set up several groupings, one in each corner: a fruit still-life, foreign dolls, some junk from local abandoned lots, an open cereal box, transistor radios and a glass of milk. Have them fill one corner themselves. Each child takes a brush, jar, and paper to paint one of the still-life groups, and then moves around the room to other groups when he or she is ready. Chat about the pictures and colors--and what they put in their corner. Show some of the pictures. Notice all the color. How was it different from the first week? Why? What is there about color? Suggest they do some felt-tip or crayon sketching in their books during the week.

Note: If there is time, you can introduce some other painting projects: design a castle to live in; plant a magic garden; draw a tired and unhappy girl; paint what it feels like outside today.

4. Group Project: Parade

Display: On the walls put a series of crowd photographs, parade paintings or photographs; books showing Chinese New Year, Carnival, or Mummers' Parade can be shown.

Materials: Newsprint, paints, felt-tip pens, charcoal, crayons.

Introduction: First, have them draw a crowd watching a parade going by. Ask a child or two to pose eating ice cream cones, waving flags, holding imaginary balloons. When this is complete, tack up the results for everyone to see. What do they think? Any criticisms or suggestions? Second, put down fresh paper. Have the children draw the parade itself. It is helpful to the children if you define the nature of the parade. So pick a day or a theme to pin down the image for them and let them begin.

Idea Exchange: Share reactions to color, style, ideas.

A Workshop in Art Appreciation

Ages: 7-12.

Number of Children: 6-10.

Time: One hour.

1. Space and Color

Materials: Colored pencils and paper.

Introduction: Ask the children to sit on the floor in an informal way, and give them pencils and paper. Ask them what art means to them. You can say what art is for you, and how we understand life through our eyes, how what we see and feel is expressed through color, line, and space. As you do this, you may want to show slides that illustrate these elements in a broad, clear way. Then move to a more specific set of concepts and illustrations from history and from children's books as outlined below:

The Home:

Jan Van Eyck, *Portrait of Giovanni Arnolfini and his Bride* (1434)

Margaret Wise Brown, *Goodnight Moon*

These represent such a contrast in old and new interiors of a home. What are they? How would you draw your own home? Give it a try.

Animals:

Greek vase, ca. 510 B.C. Harnessing a chariot.

Beatrix Potter, *The Tale of Peter Rabbit*, p. 20.

Here the feeling for and meaning of animals are very different. What are the differences? How did the artist feel and convey these differences?

Some of the elements the artist works with to make a good picture can be seen especially clearly in certain pictures.

Space:

Jan Vermeer, *Maid Pouring Milk*

Gustave Doré, *Perrault's Fairy Tales*

Vermeer's tiny, enclosed, intimate use of space contrasts strongly with the vast, echoing sense in the Doré.

Pol de Limbourg, *Les Tres Riches Heures du Duc de Berri*

Evaline Ness, *Sam, Bangs, and Moonshine*

The delicate, stage-set feeling of manuscript illustration uses space so differently from Ness's vigorous, realistic settings for Sam.

Color:

Henri Matisse, *The Purple Robe*

Henri Lamorisse, *The Red Balloon*

Here the fruits of the earth have their say: a sensual flavor and richness pervade both artists' concepts. How are they alike? How different?

Feel free to show some other examples of color and space in paintings and illustrations that either have similar purposes or display effective contrasts.

Finishing Up: Give the children time now to talk about space and color and to illustrate their own way of looking at them in pictures of their own making. Volunteers can hold up pictures and tell about them. Ask the children to sketch at home and to make drawings of space during the week if they want to.

2. Line and Rhythm

Ask if anyone sketched during the week. If anyone did and brought in his or her work, show the pictures and have a discussion about how space and color work in them. Pass out pencils (not colored this time) and paper.

Line:

Caves of Lescaux, Bison

Randolph Caldicott, *Hey Diddle Diddle Picture Book No. 3*, p. 23

Here the sense of life and motion is conveyed by a linear energy. The pictures on the cave walls show the way the animals really seem: strong, warlike, and so on. The Caldicott kicked-back lines vibrate humor as hair and cape go full blast.

Choose other examples you like from books to illustrate line and ask the children to draw a favorite subject (an animal, perhaps), concentrating in their minds on the line.

Rhythm:

Edward Degas, *The Rehearsal*

Leslie Brooke, *Johnny Crow's Garden*

Show how the rhythm of dance in the two pictures is conveyed by line and color so that it seems to be musical. The children can see how this helps to express a nineteenth-century quality of formality and elegance, too. Contrast and compare the two pictures--or painters.

Ask a child to pose doing a dance step or a yoga pose and let the others see how rhythmically they can render the pose. Then have a volunteer show and explain his or her picture. Let the model draw while another child poses.

Ask the children to look around during the week and find rhythmic poses in animals, traffic in the streets, or dance class and, if they want to, sketch some of these. Suggest a sketch book to work in now and keep, too.

3. Texture and Architectural Design

Ask who sketched during the week and then show and talk about their works. Let the children comment on the pictures and share experiences from the week. Introduce texture: What is it in painting? Can it exist in drawing? Ask them. Show some examples.

Texture:

William Turner, *Snowstorm*

Antonio Frasconi, *See Again, Say Again* books

The children can see how the paint is used to create the actual feeling of the storm in the Turner. What would it be like to put their hand right into it? In the Frasconi the watercolors suggest heat, dark, cold, contrast, stone, grass, and hills: each is touchable. Why? Show other examples and contrast a historical understanding of textures, different for different periods.

Architectural Design:

Michelangelo, *The Delphic Sibyl*

Nicholas Sidjakov, *Baboushka*

Talk about how formal design shows itself in these two pictures--the heavy sculptural quality of Michelangelo building heavy, formal relationships, the graceful counterpoint of shapes in Baboushka's kitchen giving a solid skeleton to Sidjakov's design.

4. Detail and Relationship

Detail:

Gentile da Fabriano, *The Adoration of the Magi*

Ellen Raskin, *Nothing Ever Happens on My Block*

Ask the children, one by one, to share specific details that they see. Make a long list for them on a roll of newsprint and pin it up on the wall. Have them picka detail and make a new picture equally detailed. When they are through, they can volunteer to show and talk about the pictures.

Relationship:

Thomas Hogarth, *Marriage à la Mode*

Maurice Sendak, *Zlateh the Goat* by I. B. Singer

Show the pictures, stopping after the first one to ask the children what they think the relationship between husband and wife is--between servant and master? How does Hogarth do it? Ask them what they think about the picture and what it means. The gentle Zlateh: how does Sendak convey both compassion and a sense of strain? Is that what the children see in the relationship?

Ask the children to draw a picture representing a kind of relationship (a chair and a table is good enough) so they can see for themselves how to create that feeling.

This is the last workshop. Review with the children what they've learned about the elements of art. Tape up a display of the pictures and sketches they have drawn to illustrate these elements. Show it in the children's room as an exhibit for a few weeks.

5. Visiting Day

When children come in, introduce the museum or gallery or bookstore you plan for them to visit. On arrival, before they go in, tell them a little about what they'll see--not history, but the feeling of the paintings--the use of light, for instance--or the actual things the people will be doing. This leads to historical understanding later.

After looking for a satisfying length of time, reassemble and ask the children to relate what they've seen to what they did in the first four workshops. How did the museum pictures differ from their work? In a historical sense, in a technical sense, in relation to the medium the artist used? Select one picture all the group remembers and single out its geometrical shapes, lines, and colors. Remind them they have been doing this themselves.

Note: "A Workshop in Book Creation," found in the Story chapter, would also be appropriate for introducing children to art.

Dance

A library should learn to dance.

Starting with the foundations and establishing a pas de deux with the stacks, the children's librarian should dance out the door, a Pied Piper leading the children en grand chêne.

Traditionally, the children's room has not encouraged dance, because quietness and books did not seem the right ambience for action, movement, and excitement. But actually the children's room is exactly the right place to establish a bridge between the dance world and the interested and talented children who would like to know about it. Through demonstrations, films, records, talks, posters, and books we can introduce them to all the richness they may experience by following our piper and joining the parade. Child, librarian, and local dancers will be our production staff. Here they have an opportunity to meet, learn, and exchange energy in our new setting for dance.

A way to conduct this parade, in a room supposedly given over to quiet work, is by using the materials at hand selectively, and the first of these I think of is the live demonstration. For children, to whom movement is a matter of spontaneous combustion, a must from infancy, the live demonstration will ignite their imaginations and give dance forms life in their minds. And everywhere--in the city, in small towns, and in county seats-- there are dancers who represent the various dance traditions: modern, ethnic, mime, and ballet. If asked, they may be glad to come to the library to show the children how to do it, and explain how to get started in classes. In performing and answering questions they will give an invaluable sense of immediacy to the children.

This is important because children's way of grasping dance is directly through their bodies--through rhythm, music, and movement. Watching someone in person create meaning as he or she moves through space is to catch excitement because it reminds children of themselves, skipping, jumping, climbing, and running.

Along the same lines and as a foundation workshop, yoga is a quiet available discipline and a constructive body vocabulary. Either the children's librarian or a teacher in the community can lead a simple informal workshop that gives children a chance to become a bird, a frog, or a tree, and through these *asanas*, or poses, learn some basic movements that act as a natural bridge to dance.

For exploring the dance literature itself, our libraries are rich in resources; our books, both adult and children's, our records, and our films provide a generous compendium of materials to introduce the world of the dance. Folk dance, modern dance, and ballet in all forms have been written about, chronicled musically on records, and photographed on film and video.

In addition, for exhibit and display, we have available the prints, posters, and photographs with which artists through the ages have recorded dance and dancers, their masks and festivals. Using these for workshops will bring life and color to the room and pull the dance right in with them. But before considering workshops and some books, recordings, and films useful for introducing dance, I'd like to give a brief sketch of dance history to set the scene.

Long ago, in the dawn of the world, people and animals and plants were very close to one another. Human beings stalked and crouched and climbed and ran just as the animals did.

The first dances of the community were practical and charismatic--to bring rain, bestow fertility, celebrate weddings, and mourn deaths. Dancers expressed themselves through mime in story or gesture or abstractly through a direct, physical expression of ideas and feelings. Music was rhythmically percussive and melodically static and was accompanied by a little chanting. All people danced, losing self-consciousness, freeing themselves as they became storks and snakes, swaying and stamping, telling the story, getting the animals' power. And around the world, dances of the creeper bird, the turtle, and the butterfly brought beauty, strength, and lightness to their mimes.

Then, as dance began to develop from a total community ritual to a more formal structure, some began to stand out: one or two gifted males, adept in the use of masks, began to dominate. At their lead, the shaman, the gifted and charismatic one, masked and powerful, led the choral dancers in lines and rounds, adapting the qualities of the animals or plants as symbols that worked power into the occasion. He danced out the subconscious fears and struggles of the community and the community danced with him, hypnotically, youth and age together in their mimetic celebration.

As centuries passed, the dancers still danced their eternal round of life and death, of sun to dark, of ancestors and rebirth through the spirits of plants and animals, but the early community expressions sharpened in focus. In the ancient world repetition had polished expression into a perfect dance-calligraphy, crystallizing in India by the eighth century B.C., surviving exquisitely in present-day Japan.

In the Mediterranean, a sophisticated expression of community dance evolved that further separated the audience and the performer; the dancer's role moved to a distance. Graceful adaptations of animalistic poetic forms became entertainment as individuals led the dance of life's journey. Lute and lyre played and the chorus chanted the story, criticizing, reviling, foretelling.

The festivals of primitive times metamorphosed into the Bacchanalian rites, the Dionysian catalysts of ecstasy danced by the satyr-nymphs in the Mediterranean springs of Crete and the Mycenaean world and later in the wider world of the Greeks.

Then, through early centuries and into the dark ages of the Christian era, the great split between the sacred and secular expression of life occurred. The European church rigidified, slowing down dance expression severely, the stately priest-shaman hardly moving, the young male chorus chanting organum and plainchant in severe, archaic fourths and fifths.

In the town, the folk danced as they had always danced, from generation to generation, developing slowly, varying little, celebrating their festivals in the round of their year. By the fourteenth century coupling and individuation were becoming important, and countries were evolving personal, national styles, the flamenco in Spain, pavane and galliard in France, saltarello and ballata in Italy. The charismatic dance survived in the Saint Vitus' dance, a bizarre expression of the Bacchanalian rites, danced to exorcise the plague. In style a welding was going on of the extroverted and mimetic, and the introverted and abstract modern dance was being born.

From town to town people were connected and informed by the travelers, the troubadours and trouvères, singers and storytellers who brought the news. The jongleur, their dancing brother, told his tales with mime and acting as well as singing, entertaining at court and castle and in the towns.

At the European court, as the year 1400 approached, a secondary split was occurring. The courtly dances, danced by lords and ladies for their amusement, were developing into the stately sexual refinements of the pavane and galliard, on one hand, and modest descendants of the wild stamping fertility dances, the estampie and allemande on the other.

Through the use of these courtly dances, in the fifteenth century, emerged the first tentative groupings that would become our ballet. For the first time the dances of the folk, the acting of the mime, and the leadership of the shaman merged in the artist's mind for the sole purpose of public entertainment. Ballet absorbed the traditions of image and mime, of individual and festival, thus beginning its movement toward the rich center of dance as we know it today.

The integration of sacred and secular traditions in music and dance flowered in the fifteenth century in Italy. This was a distant cousin of vaudeville called a "court entertainment" and consisted of loosely shaped skits and turns, set to the music of a formalized sequence of refined folk dances, later crystallizing into the suite. In clear, well-established sections, the suite was a compendium of short intra-European forms that composers conveniently tailored to fit the evening's entertainment. Lengthening here, taking a tuck there, they were expert arrangers.

Beginning with the landmark performance of the *Ballet de la Riene* in Italy in 1581 under the sponsorship of Catherine de Médicis, the courtly entertainment grew during the baroque period to become the court ballet in France and in England, the great Elizabethan masque. The epitome of the evolution of dance and musical tradition, these forms used everyone's talents. In England Ben Jonson wrote the scripts, Inigo Jones designed sets, and Matthew Locke and Henry Purcell wrote the music; in France, flowering under Louis XIV's patronage, the court ballet integrated the masterpieces of Jean-Baptiste Lully, the composer, the plays of Molière, and the dances of Pierre Beauchamp, the king's dancing master. Pierre Rameau's book *The Dancing Master* appeared in 1725, codifying dance techniques that had expanded to suit the new form.

This wealth of activity was leading to the need for a study center, and when Louis XIV fell in love with the dance and founded the Royal Academy of Ballet, he was creating the first such educational institution for dancers in the West; it was after this that a professional quality began to infuse the court entertainments. Lully planned, supervised, and composed them, and for the first time, under this tutelage, female dance-artists began to appear in the corps de ballet. Then, as each art in an evolving curve seems to attract the perfect proponent, Jean-Georges Noverre appeared in France. The first serious choreographer, insisting on an unaffected directness and depth of inner expression in his dancers, he was a true genius, leading the way for fifty years, first in the Opéra-Comique in Paris and, then, later transfusing his art throughout the continent and in England.

His achievements led the way for the rise of star performers, and during the nineteenth century, ballet's development was marked by their pioneering efforts. Distinguished by the work of Marie Sallé, the late eighteenth century also brought Marie Camargo's original costuming and superb techniques. In the nineteenth century Marie Taglioni gave to technique a new lightness, a spiritual vision, and dancing on toe. Her rival, Fanny Elssler, with her earthy style and character dancing, brought humor and a robust quality. Ballet was becoming an important art in itself, detaching itself from the court ballets of the past. In the nineteenth century dance gradually assumed a depth of expressive power through these gifted artists, as it grew simpler in design and more natural in its movement.

Not so visible as the virtuosi, but equally important in determining romantic style, was the writing of Théophile Gautier, craftsman and poet-leader in the French literary community. With his work *Giselle*, danced by Taglioni in 1832, the romantic period found the masterpiece that would set the artistic mood for decades: a grand design encompassing a virtuosic role. Within, an aesthetic philosophy was developing that expressed a natural mysticism, pondering the duality of animal and spirit in humanity, and worshiping the lyric beauty of woman. *Giselle* was the beginning of this rich, fruitful period in history. In Italy Salvatore Viganò was restoring the art of the mime to dance, intensifying the story by integrating it with the ballet. His choreo-drama foreshadowed the twentieth century.

Folk dancing in this century was the natural form for most people, and it had by this time, become quite decorous. People danced together in couples and the art of "ballroom" dancing was on the rise. The waltz, polka, czardas, polonaise, and march dominated the popular scene, and they were commonly used, also, by the ballet composers for their dramatic accompaniments. Subtly, the ballet scores turned out by prolific dance-suite composers such as Adolphe Adam (*Giselle*) and Leon Mincus, became infused with these dances, leaving behind the rather stiff, formal expressions of the previous period. The "mad" dance, the dance of the fools, was dying out, with the exception of the morris dancers in England. In the West these strolling players guaranteed us the continuance of a vital tradition--the antihero and skeptic, thus providing that germ of creative originality that infuses chaos with avant-garde "sense."

Then, rather abruptly, in the mainstream of ballet tradition, a major change took place in the last third of the nineteenth century: ballet became centered in St. Petersburg, the czarist capital of Russia, and the era of the Russian Imperial Ballet began. The catalyst of change this time was Marius Petipa, the great French teacher and dancer who was imported to the court. Uniquely building on the strong scaffolding of his predecessor, Charles-Louis

Didelot, over the years he provided the foundations of twentieth-century ballet, contributing *Sleeping Beauty* and *Swan Lake,* and establishing and running the royal ballet school. He set the pace for a century of distinguished work first at the Russian court and then in Europe, England, and America. Increasingly, during these years, scores by contemporary composers were being commissioned, heralding the blossoming of music for serious dance that has marked the twentieth century.

In the golden age of ballet the intuitive Michel Fokine forced a reevaluation of technique as Noverre had before him. He insisted on a true inner source for expression, and by allowing the rounded curves and extensions forbidden before and using music of excellence, music borrowed from the classic literature as well as that specially composed for the occasion, Fokine made his influence broad and far-reaching. His magical dances found life under the charismatic hand of Serge Diaghilev, master producer, and included *Petrouchka, Scheherazade,* and *Les Sylphides.* They were central to the wealth of talent in dance, music, and art brought together and paraded around the world in the Diaghilev Ballet. The twenty-five years of influence of the Diaghilev Ballet would leave the art of dance noticeably, permanently changed: musically, by the use of original scores by living composers such as Stravinsky and Prokofiev; in dance by the encouragement of experiment in form, the avant-garde, as in *Le Train bleu* of Bronislawa Nijinska; the discovery and use of dancers of outlandish talent, such as Vaslav Nijinsky, Anna Pavlova, and Fokine himself; and in art by Léon Bakst's beautiful erotic sets and costumes and the cubist originality and iconoclastic humor of Pablo Picasso. Under Diaghilev's serendipitous and powerful hand they defined the world of ballet.

These years reflected a tendency of dance style to turn away from ordinary life and people toward a sophisticated, sometimes almost epicene, expression. Then, suddenly, a strong revolt among certain dancers occurred that pulled dance expression back into a direct personal statement.

This time the shadow of dissent lay across the tough, earthy work of western America where a longing for a freer, more natural expression was being born. In Isadora Duncan's Greek-influenced, barefoot dances, and later in the oriental style of Ruth St. Denis and in Ted Shawn's exploration of American roots a new counterculture dance movement was emerging. Through their genius and unrelenting hard work their own students, Martha Graham, Doris Humphrey, and others, gave to modern American dance the form as we know it today: a dance of the earth, not escaping from it but exploring it, devoid of trappings and artificiality, danced with natural movements by a body not constricted by toe shoes and eighteenth-century techniques, danced in equality by men and by women.

Within the ballet, with the settling of the Russian ballet in New York in 1933 some years after the Russian Revolution, a slow blending of traditional dance and avant-garde modern dance began, which today can be seen in the major contemporary ballets of Gerald Arpino, Jerome Robbins, Arthur Mitchell, and Agnes de Mille, among others.

America has become the center of the dance world and the scene remains lively: new forms and techniques are continually emerging, some ephemeral, others more permanent; a burgeoning ethnic ballet, as epitomized by Alvin Ailey and Arthur Mitchell, flourishes as does the tradition of antitradition--witty, avant-garde choreography as permitted by Merce Cunningham and his group; technical wizardry, using all the extraordinary possibilities of modern technology has become important, particularly as shown by the company of Alwin Nikolais; and, always at the center, the strong traditional ballet companies in New York, epitomized by George Balanchine and the New York City Ballet.

In our grass-roots tradition, forms from the street like hip-hop and breakdance contribute idioms to dance, and in popular theater, in musical plays like *Oklahoma, West Side Story,* and *A Chorus Line,* dance has assumed a tradition of its own, vital to the storytelling and to its inner meaning.

For all these diverse forms there is music: new music of distinction, classic scores of older composers, rock music, folk music, electronic music, and, sometimes, no music at all. Starting with Michel Fokine's use of borrowed scores for dance, and Diaghilev's commissioning of new music, dance music has become a strong tradition, an inspiration to dancers and composers, alike, affording a new source of musical expression.

So has the dance evolved, slowly and powerfully, begun in history as a spontaneous expression of joy and need, working its way through the church and the courts of kings, to find a rich, theatrical new life in the art of our own day.

BIBLIOGRAPHIC ESSAY

For introducing this rich tradition I'd like to start with a handful of books on dance that set the scene for adults. Many of them are usable with children and the subjects are mirrored later in books for them. A few histories, handbooks, biographies, dictionaries, and photostudies are mentioned here, many with outstanding photographs.

Beginning our bibliographic tour is Curt Sachs's *World History of Dance,* a foundation work on the development of dance, concentrating on the early folk forms, and showing how they express the real need of people for sexual expression, ritual, magic, and celebration. Then, in a grand sweep, he traces their growth through the primitive world to theater dance in China, ballet in France, and modern dance in America. In contrast, Walter Sorrell's *Dance through the Ages* is a slide show, a readable visualization of the slow evolution of the dances of the world's peoples.

Spicing the historical pot are fascinating documents like Jean-Georges Noverre's *Letters on Dancing and Ballet* (c. 1760), impassioned views on the importance of the inner world to a dancer, and Pierre Rameau's *Le Maître à dancer* of 1725, a priceless handbook of dance forms and ballet positions written in a witty, opinionated style. In addition, for browsing and display I found some cheerful companions to the times of the nineteenth century in the old Victorian mellowed-out volumes about dance that line the shelves of some of our older libraries, with pictures and illustrations or daguerreotypes which give pleasure and insight to the period.

There are many histories of specific forms that are excellent, like Joan Lawson's *History of Ballet and Its Makers,* which chronicles the development of ballet in England; Cyril Beaumont's *The Complete Book of Ballets,* in which the grand old English balletomane discusses the productions of the great period ballets with loving authority; and George Balanchine's *Complete Stories of the Great Ballets* which gives synopses of works up to 1970 with an interesting emphasis on music and ensemble.

In warm, familiar style Walter Terry, New York dance critic for many years, traces modern dance history in *The Dance in America,* and a fascinating companion to it is Louis Horst's *Modern Dance Forms in Relation to the Other Arts.* For fifty years an active composer-performer, Horst was the musical pioneer of the modern dance movement, and his original mind explores its various styles and forms in these unusual essays.

Contemporary essays on dance can offer valuable insight, too, and in *The Dance Has Many Faces* Walter Sorrell gives us a compendium of writing by dancers, choreographers, and critics of the twentieth century. In contrast to the faded-flower charm of his writing are the insightful, intellectual *Afterimages* of Arlene Croce, at present dance critic for the *New Yorker* magazine. She is a gifted writer, and a whole world of contemporary dance and dances seems to spring to view under her pen.

As to the choreographers themselves, most "wrote" their dances, not books, but there are exceptions. *The Notebooks of Martha Graham* explores poetically the process of creation, bringing plots to life and charting dance movements with a clarity of detail that exposes the gigantic task of the choreographer in trying to achieve meaningful self-expression. Doris Humphrey, in *The Art of Making Dances*, sets the reader on the path of understanding the development of choreography in a straightforward detailed study.

Personal history is important, too, and autobiography gives a special quality of light to the understanding. Michel Fokine, the bringer of emotive gesture to classical ballet, gives an intimate, gossipy account of his life and times with the Diaghilev Ballet in his *Autobiography*, and Irene Rogers writes touchingly of her years as *A Duncan Dancer*, describing the beginnings of modern dance in America. Katherine Dunham, in *Touch of Innocence*, gives a painful account of how she wrought success from a deprived and unrelentingly stressful childhood in the South, and Agnes de Mille's *Dance to the Piper* is an important book, a liquid, absorbing chronicle of her path from gifted childhood to successful adult. The endless task of work, of perseverance under stress, of balanced power in the struggle is shared by them all, though the stories differ so much.

Another mode of presentation that is crucial to a grasp of dance for adult and child equally is photographs, which along with demonstration and autobiography are essential stepping-stones to understanding. Adult photography books of dance are beautiful, and some can be found in almost all libraries. For display they can provide illumination and be a solid teaching guide. Several of these are noted in the bibliography at the close of the chapter, but I will list here three outstanding ones: Jack Anderson's *Dance*, for instance, is a unique study of history of dance, both in color and in black and white, through paintings, masks, and photographs of ancient rites. Richard Philip's *Danseur: The Male in Ballet* could be an inspiration to boys who are wary of the dance world because they have heard rumors of male effeminacy. Original and strong in image, the book explores the history of the male role in dance. Finally, in *The Dancer's Image*, Walter Sorrell highlights dance history through photographs of the painters, set designers and costumers who have been important to it. These speak directly to our understanding, illuminating design and clarifying movement.

Less glamorous but essential companions on our tour are the handbooks, encyclopedias, teaching guides, and bibliographies that are the backbone of the reference shelf. Reflecting a contemporary surge of interest in dance, there are some new, lively handbooks including the *Illustrated Ballet Dictionary* with definitions of dance for children.

Books that seem indispensable start with Anatole Chujoy's *The Dance Encyclopedia,* an exhaustive survey, including forms of dance, short biographies of famous dancers and companies, and the literature of dance. Written by experts, with brief histories of various kinds of dance, it was brought up to date in 1978 and includes entries on dance education.

There are several useful dictionaries like *The Concise Oxford Dictionary of Ballet* (1972), especially comprehensive, and G. G. Naffe's *Dictionary of the Dance,* which emphasizes folk and ethnic history and includes geographical indexes.

For anyone doing research or looking for additional materials on dance, the *Bibliographic Guide to Dance* (1975 and annually thereafter) is especially useful, being a unique catalog of each year's additions to the dance collection of the New York Public Library, a formative resource.

Reference books dealing with presentation of dance technique include the valuable *Book of Ballet* by Genevieve Guillot and Gus Giordano's *Anthology of American Jazz.* The first book diagrams dance technique in handbook form in an exhaustive study of leaps, steps, positions, and turns, and Giordano chronicles jazz in history, including many photographs and a teaching section with steps in diagrams.

Finally, an unusual contribution, Terri Loren's *The Dancer's Companion: The Indispensable Guide to Getting the Most out of Dance Classes* is an enthusiastic work for the young dancer by a dance education expert. She describes varieties of dance, how to select one, the special benefits of each, and what to wear to class.

A little book by Leon Harris, *The Russian Ballet School,* is a study of their curriculum, life-style and training done clearly and well in a mixed format of works and photographs. It would be suitable for both younger and older children and, would be interesting to pair with a videotape, the beautiful *Children of Theater Street.*

An outstanding book on ballet and modern ballet for young adults or younger balletomanes is Agnes de Mille's *To a Young Dancer: A Handbook for Dance Students.* It takes up where the technical books leave off, discussing the problems facing the beginning student/dancer, aspects of performance, ballet lessons, inner attitude, technical progress, and choreography. The stress is on that concept of inner discipline and creative perseverance that mark the serious artist, becoming for him or her the golden thread. De Mille writes direct, compelling prose, bending her years of professional experience to a minute dissection of the daily problems faced in the pursuit of a dance career.

Synopsizing the great ballets of history are quite a few picture books, of which the best is Donna Diamond's treatment of *Swan Lake,* by Peter Ilich Tchaikovsky. The story is told in a contemplative, serious way, sympathetically accompanied by her evocative and sensitive drawings. These are done in such a way as to lead one directly into the heart of the dance, into Odette-Odile's joy and despair. *Swan Lake* would make a good read-aloud introduction to a child's first ballet. Others of this genre seem to tend toward distinguished drawing marred by a trivial, sentimental text. *Swan Lake,* adapted by Eriko Kishida and illustrated by Shigen Hatsuyama, and *Giselle,* by Violette Verdy with Marcia Brown's expressive woodcuts, typify these.

Turning from ballet to folk dance, again there are few books. Elizabeth Burchard's classic study *Folk-Dances and Singing Games* is a wonderful old source book for folk-dance projects, which illustrates and carefully describes twenty-six dances from all over the world, with simple piano accompaniments. Jane Harris's *Dance a While* is a beautifully clear, well-organized handbook, including dance fundamentals, square dance, folk dance, and sections on teaching and recreational dance with an indispensable set of directions for many American dances. *Folk Dancing* by Lydia Anderson is more up-to-date than either of these but lacks the richness of character of the earlier works, acting more as a serviceable guide to all sorts of dances from the Far East as well as those from America and Northern Europe.

An odd work that falls into no particular category is Johana Exiner's *Teaching Creative Movement,* particularly useful for production and teaching. Starting from the child's experience and moving out, she explores how a teacher can guide a child into movement through body awareness, activities, space, time, and theme. Many illustrative photographs are included.

In modern dance Stephanie Sorine has contributed two appealing, useful photographic studies, *Imagine That! It's Modern Dance* and *That's Jazz,* which show children engaged in these contemporary forms. The large clear pictures and light captioned text offer a kind of mirror for them, forging a sense of kinship and possibility.

In the fiction collection one can find several books attempting to deal with the subject of becoming a dancer. So far they are disappointing. The very subject seems to induce in authors a style of tattered cliché and the sentimental, unrealistic point of view that often accompanies it. Streatfield's *Ballet Shoes,* Catherine Blanton's *Hold Fast to Your Dreams,* and the Zindels' *A Star for the Latecomer* are all, in one sense, the same book: young girl aspires, faces stiff competition, excels easily, goes forward rapidly despite dreadful problems courageously faced, and then fades into the plastic-pink sunset.

This kind of soap opera is apt to raise high expectations in someone who is then shocked and disappointed when the hard work, discipline, and real competition of the dance world become clear. Thus, the real thing, as presented in biography and autobiography, assumes great importance in proportion. By showing the actual steps along the way, a good writer lets glamorous unreality recede in the light of personal truth, leaving a valuable sense of distant but real possibility. When they are good reading, colorful and well written, good biographies can inspire children and still show a balanced view of the dancer's life.

Robert Maiorano's *Worlds Apart* is an excellent example. For many years a top dancer with the New York City Ballet, Maiorano's childhood was intense and colorful. Growing up in poverty, and the son of an ambitious, artistic mother, Maiorano faced daily anxiety on the streets and mockery from his peers for his dancing--and yet his inner life was rich and happy, his dancing ecstatic and successful. He is a gifted writer and evokes the very smells of his childhood Brooklyn, the pain of his sister's rebellion, the excitement and happiness of his dance career.

For younger children *Arthur Mitchell* by Tobi Tobias is well done, showing the great dancer's childhood environment minutely, warmly chronicling his difficult struggle to the top and, finally, his creation of the famous Dance Theater of Harlem. *African Rhythm, American Dance* is the biography of Katherine Dunhan. Terry Hernon glosses over a good deal of the pain and loneliness of Dunham's southern childhood, but her telling of the story of effort in the service of great talent, of fortitude in the struggle to develop it, is warm and sympathetic to children.

Agnes de Mille's *Dance to the Piper,* already reviewed, is an excellent choice for older boys and girls as well as adults. Her style is colorful and sympathetic and she has a way of presenting the depth of feeling involved in her work, the glamour of the life, her view of her own remarkable Hollywood family, and the homely details of the artist's life that is deeply engaging.

Finally, *Contribution of Women: Dance* by Carol Fowler is an attractively presented group of short biographies. In it she gives sketches of Isadora Duncan, Martha Graham, Agnes de Mille, Twyla Tharp, and Gelsey Kirkland. Children can identify with the informal presentations and imagine their own future possibilities through these well-presented stories.

A fresh approach to dance literature altogether is Helen Plot's *Untune the Sky,* poems from many periods and countries, which remind us of the essential personal experience of movement. These dance poems are young adult in orientation, useful as adjunct to a workshop, and can stimulate children to find their own poems about dancing or to write them. Then for pure subversion, try some preschool starters like Rachel Isadora's wonderful *Max* or *My Ballet Class,* or Elaine Edelman's *Boom-de-Boom,* picture stories that give a beginning look at dance a certain magic.

Through these excellent books, children can begin to feel the history of dance as a living thing. *The Dance of Africa, Worlds Apart, A Very Young Dancer, Swan Lake*--these kinds of books bring past and present vividly into the child's mind and help set a firm background for engagement.

Among the books published for children is Arnold Haskell's *Wonderful World of Dance,* in which he attempts to bring the dances of the world to children, as Curt Sachs did for adults. He takes primitive dances from their origins through their development and formulation into the mainstream of contemporary movements. His writing is cheerful and readable, transmitting information clearly, and he includes many photos, prints, and drawings. A comprehensive glossary in simple terms is a valuable addition.

Melvin Berger's *World of Dance* is a complement to it and a refreshing treatment of dance forms. In an easy informal style he takes regional forms of dance and gives an idea of their basic composition and style. Greek, Chinese, primitive, ballet, modern, and social dancing are all part of this attractive history.

The exploration of primitive music, itself, hasn't gone very far for children, but Lee Warren attempts it in *The Dance of Africa*. She tells a little of the ritual, recreational, ceremonial voice of the dance heritage and also shows the tribal use of masks and diagrams a few dances. Along with this, *Dancing Masks of Africa* by Christine Price is a rhapsodic, poetic celebration of masks, short, lively, and poignant. It could be used with down-to-earth factual material or with a film as part of an ethnic dance workshop.

At the roots of dance technique is pantomime, and there are a few books on that for children. Supposedly for little ones, three to five, but probably for all of us, George Mendoza's *Marcel Marceau Alphabet Book* shows us vivid photographs of Marceau miming his way through the alphabet in an elegant revelation of the essence of his art. For older boys and girls Douglas Hint and Kari Hunt's *Pantomime, the Silent Theater* is a model of simplicity and clarity of presentation. In a brief, well-organized history of theater, the authors define the silent art, exploring it thoroughly from the Greeks to the days of silent films. Along with it, an in-depth technical study for children is *Exploring Mime* by Mark Stotzenberg. This is a careful, well-photographed guide, minutely tracing the movements and sequence of movements involved in mime technique. "The Robot," "The Mechanical Person," and "The Wall" are among the personas explored in an easy, engaging style.

Another source discipline for dance is yoga, and there are some good books on it to show the children: Elaine Landon's *Yoga for You* is a gentle, clear study for ages nine and up. She leads the asanas, and includes a chapter on meditation and diet. For younger children *Be a Frog, a Bird or a Tree* by Rachel Carr is a simple, boldly presented series modeled by a child, easily introduced and emulated.

In ballet we find the star of the dance books for children: Noel Streatfield's *Young Person's Guide to Ballet* (1978). It was a relief to find this painstakingly researched book, well presented in a book design that combines drawn figures illustrating positions and steps with verbal description and appropriate photographs. The historical sequence is clear and the punctuation provided by prints of old drawings brings life to the account.

Mrs. Streatfield understands and is sympathetic to children, writing directly to them, and the book has impact: technical expertise, imaginative book design, and a lucid style.

Equally good, although more traditional, is Anthony Dufort's *Ballet Steps: Practice to Performance,* an exhaustive guide to ballet positions, the vocabulary of dance. It is originally illustrated by a generous accompaniment of carefully rendered drawings, with occasional set-in photographs. Well organized, thorough, and serious, the book is written in engaging prose, well adapted to ages nine and up.

A companion in contemporary excellence is *A Very Young Dancer,* welcome exponent of the expressive teaching power of photography for children. Photographed at George Balanchine's School of American Ballet by Jill Krementz, it tells the story of ten-year-old Stephanie, how she started in dance, what her day is like, how she feels, immersed in the world of dance and dancers. The human feeling of the book is as welcome as the realistic attitude that pervades the absorbing story.

For older children, Suzanne Merry, a New York dance critic, has brought an incisive professional skill to the study of a young dancer's day-to-day life from the time of her leaving her native western home through her studies in New York and then her work with the Joffrey Ballet II, in the city and on tour. *Dancer's* photographs are perfectly meshed with the story which is told in clear, warm prose, and they are very revealing of what it takes to become a dancer and the homely details of the daily life.

There are quite a few older how-to books on how to do it and these are frequently asked for by curious children as an introduction to technical training in ballet. *Ballet for Beginners* by Nancy Draper and Margaret Atkinson is a clear, flexible arrangement of photos and description, and there is a brief history, some short biographies, and synopses of famous ballets. More recent and very welcome after the early "stiff and proper" books on ballet is *I Can Dance* by Brian Bullard and David Charlsen. Accompanied in the current style by matching illustrative photographs, positions, tendus, stretches, and combinations are described in easy narrative style. This is an excellent guide for an interested child and a possible handbook for use with the videotape *Video Dictionary of Classical Ballet.*

Although there are no periodicals on dance especially for them, children may enjoy browsing through the adult magazines for the photographs, star profiles, and so on. The most readily available of several possibilities is the *American Dance* magazine, a cheerful catch-all loaded with photographs, which gives a lively look at the scene around us and includes reviews, classified ads, educational listings, and an annual publication in addition. More scholarly are *Dance Chronicle,* a social survey published in New York, and the now-defunct *Dance Observer,* Louis Horst's magazine of modern dance published between 1933 and 1964. There are many others, and children may especially like the old playbills and striking accompanying photographs of *Dance World,* an American annual including brief biographical sketches.

Next is our magic resource: the paintings, prints, and posters for display that please our eye and can cause a child's imagination to light up, the perfect setting for a dance workshop. To find these, the children's librarian can explore the collection of the library to locate the books and prints of painters and sculptors who have interpreted dance worlds in art. Seurat, Degas, Matisse, Toulouse-Lautrec, Picasso, and Goya are outstanding, and there are works of great beauty by many individual, lesser-known artists.

Books that set out to present a history of dance in art, however, are few and disappointing. Exceptional is *Dancing in Prints,* a sensitive selection by the New York Public Library's Dance Collection staff, a portfolio of etchings and engravings from 1634 to 1870, impish in feeling, exquisite and airy in expression. Elli Lohse-Claus's *The Dance in Art* includes forty-six plates of sculpture, painting, and frescos from all over the world, from celebrative Eskimos to Greek lovers, but it is marred by poor printing and is not child-sympathetic in approach. It might be useful historically or to suggest further access of approach in the library itself.

A helpful bibliography is Virginia Carter Bail's *Dance in Art,* a selected list of representational paintings, drawings, and other art forms, published by New York University, and a beautiful book in paperback is *One Hundred Years of Dance Posters* by Walter Terry and Jack Rennert, fresh in design and enjoyable for adult and child alike.

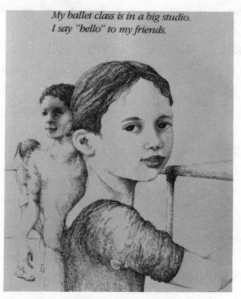

Illustration from *My Ballet Class.* © 1980 by Rachel Isadora. By permission of Greenwillow Books (a division of William Morrow).

71

BIBLIOGRAPHY

General

Anderson, Lydia. *Folk Dancing.* New York: Franklin Watts, 1981.

Berger, Melvin. *The World of Dance.* New York: S. G. Phillips, 1978.

Breakdancing: *Mr. Fresh and the Supreme Rockers.* New York: Avon Books, 1984.

Bullard, Brian. *I Can Dance.* New York: G. P. Putnam & Sons, 1979.

Burchard, Elizabeth. *Folk-Dances and Singing Games.* New York: G. Schirmer, 1909, 1938.

Carr, Rachel. *Be a Frog, a Bird, a Tree.* New York: Doubleday, 1973.

De Mille, Agnes. *To a Young Dancer: A Handbook for Dance Students, Parents and Teachers.* Boston: Little, Brown, 1960.

Draper, Nancy, and Margaret F. Atkinson. *Ballet for Beginners.* New York: Knopf, 1951.

Dufort, Anthony. *Ballet Steps: Practice to Performance.* New York: Clarkson N. Potter, 1985.

Fowler, Carol. *Dance: Contributions of Women.* Minneapolis: Dillon Press, 1979.

Freeman, Mae Blacker. *Fun with Ballet.* New York: Random House, 1952.

Hammond, Mildred. *Square Dancing Is for Me.* Minneapolis: Lerner Publishing, 1983.

Hanson, Rosanna. *The Fairytale Book of Ballet.* New York: Grosset & Dunlap, 1980.

Harnan, Terry. *African Rhythm-American Dance: A Biography of Katherine Dunham.* New York: Knopf, 1974.

Harris, Leon A. *The Russian Ballet School.* New York: Atheneum, 1970.

Haskell, Arnold. *The Wonderful World of Dance.* Garden City, N.Y.: Doubleday, 1969.

Howard, Vernon. *Pantomimes, Charades and Skits.* New York: Sterling Publishing, 1974.

Hunt, Douglas, and Kari Hunt. *Pantomime: The Silent Theater.* New York: Atheneum, 1964.

Jaffe, Evan. *Illustrated Ballet Dictionary.* New York: Harvey House, 1979.

Landon, Elaine. *Yoga for You.* New York: Messner, 1977.

Lawson, Joan. *Ballet Stories.* New York: Mayflower Books, 1978.

Loren, Teri. *The Dancer's Companion: The Indispensable Guide to Making the Most out of Dance Classes.* New York: Dial, 1970.

Lowe, Jacqueline, and Charles Selber. *The Language of Slow Dancing.* New York: Charles Scribner's Sons, 1980.

Maiorano, Robert. *Worlds Apart.* New York: Coward, McCann & Geoghegan, 1980.

Mara, Thalia, and Lee Wyndham. *First Steps in Ballet.* Garden City, N.Y.: Doubleday, 1955.

Mendoza, George. *Marcel Marceau Alphabet Book.* Photographs by Milton H. Greene. Garden City, N.Y.: Doubleday, 1970.

Plotz, Helen. *Untune the Sky.* New York: Thomas Y. Crowell, 1957.

Price, Christine. *Dancing Masks of Africa.* New York: Charles Scribner's Sons, 1975.

Sorine, Stephanie. *Imagine That! It's Modern Dance.* New York: Knopf, 1981.

_____. *That's Jazz.* New York: Knopf, 1982.

Stoltzenberg, Mark. *Exploring Mime.* New York: Sterling Publishing, 1979.

Streatfield, Noel. *A Young Person's Guide to Ballet.* London: Frederick Warne, 1978.

Terry, Walter. *Frontiers of Dance: The Life of Martha Graham.* New York: Thomas Y. Crowell, 1975.

Tobias, Tobi. *Arthur Mitchell.* Illustrated by Carole Byard. New York: Thomas Y. Crowell, 1975.

Verdy, Violette. *Giselle; or the Wilis.* Adapted from Théophile Gautier. Illustrated by Marcia Brown. New York: McGraw-Hill, 1970.

Wakenfield, Eleanor. *Folk-dancing in America.* New York: J. L. Pratt, 1966.

Warren, Lee. *The Dance of Africa.* Englewood Cliffs, N.J.: Prentice-Hall, 1972.

Picture Books about Dance

Ancona, George. *Dancing Is.* New York: Dutton, 1981.

Bornstein, Ruth. *The Dancing Man.* New York: Seabury, 1978.

Edelman, Elaine. *Boom-de-Boom.* New York: Pantheon, 1980.

Isadora, Rachel. Max. New York: Macmillan, 1976.

_____. *My Ballet Class.* New York: Greenwillow Books, 1980.

_____. *Opening Night.* New York: Greenwillow Books, 1984.

Maiorano, Robert. Backstage. Illustrated by Rachel Isadora. New York: Greenwillow Books, 1978.

Shannon, George. *Dance Away.* Illustrated by José Aruego and Ariane Dewey. New York: Greenwillow Books, 1982.

Wallace, Ian. *Chin Chiang and the Dragon's Dance.* New York: Atheneum, 1984.

CHRONOLOGICAL DISCOGRAPHY

Ethnic Music

Primitive Music of the World. 2-Folkways 4581.

Songs and Dances of Africa. Folkways 8852.

Drum, Chant, and Instrumental Music: Africa. Nonesuch 72073.

Dances of the World's Peoples:
    Balkans and Near East. Folkways 6501.
    Caribbean and South American. Folkways 6503.
    Turkey, Greece, Middle East. Folkways 6504.

Far East, India, Africa, the Americas, Continental Europe. Nonesuch
    Explorer Series H7-11.

Greece, Japan, Crete, Egypt

Gail Laughton: Harps of the Ancient Temples. Laurel 111.

Music for the Balinese Shadow Play. Nonesuch Explorer Series 72037.

Christian Era (to 1200 A.D.)

Gregorian Chants: Benedictine Monks (Luxembourg). Philips Sequenza
    6527073; TC 7311073.

Plainchant and Polyphony. Nonesuch 71312.

Schola Antiqua, Blackley--10th c. Liturgical Chant in Proportional Rhythm.
    Nonesuch 71348.

Early Music: Ars Antiqua. Telefunken 641928; TC 6-35010.

Middle Ages (1200-1400)

Troubadour and Trouvere. Russell Oberlin. EA12E.

*Antique Provençal Instruments: Instrumental and Troubadour 12th-14th
    Centuries.* Arion 90413.

Music of the Middle Ages. Lyrichord 785E.

Art of Courtly Love: 14th-early 15th. 3 vols. David Munrow. Seraphim
    SIC-6092.

History of Music: Middle Ages to Baroque. 3-Lyrichord 7278.

Music of the 100 Years War. Philips 85973.

Music of the Crusades. Argo ZRG-673.

Les musiciens de Provence: Medieval and Renaissance on Antique Instruments. Peters PLE-098.

Sacred music c. 1400. Telefunken 641221.

Late Medieval Music: 1300-1400. Pleiades 250.

Instruments of the Middle Ages and Renaissance. Angel SBZ-3810.

Medieval and Renaissance Sounds. Vols. 1-6. Musica Antiqua. Desto 7183, 7184, 7190, 7192, 7200, 7201; TC 47183, 47184, 47190, 47192, 47200, 47200.

Renaissance

Renaissance Dances. Odyssey 32160036; TC YT-60036.

Renaissance Festival Music. MLA 2511.

Sixteenth Century French Dance Music. Philips 6500293.

Sixteenth Century Italian Dance Music. Philips 6500102.

Dance Music of the Renaissance. Ragossnig, Ulsamer/Collegium. CD DG ARC 41594-2.

Dances of the Court and Villages: Sixteenth Century. Malgoire/Grand Écurie and La Chambre du Roy. Odyssey 34617; TC YT-34617.

To Entertain a King: Henry VIII. Argo ZRG-568.

Pleasures of the Court: Dances by Susato, Byrd, Dowland, and others. Angel S-36851.

Baroque (1600-1750)

Collections

Masque Music (Stuart). Nonesuch 71153.

Dance Music of the Early Baroque. Ragossnig (lute). DG ARC 2533150.

Dance Music of the High Baroque. DG ARC 2533172.

Dance Music of the Renaissance. DG ARC 2533111.

The High Renaissance. DG Archiv 14653.

Suites for Harpsichord. RNH 4057.

Bach, Johann Sebastian (1685-1750)

Suites for Orchestra. Marriner/Academy of St. Martin in the Field. 2-London 414248-1; TC 414248-2.

Suites for Lute. North (baroque lute). Amon Ra SAR-23; CD KTC-23; TC SARC-23.

Suites for Cello Unaccompanied. Casals (rec. 1936-39). 3-Angel 3786(m); Yo Yo Ma. 2-CBS CD M2K-37867.

Suite no. 2 for Flute and Strings. Galway/Solisti di Zagreb. RCA AGLI-5445; TC.

Couperin, Francois (1668-1733)

Concerts Royaux. A. and C. Nicolet (flutes), Holliger (oboe), Brandis (violin). DG 415785-1; TC 415785-4.

Gluck, Christoph Willibald (1714-1787)

Iphigenie en Aulide. Bavarian Orchestra and Chorus. 2-RCA ARL 2-1104.

Don Juan (ballet). Marriner/Academy of St. Martin-in-the-Fields. 2-London 1285.

Handel, George Frideric (1685-1759)

Harpsichord Music. Kipnis. Nonesuch 79031; CD 79032-2; TC 79037-4.

Terpsichore (ballet). Devos/Pasdeloup Orchestra. Nonesuch 71164.

Amaryllis Suite (ballet music from Handel operas, arranged by Sir Thomas Beecham). Menuhin/Royal Philharmonic. MCA-6186; CD MCAD-6186; TC MCAC-6186.

Locke, Matthew (1621/2-1677)

The Tempest (a masque). Hogwood/Academy of Ancient Music. Oiseau-Lyre OSLO-507.

Consort no. 6 for viols. New Music Quartet. Bartók 913(m).

Lully, Jean-Baptiste (1632-1687)

Le Triomphe de l'amour. Weissberg/Vienna Symphony. Audio-Fidelity 50079.

Alceste (1674). Malgoire/Grande Écurie and La Chambre du Roy. 3-CBS M3-34580.

Armide. Yakar, Gari, Vandersteene, Borst, Herreweghe/Royal Chapel Ensemble. 2-Erato 71530.

Purcell, Henry (ca. 1659-1695)

The Fairy Queen. Deller Consort. 3-Harmonia Mundi 231.

King Arthur (1691). Smith, Fisher, Priday, Stafford, Gardiner/English Baroque Soloists, Monteverdi Choir. 2-Erato 75127; TC.

Suites (Abdelazar, The Old Bachelor, The Gordian Knot Untied). Leppard/English Chamber Orchestra. CBS IM-36707; TC.

Rameau, Jean Philippe (1683-1764)

Anacreon (ballet). Christie/Ensemble "Les Arts Florissants." Harmonia Mundi 1090; TC 401090.

Le Temple de la gloire. Candide CE 31012.

Pièces de clavecin. Christie. 2-Harmonia Mundi 1120/1.

Classical (1750-1820)

Adam, Adolphe-Charles (1803-1856)

Giselle. Bonynge/Monte Carlo Opera Orchestra. 2-London 2226.

Giselle (suite). Martinon/Paris Conservatory Orchestra. Price-Less TC C 87743.

Auber, Daniel-François (1782-1871)

La Muette de Portici (1828) (ballet). Marco, Spadd/London Symphony. London 6923.

Beethoven, Ludwig van (1770-1827)

The Creatures of Prometheus (excerpts). Mehta/Israel Philharmonic. London 6660.

Contradances (12), G. 141. Marriner/Academy of St. Martin-in-the-Fields. Angel S-37044; TC.

Romantic (1820-1900)

Composer-Compilers

Drigo, Riccardo (1846-1930)

Les Millions d'Arlequin.

Minkus, Alois (Louis) (1826-1917)

Don Quixote. Lanchbery/Melbourne Orchestra. Angel S-37008.

Pugni, Caesare (1820-1870)

La Fille du marble (1847).

The Artist's Dream (1848).

Beginnings of Original Work

Delibes, Léo (1836-1891)

Coppélia (complete ballet). Bonynge/National Philharmonic. 2-London 414502-1; TC 414502-4.

Coppélia (suite). Ansermet/Orchestra of the Suisse Romande. London 6185.

Herold, Louis Joseph F. (1791-1833)

La Fille mal gardée. Lanchbery/Royal Opera House Orchestra. 2-London 410190-1; TC 410190-4.

Tchaikovsky, Piotr Ilyich (1840-1893)

Nutcracker, op. 71 (1892) (complete). Abravanel/Utah Symphony and Chorus. 2-Vanguard S-168/69; TC CSRV-168/69.

Nutcracker Suite. Bernstein/New York Philharmonic. CBS MY-37238; TC.

Sleeping Beauty (Petipa; 1890) (complete). Previn/London Symphony. 3-Angel AE-34442; TC.

Swan Lake (Petipa; 1895) (complete). Abravanel/Utah Symphony. 2-Vanguard S-223/4.

Swan Lake (excerpts). Karajan/Berlin Philharmonic. Angel S-35740.

Modern (1900-)

Chopin, Frederic (1810-1849)

Les Sylphides (Fokine; 1908). Karajan/Berlin Philharmonic. DG 136257.

Debussy, Claude (1862-1918)

Jeux (Nijinsky; 1912); *Prelude to the Afternoon of a Faun* (Nijinsky; 1912). Boulez/New Philharmonia Orchestra. CBS MY-37261; TC.

Prokofiev, Serge (1891-1953)

Pas d'acier (Massine; 1927).

Ravel, Maurice (1875-1937)

Daphnis and Chloe (Fokine; 1912) (complete). Boulez/New York Philharmonic. Columbia M-33523.

Rimsky-Korsakoff, Nikolai (1844-1908)

Scheherazade (Fokine; 1910). Stokowski/London Symphony. London 21005.

Rossini, Gioacchino (1797-1868)

La Boutique fantasque (Massine; 1919).

Satie, Erik (1866-1925)

Parade (Massine; 1917). Abravanel/Utah Symphony. 2-Vanguard C-10037/8; TC.

Stravinsky, Igor (1882-1971)

Firebird (Fokine; 1910). Ozawa/Boston Symphony. Angel CD CDC-47017.

Petrouchka (Fokine; 1911). Monteux/Paris Conservatory Orchestra. London TC 417037-4.

Le Sacre du printemps (Nijinsky; 1913). Boulez/French National Radio Orchestra. Nonesuch 71093.

Apollon Musagète (Balanchine; 1928). Ansermet/Orchestra of the Suisse Romande. London STS-15028.

Music Borrowed for Ballet from Classical Composers

Bartók, Béla (1881-1945)

Miraculous Mandarin (suite) (Strobach; 1927). Ozawa/Boston Symphony. DG 2530887.

Bizet, Georges (1835-1875)

Symphony no. 1 in C (Balanchine; 1948). Marriner/Acadamy of St. Martin-in- the-Fields. Argo ZRG-719.

Brahms, Johannes (1833-1897)

Liebeslieder Walzes (Balanchine; 1960). Guzeliman, Herrera/LA Vocal Arts Ensemble. Nonesuch 79008; CD 79008-2.

Britten, Benjamin (1913-1976)

Fanfare (Young Person's Guide to the Orchestra) (Robbins; 1953). Ormandy/Philadelphia Orchestra. Odyssey Y-34616; TC YT-34616.

Les Illuminations (Ashton; 1950). Harper, Marriner. Angel S-36788.

Chabrier, Emmanuel (1841-1894)

Bourrée fantasque (Balanchine; 1949). Bourgeot (piano). Coronet 1719.

Chausson, Ernest (1855-1899)

The Lilac Garden (Poème) (Tudor; 1951). Oistrakh (violin), /Moscow Radio Symphony. Melodiya/Angel S-40077.

Debussy, Claude (1862-1918)

Prelude to the Afternoon of a Faun (Robbins; 1953). Boulez/New Philharmonia Orchestra. Columbia MS-7361.

Druckman, Jacob (1928-)

Animus II. de Gaetani. CRI S-255.

Gluck, Christoph Willibald (1714-1787)

Orpheus and Euridice (Balachine; 1937). Horne, Verrett, Solti/Royal Opera House Orchestra, Covent Garden. 2-London 1285; Speiser, Gale, Baker, Leppard/London Philharmonic. 3-Erato 750422.

Ravel, Maurice (1875-1937)

Mother Goose Suite (Bolender; 1948). Boulez/New York Philharmonic.

La Valse (Nijinska; 1928 and Balanchine; 1951). Ansermet/Orchestra of the Suisse Romande. London STS-15092; CD 414046-2.

Shostakovitch, Dmitri (1906-1975)

Quattuor (String quartet no. 1) (d'Amboise; 1964). Gabrieli Quartet. London STS-15396.

Tchaikovsky, Piotr Ilyich

Serenade for Strings (Balanchine; 1935). Karajan/Berlin Philharmonic. DG 25321-2; CD 400038-2; TC 3302012.

Webern, Anton (1883-1945)

Episodes (Six Pieces) (Graham-Balanchine; 1959). Karajan/Berlin Philharmonic. 4-DG 423310-1.

Music Originally Scored for Modern Ballets

Bernstein, Leonard (1918-)

Fancy Free (Robbins; 1944). Bernstein/New York Philharmonic. 2-Columbia MG-32174; TC MT-6677.

Carter, Elliott (1908-)

The Minotaur (Taras; 1947).

Copland, Aaron (1900-)

Billy the Kid (Loring; 1938); *Rodeo* (de Mille; 1942). Bernstein/New York Philharmonic. Columbia MG 30071; TC MGT 30071.

Ellington, Duke (1899-1974)

The River (Ailey). Schuller/New England Conservatory Jazz Repertory Orchestra. Golden Grest 31041.

Gould, Morton (1913-)

Fall River Legend (de Mille; 1948). Mitropolous/New York Philharmonic. New World 253(m).

Hindemith, Paul (1895-1963)

Four Temperaments (Balanchine; 1946). Rosenberger, DePriest/Royal Philharmonic. Delos 25440; CD DCD-1066.

Macero, Teo (1925-)

Opus 65 (Sokolow; 1965).

Mayasumi, Toshiro (1929-)

Olympics (Arpino; 1966).

Prokofiev, Serge (1891-1953)

The Prodigal Son (Balanchine; 1950). Rozhdestvensky/USSR State Symphony. Vox Cum Laude 90936; TC.

Romeo and Juliet (Ashton; 1955). Solti/Chicago Symphony. London CD 410200-2; TC 410200-4.

Peter and the Wolf (Bolm; 1946). Karloff, Ormandy/Philadelphia Orchestra. RCA ARL1-2743.

Cinderella (Sakharov; 1945). Rozhdestvensky/Moscow. 2-Melodiya-Angel S-4102.

Schuman, William (1910-)

Undertow (Ashton; 1945). Levine/Ballet Theater Orchestra. New World 253(m).

Stravinsky, Igor (1882-1971)

Orpheus (Balanchine; 1948). Stravinsky/Chicago Symphony. Columbia MS-6646.

Appolon Musagète (Balanchine; 1937). Stravinsky/Chicago Symphony.

Thomson, Virgil (1986-)

Filling Station (Christiansen; 1938).

Walton, William (1902-)

Façade (Ashton; 1931). Sitwell, Prausnitz. Odyssey Y-32359(m).

Music Originally Scored for Modern Dance*

Barber, Samuel (1910-1981)

Medea's Meditation and Dance of Vengeance: Cave of the Heart (Graham; 1947). Schippers/New York Philharmonic. Odyssey Y-33230; TC YT-33230.

Britten, Benjamin (1913-1976)

String Quartet (Humphrey; 1953). Allegri Quartet. London STS-15303.

Cage, John (1912-)

Winter Music for 1-20 Pianos; Winterbranch (Cunningham). Flynn (4 piano version). Finnadair 9006.

*Although many scores have been commissioned for modern dance in recent years, few, if recorded at all, have remained in print: a search for these is indicated.

Copland, Aaron (1900-)

Appalachian Spring (Graham; 1944) (suite). Copland/London Symphony. 3-CBS D3M-33720.

Day on Earth (Piano Sonata) (Humphrey; 1947). Silverman (piano). Orion 7280; TC 691.

Feldman, Morton (1926-)

Summerspace (Cunningham; 1966).

Hopkins, Kenyon

Rooms (Sokolow; 1955).

Hovhannes, Alan (1911-)
  Circle (Graham; 1963).

Johnson, Hunter (1906-)
  Letter to the World (Graham; 1946).

FILMOGRAPHY-VIDEOGRAPHY

Films

Films are a natural, direct method of showing dance to children. Next to the live demonstration they best communicate the celebration of the body's play with space through time that is dance; colorful, alive, and absorbing.

Being such a recent art, and a recent edition to the archives, there are not a great many films of excellence for children, and these group themselves rather closely into those appropriate for small children, largely short fantasy and funny films, and those best suited to older boys and girls: clips of live performances, dances of the world's peoples, and more sophisticated fantasy. The tone of the films is artistic, movement as play, rather than historical or pedagogical, although there are exceptions.

Beginnings. 26 min. Color. Lightworks.

For children interested in ballet, this lively film, which combines interviews with students and faculty of the School of American Ballet and a New York City Ballet performance of *Coppelia,* is a satisfying blend of introduction to student life and actual performance.

A Chary Tale. 10 min. B/W International Film Bureau.

Norman McLaren's *A Chary Tale* is one of several of his short zany animations for the dance that draw children right into the center of his idea. Here a man and a "girlish" chair have a hilarious pas de deux of approach, resistance, innuendo, and respite that ends in a wild slapstick dance. The perfect example of dance as nonverbal communication and as comedy, *A Chary Tale* is also fun for children, who long to identify with a triumphant rebel.

Chinese Shadow Play. 10 min. Color. Pictura.

Chinese Shadow Play illustrates the use of mime in the service of drama, showing children how it works. The narrator tells of White Swan and Black Snake, ladies of ancient China, engaged in a tale of intrigue that is infused with a natural mysticism. As he speaks, the exquisite, paper-thin puppets act out the story as they are manipulated magically from behind. The mood is quiet, intense, and calm, with evocative color and music.

Karate. 10 min. Color. Pyramid.

Karate emphasizes karate as a nonviolent martial art and is sympathetic with Mitchell's thesis that dance is for boys and for men as well as girls. "The Way of the Empty Hand" has an expressive beauty that the pragmatic use of the technique cannot disguise. Despite the rather crude editing, the film's message of strength and beauty in movement is clear and unequivocal.

Matrioska. 5 min. Color. McGraw-Hill.

Matrioska concerns a whirring, turning, endearing family of archaic painted dolls, which emerge from their collective self to dance separately in a crude lively polka. A delicious sense of fun pervades their mischievous antics, obscuring the rather sophisticated dance techniques they are displaying: turns, jumps, holds, and so forth.

A Modern Ballet. 29 min. Color. I.U.

A Modern Ballet is for young adults or those children already fascinated with ballet. Put together colorlessly and a little stiffly by Martha Myers, a Smith College professor, it is a historical approach to the development of twentieth-century ballet as found in the dances of Anthony Tudor, the English choreographer. It is recommendable for the performance of Nora Kay: illustrating some of the developments in contemporary dance, she is so moving, and her technique and style so intense, that a didactic clarity is achieved, despite the slow pace and mildly self-conscious quality of the film.

Rhythmitron. 40 min. Color. Phoenix.

Rhythmitron, Arthur Mitchell's film showing the young dancers of his Dance Theatre of Harlem, is uniquely valuable in that it is a film manual of dance education, especially helpful to a teacher or librarian who has no access to a live demonstration. Showing the techniques of ballet step by step with engaging humor and superb technique, Mitchell radiates an infectious enthusiasm and expertise. Older children and young adults will be interested to find out what ballet students learn, what they do, and how a studio looks, and they will enjoy the three striking dances performed by the company to illustrate his introduction.

Walking. 6 min. Color. LCA.

Walking is for a slightly older child, perhaps five and up. Life-figure animation to a lively pop-jazz score shows how walking becomes dancing as people pass by on a city street. Showing styles of movement of men, women, and children, *Walking* illustrates self-acceptance and shows how bodies become expressive in movement. It's an original, absorbing film.

Why the Sun and Moon Live in the Sky. 11 min. Color. ACI Films.

Developing the pantomime theme for younger children is *Why the Sun and Moon Live in the Sky.* Celebrating the use of masks in solemn procession, Blair Lent's animals march by on the way to the house Sun and Moon built before Water moved in and sent them to settle in the sky. Lent's distinctive illustrations for the African legend are animated and narrated with fluid brilliance, and the use of masks is particularly successful, illuminating design and function.

Discovering Indian Music. 22 min. Color. BFA.

Discovering Indian Music is a teaching film for older children. It endeavors to explore the dance and music of Native Americans. In the solemn tones of the National Geographic, short clips of dances of the Navajos in Arizona, the Pueblo tribes of New Mexico, the Cheyenne, and the Ute are shown in their natural settings. The gorgeous Eagle Dance, various war dances, and community ritual dances are accompanied by a sharp, percussive music and chant, illustrating ethnic roots and giving children a chance to share their heritage.

He Makes Me Feel Like Dancing. 51 min. Color. Direct Films.

Jacques d'Amboise, principal dancer with the New York City Ballet, has been a charismatic force for children in that city's dance world for some years. He has propelled them into dance in myriad ways through his teaching, and this film explores the children's progress, their failures, and their successes in a lively, expressive documentary, allowing the audience to discover what this world can mean to them.

Keith. 10 min. Color. Budd.

Keith brings home Marceau's teaching in an appealing film for children. Keith, a fifteen-year-old bored in the city on a summer's day, dons whiteface at a minipark. He assumes a mime position on a nearby pedestal and then develops delicately a dance act around the fountain to a gentle, rhythmical piano score. The pantomime is so clear and clean, the film so brief, that it has the quality of brilliance that oriental artists achieve in three-line drawings.

Mime of Marcel Marceau. 23 min. Color. LCA.

The Mime of Marcel Marceau is another documentary that attempts to pass on the ancient tradition of shaman and mask. Sadly, it is choppy, the telling marred by sentimentality; yet, with so few available to us, it is valuable in showing this narrow theater art. Marceau's natural storytelling, his delicious humor, will captivate some children: he is a snake, he is in love, he is a fencer--each mode becomes a jewel of expression.

Mixummer Daydream. 10 min. Color. ACI.

Mixummer Daydream's colorful ghosts dance through their summer garden out of the house and into the forest, abstractions giving life to the daydreams of the young composer within. A little removed from actual storytelling,

Mixummer Daydream seems to comment on dance, on the function of music for dance, in a far-flung fantasy in ravishing color. There's a jazzy carefree score that's a little mocking, which children will like.

Myra. 3 min. Color. Churchill.

While the other children in her dance class lope along properly in their little line, pretending, Myra turns herself *into* each animal, thus exquisitely discommoding her teacher and peers, and delighting her audience. All too short.

Then there is a group of films for older children that simply record the ballets directly. I have chosen one or two as examples that I found to be of superior quality, but there are many, and television's public stations are responding to twentieth-century enthusiasm for the dance by showing many of the great companies at frequent intervals.

Ballet Adagio. 10 min. Color. Pyramid.

The solemn beauty of Albinoni's adagio movement for strings gives exquisite depth to Norman McClaren's filming of a pas de deux: stark, compelling, and beautiful, the dance is a perfect teaching medium, illustrating the basics of techniques in flawless performances for which the slow tempo is a natural foil. The two dancers are rather heavy in body build and their performance is very clear, lending a slight quality of archetype to a film that is pure in its classicism.

Fall River Legend. 15 min. Color. ACI.

Agnes de Mille's Fall River Legend tells the story of Lizzie Borden, of how the stern repressiveness of her New England elders creates a gathering storm of rage in a lonely, frustrated young girl until she is driven to murder. The quality of modern ballet is that it is danced from the inside out rather than from an imposed set of rules, and the power that this gives the dancers' interpretation of character is impressive as they dance the fast-paced choreography that builds to painful climax. Filmed in New England out of doors, the warm, intense colors are in startling contrast to Lizzie's agony of spirit.

Video

Videography brings up a very different world--home viewing and all that that entails. Longer films are possible than could be used in a workshop, and certain films that could be partially viewed or talked about in the process.

Children of Theater Street. 92 min. Color. Kultur.

Children of Theater Street, narrated by the late American actress Grace Kelly, is the story of children at the Imperial Ballet School in Leningrad, in training for the Russian ballet. Filmed at the Kirov and Bolshoi theaters, Theater Street is a completely absorbing description of the stringent entrance process, the daily life and schooling, the slow emergence to the state of effortless grace that years of patient effort, great talent, and dazzling example can bring a dancer. The hints of history in the script and the clips of Nijinsky, Pavlova, and others are particularly precious.

I Am a Dancer. 90 min. Color. Thorne.

The emphasis on the dedication and hard work necessary to bring a dancer's life to excellence is very welcome in this British documentary of Rudolph Nureyev's life and art. This fact together with the entrancing scenes of dance with Carla Fracci and Dame Margot Fonteyn could make this rather long film a choice for older boys and girls who are already somewhat versed in the foundations of ballet. In its emphasis on bar technique and actual dances Nureyev's *I Am a Dancer* could be a useful guide to an older child who is already interested.

In a Rehearsal Room. 11 min. Color. Films, Inc.

For older children who know dance, *In a Rehearsal Room* is a nondidactic, beautiful presentation of classical dancing à deux. Cynthia Gregory, in impeccable style, falls in love with her waiting partner at the theater, and they dance together in the bare polished room--a passionate, quiet, romantic statement.

The Video Dictionary of Classical Ballet. 270 min. Color. Kultur.

The Video Dictionary of Classical Ballet is a no-nonsense, four-part visual directory of dance technique, illustrated with impressive facility by members of the New York City Ballet, the American Ballet Theater, and others, who meticulously demonstrate positions, and then move through an increasingly complex set of movements, such as center practice, allegro, pointe, and leaps. The film illustrates the remarkable facility of video for teaching, and its adaptability to home, class, and workshop setting.

These brief critiques will give some idea of the style and variety of dance films available for children, and suggest their vitality and wonderful ability to cut across age and background and show the dance directly.

To close I'd like to suggest widening the possibilities for introducing dance to children by taking advantage of the neighborhood movie house, community theater, videotapes, sometimes the family television--especially public television. Movies like *Fame, Flashdance,* and *A Chorus Line,* contemporary films that use dance as a central form, can be valuable. They seem close to home and give a sense of real life and possibility to the young.

Here the parade is over: we have piped our children to attention and danced them out the door into their own world of dance with our books and music and films, giving them a library tour to wing their feet and ready their minds for flight.

WORKSHOPS

Note for Special Children:
Although deaf children cannot hear music, they are often very sensitive to rhythm and movement. These workshops can be useful to them in strengthening these abilities through what they see in following the dancer. Children in wheelchairs can enjoy everything as audience if not as dancers. If a whole group of deaf children is present, a sign language specialist can be asked to translate the story of the dance, the dancer's words, and the meaning or description of the music to be played.

For those who are visually impaired, include some verbal description of the dances. Music will be helpful for their understanding of the rhythm and the mood of each dance. If a dancer is presenting the workshop, he or she might want to spend a little time actually moving together with the child through the dance steps.

Preschool Workshop

Ages: 2-5

Time: Twenty minutes.

Space: Bare hardwood or linoleum floor, swept clean of furniture, books, pictures, and clutter.

Materials: A drum, film projector, record or tape player.

With children sitting on the floor in a circle, begin with some basic poses of yoga, such as the frog, the stork, the locust, and so on. Demonstrate the poses and then have the children try them out.

Then with someone drumming rhythmically, let them circle around the room: walk/skip/jump/hop/run/slow/walk/stop. Have them close their eyes and feel their center in their stomach. Coming from the center, they can be a live bird or frog or tree that really moves instead of just posing. Let each child try one he or she likes in order to show the others its form. It might be a flower opening, a frog jumping, a snake creeping, a bird flying. As the special movement begins to form, let a special drum effect be the theme of the movement, one for the flower, for the frog, for the snake. Coming back to quiet and into the circle, have them sit down.

If the children are still with you, try a short film, such as *Matrioska* or *A Chary Tale.*

Ballet Workshop

Ages: Middle grades, or 8-12.

Time: One hour.

Environment: Costumes, toe shoes, tutus on display; posters of dance and dancers, such as those by Degas, Goya, and Picasso; books of photographs and art books arranged in clear view; sculpture, if obtainable; records for check-out later.

Materials: Film projector, record player.

With a Dancer Present:

Introduction: Tell something about the story of dance; either the children's librarian or the dancer can do this. Then let the children stretch and relax in place.

Book Talk: Make this brief. A good-humored start is to read aloud *Max* by Rachel Isadora, *The Wonderful World of Dance* by Arnold Haskell, *Young Person's Guide to Ballet* by Noel Streatfield, *A Very Young Dancer* by Jill Krementz.

Film: Fall River Legend could be shown.

Demonstration I: The dancer alone gives a short program.

Demonstration II: With the children some possibilities you might want to consider with your dancer include him or her demonstrating the five positions and encouraging the children to try them; or perhaps showing some jazz or Afro-jazz variations and explaining some of the movements that have emerged in contemporary dance.

Questions and Discussions: Children always have lots of questions: How do you become a dancer? What is the training? Where do you get it? How long does it take? Local dance studios and teachers can be mentioned.

Note: A useful technique for this kind of workshop is setting up a dance film program--for instance, *Mixummer Daydream, Rhythmitron,* or *Ballet Adagio*-- the week before.

For a Librarian Alone:

Let children stretch and relax in place before settling down.

Introduction: A short film, such as *Ballet Adagio* or *Mixummer Daydream.*

Informal History: This can be made lively and engaging by using books of photography to help trace ballet through its important stages: primitive, medieval, renaissance, baroque, classic, romantic, and modern. In addition, records from the companion discography can be played to illustrate them.

Questions and Discussion: During your discussion be sure to include a list of local dance studios and teachers, with phone numbers and addresses.

Conclusion: Encourage the children to check out all available pictures, records, books, and films.

Modern Dance Workshop

Ages: Middle grades, or 8-12.

Time: One hour.

Environment: Posters by Matisse, Picasso, or Toulouse-Lautrec, or those showing Duncan or Graham, illustrating contemporary dance in one form or another.

Materials: Record player and film projector or video recorder.

With a Dancer Present:

Let the children stretch and relax in place before sitting down.

Introduction: The children's librarian can introduce the dancer and the history of modern dance can be traced by either leader.

Demonstration: By guest dancer with some active involvement of the children.

Questions and Discussion. Let the children ask the dancer any questions they might have.

Book Talk: Brief comments on a yoga book, a biography, or a history.

For a Librarian Alone:

Let children stretch and relax in place before sitting down.

Introduction: Explain historical roots in America via primitive dance and briefly trace the growth of modern dance in this century. If yoga is a familiar discipline, illustrate this talk by some asanas for the children as introductory to modern dance. Let children try the poses, individually or together.

Book Talk: Tell the children briefly about *Be a Frog, a Bird or a Tree* by Rachel Carr; *Wonderful World of Dance* by Arnold Haskell. Biographies include those of Martha Graham, Katherine Dunham.

Record Sampling: Good for dance are brief excerpts of music from primitive, jazz, modern scores such as *Appalachian Spring* by Aaron Copland, electronic works such as Jacob Druckman or Brian Eno, rock selections.

Films: Walking; Keith; a film of live modern dance from such a collection as that of Alvin Ailey or Martha Graham.

Folk Dance Workshop: The Virginia Reel

Ages: Middle grades, or 7-12.

Time: One hour.

Space: Large, uncluttered space, preferably hardwood floors. Folk dance books, photographs, and records can be displayed around the room.

Materials: Record player.

As children enter, have them line up facing each other about eight yards apart. As they wait, explain that this will be a live workshop led by called directions and music, illustrating an American folk dance.

Begin:

First call: Honor your partner: walk over, bow, walk back, and twirl.

Second: Swing your partner, linking elbows, right one time around and skipping back into place.

Third: Dosey-do: Skip your partner, go around him or her and skip back into place. Repeat.

Fourth: Front couple joins hands and skip-gallops (sashays) down the line and back as everyone claps to the music.

Fifth: Front couple swings right arm around one and a half times and then alternates this motion first with boy or girl in line, then with partner, left arm to right arm, sashaying back to the place at the head of the line.

Sixth: Both lines turn, facing front couple and promenade: leaders skip around the outside leading their line around, meeting at the bottom and forming an arch under which each couple goes, the first to become the new lead couple. Drop hands. Repeat sequence till all couples have played lead couple once.

Allow children to rest, sitting on the floor where they are, and talk with them about the background and traditions of American folk dance. You can introduce some books and records:

Books: Folk Dancing in America by Eleanor Wakefield; *Folk-dances and Singing Games* by Elizabeth Burchard.

Records: Big Circle Mountain Dancing, Glen Bannerman (two records); various records of your choice of American folk dance music.

World Dance Workshop: African Dance

Ages: Primary or middle grades, or 6-12.

Time: One hour.

Environment: This workshop will be based on the dance traditions of a chosen country, so display the art, costumes, photography books that will best show off the culture and the people of that country.

Materials: Film projector, video recorder, record player.

With a Dancer Present:

Children should stretch and relax in place.

Introduction: The children's librarian can introduce the dancer and give a brief descriptive background of African dance tradition.

Demonstration: A guest dancer can show some of the collection of costumes, masks, and instruments brought in for the workshop in a living context. Records can be played as a setting for dancing. If there is enough space, children can actively participate in some parts of the dance and get a feeling for the artifacts.

Book Talk: Give a brief talk on suitable books (listed below) and offer the children a chance to check out books.

Discussion: Children will want to ask questions of your dancer, and discuss this kind of dance and its world. They should be given the opportunity to examine and touch the costumes and artifacts.

For a Librarian Alone:

Children should stretch and relax in place.

Introduction: Explore with them the role of dance in an African country such as Nigeria, the interplay of dance with spiritual life, storytelling, courtship, and festival, and how these forms have affected and become interwoven with our own modern, jazz, Afro, and ballet music and dance. Costumes, sculptures, masks, or photographs can enrich this presentation.

Film: Some possibilities are *Africa Dances* or *Why the Sun and the Moon Live in the Sky* (masks).

Book Talk: Discuss briefly *The Wonderful World of the Dance* by Arnold Haskell; *Dancing Masks of Africa* by Christine Price; *The Dance of Africa* by

Lew Warren; or *African Rhythm, American Dance* by Terry Harman. Choose only one or two of these for your younger children.

Records: Play some examples of native African music for them.

Costumes, Masks, Sculptures: Children's inspection and handling of these cultural artifacts can help them think creatively by making the country real. If possible, arrange to have the children try on masks and costumes and to take these home. Let them try out some dance movements and check out books and media materials.

Discussion: Let this emerge naturally from the context of the movements they've tried, the book talk, and your display.

Movement Exploration Workshop

For a Librarian Alone, or with a Dancer Present:

Ages: Middle grades, or 8-12

Time: About an hour.

Space: Large, uncluttered space, hardwood floor preferable.

Materials: Cassette player with speaker, a small drum.

Special Preparation: To create a tape for the central section of this class, gather up available records from your own collection, the library's, or your friends'. Splice at one-minute intervals as many as a dozen different styles: African contemporary (such as Olatunji), jazz, Irish jig, polka, eighteenth-century European dance suite (such as Bach), slow dancing, rock, electronic, Chinese dance or theater music, Gregorian chant, ethnic drumming or chanting, nineteenth-century romantic (such as *Swan Lake* by Tchaikovsky), Prokoviev, twentieth-century American (Copland's *Appalachian Spring*, for example, or Samuel Barber's *Adagio for Strings*), or Indian Raga music. Choose any well-defined, characteristic dance styles from various cultures. Begin your tape with a few minutes of meditative calm background music of the "Music from the Hearts of Space" kind, or any sound/environment music. Then, on the reverse side of the tape, splice together three or four specific musical styles for a longer interval of five minutes each. Pick vigorous, well-known kinds that are somewhat familiar to the children: African, jazz, European ballet, or American modern, for instance.

As the children file in, wearing loose, comfortable clothes, have your background music playing. Ask them to pick a space nearby with enough room to move freely. What direction are they facing? Who is sharing this space? Can a person carve space? How far out does space extend? Can they use arms, hands and fingers to carve space? Legs or feet? What works? Have them try swinging their head, arms, now their legs, feet, fingers and toes, and even the torso. Ask them to show the rhythm of the music in their movement.

Now, beginning the central, many-faceted portion of the tape, ask them to express the feeling of each kind of music with their bodies in their own way, changing each time the music changes. Be aware of others only so as not to collide with anyone. Notice *what* wants to work--hands only? torso? legs? head?

When the one-minute portions of the tape are complete, ask them to stand where they are. What did they notice about how their bodies responded to different kinds of music? Allot a few minutes for sharing responses.

When the tape is done, after a resting time, suggest they use the last minutes of the workshop to let themselves create freely a merging of the different styles, "just dancing," moving as they choose. Here your own drumming might be the best, nonspecific way to release them into their own sense of movement.

Before they leave, suggest they dance at home, when they feel like it and the space is theirs, to tape or records they might have.

> Workshop designed by Barbara Kohn
> and Cheryl Yonker
> Adapted by Lea Burroughs

Music

And Sadko played on his dulcimer and sang.

He sang of Novgorod and of the little river Volkhov which he loved . . . and there was the sound of wind over the lake in his song, the sound of ripples under the prow of the boat, the sound of ripples on the shore, the sound of the river flowing past the tall reeds, the whispering sound of the river at night. And all the time he played cunningly on the dulcimer. . . .

Never had the Tzar of the Sea heard such music.

"I would dance," said the Tzar of the Sea, and he stood up like a tall tree in the hall.

--Arthur Ransome, *Old Peter's Russian Tales*

Each time music enters children's literature you get a key to the powerful secret world that it is for children. A language of feeling releases children from the square, rigid structures of words into a generous, liquid realm.

101

Sometimes, as the children of Hamlin found out in their wild pursuit of the Pied Piper, music can be used as magic to take one on a strange and transforming journey. At the same time it is private. Music suggests, evokes, jokes, and dances but never lectures or demands, never pontificates or admonishes. Instead, as Oscar Wilde said, "Art says nothing, art expresses everything."

In this language of pure expression, children relax and play, dancing and singing and learning by doing while the music expands their inner world. At the very beginning of things, as in P. L. Travers's *John and Barbara's Story,* the language of sun, the patterns of wind on the cheek, the meaning of Sparrow's petulant chirping at the window sill are the music of infants, nonverbal language, quite clear in meaning to them, just not speech--a different way. This direct language of feeling is not really forgotten later, though it seems to be (who says they can understand the language of the wind?); instead, it becomes the language of music, a distillation of the feeling world, a human translation of sun and wind and sparrow. As children grow, responding to music in hopping, skipping and playing, sometimes in dancing or singing jingles or tunes or singing along to music at home, this deep symbolic early meaning begins to translate into outer expression.

For some children, like Louretta, in *Soul Brothers and Sister Lou,* expression of this language is a talent for them, and through it they begin to take hold of their life's journey. For others, like Tom in *Jazz Country,* exploring the practical, immediate world of music and musicians as a teen is a rite of passage, an exploration of the adult world while protected, in a sense, by the familiar childhood language of music, the perfect transition.

But for almost all of us, just listening as we grow up is the uncomplicated natural way of understanding music, and it presents us with an unspoken but profound set of archetypes: Sadko plays for a dance at the Church Fair; Apollo's lyre sounds its themes of love in our backyard; far away we may hear the Siren's warning, and at our most creative, we too become Vainamoinen, singing up the mountains.

Children sense power in music and it draws them into a playful involvement in making it; then, as they begin to explore this rich and seamless world, they find an intricate and multifaceted set of inner works-- the elements of music. Music's "words" are notes, for instance; when they are shaped to a phrase or sentence they become a melody; melodies themselves move in a characteristic set of durations or rhythms; and when they come to rest with an accompanying set of notes, they generate a series of tones together called harmony. When melodies are put out to flight with other melodies, this moving fabric is called a counterpoint, and either way the tones must be generated by some kind of media, or instruments. These last can be voice, drums, computer, electronic generators, or a symphony orchestra; the choice of instrumental color is up to the composer. What they add up to is texture, the characteristic interweaving of different kinds of sounds special to each piece.

And perhaps it should be said that all of this is useless if there is no one to hear it, so that audience is the hidden and completing element of music. Whether in a concert hall, on the dance floor, or at home near the stereo, the auditor completes the sequence. In the end it is what we make of music that gives it its life and importance.

Children's way of listening, of gathering in these elements, is to join in, and as music isn't verbal they do so even as babies, attempting without inhibition to play instruments at an early age, to sing melodies (though awkwardly at first), and to skip and play rhythms. Spontaneous and not characteristically self-conscious, small children make lively performers and a responsive audience.

Melody, the song in music, is the phrase at the heart of things. At the beginning of human music making, the natural world was already deep into it; bird song, the spring mating calls that sounded through the forests and soared overhead, suggested melody to our ancestors, who imitated the birds with their voices, giving sound to feelings of joy or sorrow or nostalgia, expressing every shade and meaning.

Later, as communities came together in their work of the day, clearing the forests or planting the fields, the individual singers created joint melodies in work songs that were the first choral music, strong and rhythmic. Later still, as societies developed increasingly codified and separate rites, melody expressed and accompanied people's activities in new ways. During the Middle Ages in Europe, for example, melodies to celebrate God blossomed in the monodic and antiphonal choirs of the Christian church. Outside of it, the troubadors sang their stories of love, politics, and passion in their secular, message-bearing songs. Folk tunes of love and work were sung everywhere, and as people grew increasingly sophisticated, they invented and refined instruments and styles to communicate musically--martial songs for marching bands, dirges for funerals, dance tunes for festivals, songs for the theater. Crudely carved wooden reed instruments like recorders and drums and simple stringed instruments like the lyre, developed over the years into the sophisticated combinations of a string quartet or jazz ensemble.

Thus melody has expanded to meet the needs of a world of growing awareness and understanding, yet melody and music are still expressive of basic feelings, and love, and work, as in the beginning.

Rhythm, children's friend, is the body's way of expressing music. A hawk sustaining a still flight is like a tone of long duration ⌀ and its quick winging to go up again suggests very rapid notes, sixteenth or thirty-second ♫♫♪ . Sometimes, when ducks are whisking water off their wings the motion even resembles a trill ♪ . Whether it be birds or people, rhythm is the body giving life to the inner design of the piece. For a marching band this is a square emphasized set of durations ♩♩♩♩|♩♩♩♩, and for a pair of waltzing partners the music gives off a three-cornered beat that makes them sway and pick up again ♩♩♩|♩♩♩. In jazz the complex syncopated rhythmic interaction of the instrumental melodies is what gives it the secret texture, part joke and part storytelling, that is its style.

Rhythm has great power in its physical sense: Bach writing in a pastoral mode used a quiet, repetitive rhythmic structure to suggest tranquility; a twentieth century composer, like Luciano Berio in his *Folk Songs,* erupts in an abrupt, jagged set of rhythms that express the fierce anxiety of our time. And it is tempo that carries the rhythm along, now faster, now slower, as befits the mood and meaning of the piece. Each set of rhythms has a pace that is natural to it. If Bach's pastorale is measured, grave, and moderate, so Berio must be rapid and sharp in tempo, to convey his intensity. The marching band sets out at a good pace, an allegro, not too fast or too slow. Children feel the rhythmic structure of a piece even in the preschool years, adapting and evoking both design and pace in their spontaneous dancing.

When rhythmic melodies begin to play with one another, two, three, or four of them, this shifting weaving of sounds is called the counterpoint of the piece. Note sounds against note and line against line, and as instruments play melodies together, they set up a rich texture. Thus counterpoint is really a kind of conversation, in which first one voice stands out and then another. As they move along they appear to develop the thoughts of the composer. Listening to voices sing a simple round like "Five Coral Bells," playing duo-piano, or listening to the slow movement of a string quartet will make the counterpoint conversation come clear and seem engagingly simple.

But of all the elements of music it is probably the least simple. Many hundreds of years of song and chant and experiment passed before, in Europe, Johann Sebastian Bach took hold of the modest body of counterpoint that had come before him and turned it into his own, making it central to the music of all composers. The forms of jazz music and twentieth-century chamber music may be freer and the texture more dissonant, as in John Coltrane and Béla Bartók's work, but the sense of a conversation going on is still central to counterpoint. In fact, it is exactly this conversation, this sense of a community of "speakers" that make counterpoint the most human of music's elements. By playing an instrument or singing with others, children can take part in this conversation for themselves and thus work their way into the fabric--understanding by participating.

The element that provides an environment for all the interplay of counterpoint and rhythm is harmony, the sounding together of several tones, a springing up of color. These groups of sound are called chords, and when they are played one after another, they make progressions. The understanding of chordal structure, the "grammar" of music, came into focus late in musical history in the eighteenth century, and the idea of groups of tones progressing in orderly fashion was immediately appealing to composers and audience alike.

From the first, harmony has had a rare ability to express setting, to evoke mood in a way rhythm and counterpoint cannot. In very harmonic music like that of Richard Strauss or our own blues, the feeling is rich and emotional. When Billie Holiday sings, the nostalgia and heat and sadness of the urban world seems to surround us. The opera *Der Rosenkavalier*, written by Strauss in 1911, plunges us into the ornateness and decadence of pre-World War I Vienna.

But whatever the time or the setting, the harmonic part of music is something easily grasped and appreciated by children. They understand it intuitively quite well, although the theory may be difficult (or perhaps unnecessary), and their way to that understanding may once again be through an instrument, the guitar, perhaps, or the piano. The progressions of harmony become clear to them as they sit down and play through chords, experimenting, listening, and absorbing the sense of the progressions.

As their bodies sense rhythm and their voices realize melody, so children make harmony understandable to themselves by playing an instrument in a school orchestra or rock group, by singing in a chorus, or by playing a simple string or keyboard instrument and singing an accompaniment. So instruments are vitally important to children. They come to understand music's elements through playing them. But they are also a key to making music personal, to expressing it and having fun.

Instruments, based at first on the human voice, a very beautiful instrument in itself as Andersen describes so eloquently in *The Emperor's Nightingale*, have expanded way beyond the vocal range, but their simple single-voicedness is still characteristic. Instruments as solo players convey melody. Whether they are oboes, thin and penetrating, or a massed set of strings, they set the tone of the piece. They set the pace as well. Instruments immediately establish rhythm and tempo firmly. They say whether it is song or dance we are hearing.

In addition, they are completely in charge of texture. Spare medieval church music has a quiet, smooth texture, but Jacques Ibert, in his piece for twenty saxophones, creates a bubbling texture that's berserk and off-balance, as was the intention. An avant-garde composer like Meredith Monk can use a combination of voice and electronics that shocks you and almost hurts, the texture is so harsh. Either way, texture's the sensual aspect of music. Some composers, like Mahler or Berlioz, have been so in love with it they rarely used any instrument but the symphony orchestra, the richest and most lush of all.

Instruments convey mood and color, too. The organ's massive pipes and intricate keyboards were designed to evoke a religious feeling; the hornpipe literally sets your feet dancing; string quartets of any period elicit intimacy; and drums set a martial mood. Some instruments seem to suggest a given mood regardless of their setting, whereas others, like the voice or the piano, have a tremendous range and subtlety of color.

All this color--color of instruments, harmonic color--textures, and shifting mood reach children with no trouble at all. Children are an audience open to everything in music except sitting still too long or being made to listen a certain way. As Leonard Bernstein discovered when he led the New York Philharmonic through many years of successful children's concerts, they are a fresh, enthusiastic, and iconoclastic audience, and very ready for the new and contemporary.

But whether child or adult, the audience completes the intention of music, setting off in each listener's mind an individual meaning that starts a new life from the old, as the listener interprets and redefines the material for him- or herself. Children can begin very young; programs for toddlers and parents, with singing and Autoharp, or a few guitar-accompanied preschool story hours--both are common practice now in our children's rooms and they give a strong, colorful beginning for children's musical awareness. As they get older they can be helped to understand and grasp music concretely by painting or coloring as they listen to a piece, by dancing it out, or by "storytelling" with their pencils and pens. If you are introducing an orchestral piece, just give the children some crayons to show the colors, and watch the piece take shape.

So it seems that children have a natural affinity for music, and it can be brought to life in the children's room. But what of the library's more traditional role, its natural materials, to give some sense of this glorious but intrusive art?

Here, as I suggested earlier, the expanded role of the library as a media resource can become a cornerstone of introducing music to children. Before this century, music lay trapped between the covers of books, which, with the exception of books of folk songs, lullabies, and the like, were and are rarely checked out of our libraries. Mostly useful as part of a musical study program or an individual child's instrumental work, even the most excellent book about music can have only a peripheral role in a child's understanding of music itself. Words are not a substitute for music. But records and tapes present music directly--every period and every country, every kind of music from folk to electronic, and every sort of instrument in the world.

Recordings can form the introduction to each aspect of music and provide a firm basis for a workshop introduction to music's elements or to one in instrument making or history. The records used can be expanded from the traditional children's records, mostly folk songs and holiday celebrations, to include appropriate music of all kinds from around the world.

I think that we underestimate children's capacity to listen broadly; given a sensitive approach, they are quite capable of appreciating a wide range of musical expression. Whether they have access to a listening section of the library or check out records and cassettes to play at home, the opportunity for children to experience different kinds of music is at our fingertips and theirs and needs only an introduction.

Films are a useful adjunct to records in deepening an appreciation of music. There are now several films on instruments, and on music of different cultures, and a handful of folk song films, like Pete Seeger's *Foolish Frog,* provide a magnificent introduction for small children.

Books need to be brought into play in a tactful way. Suggest them to a child who plays an instrument, for instance, or a member of an orchestra who would like to understand the nature of other instruments as well as his or her own. Books provide a backup for history and for understanding theory; even a book on how to play an instrument in certain cases can be just the right thing. Last--and if only there were more of these in a fully contemporary mode--are song books and musical scores that a child can check out to play or experiment with on an instrument at home. This way the library brings music right into the child's home world--harmony, melody, rhythm, and all.

At the library, these elements can be the basis of a rich workshop, using records or tapes along with books to demonstrate clearly the various elements of the musical language we've been discussing. And young people can demonstrate instruments themselves. Local teachers may be happy to bring their pupils for performance and demonstration, too, and older brothers and sisters may be part of a New Wave or rock group that would love to come in and show off a little. Local churches are a good resource, and the music department of a local university or community college may well have students eager to come to the library and show the children what kind of new music is in the works and what they can do with it.

Closely related to this experience is the fun of an instrument-making workshop. Getting down to work and actually constructing a noise-making machine can be a liberating experience. Simple forms of drums and reed and stringed instruments are easily made out of found materials and can be completed during the length of an afternoon's workshop time. Working with group improvisation, one child playing "Three Blind Mice" on her new panpipes accompanied by another elaborating on his drums or pebble-box tambourine translates the abstract into a living thing and sets the way for musical composition.

Thus, using the resources of the library materials and the community allows teachers and librarians to expand their role. Elements of live performance during story hours, workshops, and the sensitive introduction of materials--records, tapes, books, and films--can bring music to children in a direct, unregimented way that leaves them receptive and responsive to the deep enjoyment of music's transforming journeys.

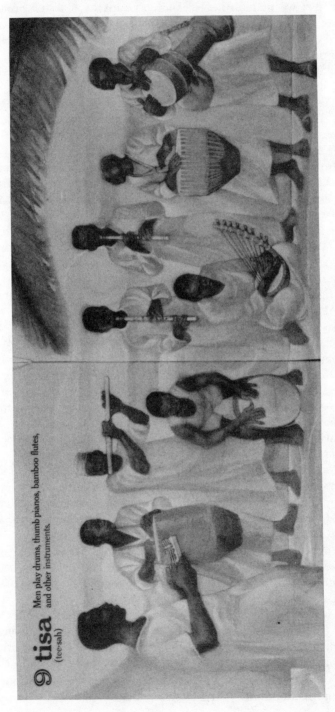

9 tisa
(tee-sah)

Men play drums, thumb pianos, bamboo flutes, and other instruments.

From *Moja Means One: Swahili Counting Book* by Muriel Feelings, pictures by Tom Feelings. Text © 1971 by Muriel Feelings. Illustrations © 1971 by Tom Feelings. Reprinted by permission of the publisher, Dial Books for Young Readers.

BIBLIOGRAPHY

A Basic Introduction

Britten, Benjamin, and Imogen Holst. *The Wonderful World of Music.* Garden City, N.Y.: Doubleday, 1968.

Theory

Collier, James Lincoln. *Practical Music Theory: How Music Is Put Together, from Bach to Rock.* New York: Grosset & Dunlap, 1971.

History

Bess, Nancy Wise, and Stephanie Grauman Wolf. *The Sounds of Time: Western Man and His Music.* Philadelphia: J. B. Lippincott, 1969.

Bierhorst, John. *A Cry from the Earth: Music of the North American Indians.* New York: Four Winds Press, 1979.

Boeckman, Charles. *Cool, Hot and Blue: A History of Jazz for Young People.* Washington, D.C.: Robert B. Luce, 1968.

Hughes, Langston. *The First Book of Jazz.* New York: Franklin Watts, 1955.

Krishef, Robert K. *Introducing Country Music.* Minneapolis: Lerner Publishing, 1979.

Matthews, Thomas. *The Splendid Art: A History of the Opera.* New York: Crowell Collier, 1970.

Myrus, Donald. *I Like Jazz.* New York: Macmillan, 1964.

Palmer, Geoffrey. *Music Tells the Tale: A Guide to Programme Music.* New York: Frederick Warne, 1968.

Rublowsky, John. *Music in America.* New York: Crowell Collier, 1967.

Siegmeister, Elie. *Invitation to Music.* New York: Harry Howe, 1961.

Stambler, Irwin, and Grelun Landon. *Golden Guitars: The Story of Country Music.* New York: Four Winds Press, 1971.

Vander Horst, Brian. *Folk Music in America.* New York: Franklin Watts, 1972.

Wechsberg, Joseph. *The Pantheon Story of Music for Young People.* New York: Random House, 1968.

Instruments

Anderson, David. *The Piano Makers.* New York: Pantheon, 1982.

Ballantine, Bill. *The Piano: An Introduction to the Instrument.* New York: Franklin Watts, [1971].

_____. *The Violin.* New York: Franklin Watts, [1971].

Berger, Melvin. *The Photo Dictionary of the Orchestra.* New York: Methuen, 1980.

Dietz, Betty Warner, and Michael Babatunde Olatunji. *Musical Instruments of Africa.* New York: John Day, 1965.

English, Betty Lou. *You Can't Be Timid with a Trumpet: Notes from the Orchestra.* New York: Lothrop, Lee & Shepard, 1980.

Etkins, Ruth. *Playing and Composing on the Recorder.* New York: Sterling, [1975].

Gilmore, Leo. *Folk Instruments.* Minneapolis: Lerner Publishing, 1962.

Huntington, Harriet. *Tune Up: The Instruments of the Orchestra and Their Players.* New York: Doubleday, 1942.

Kettlekamp, Larry. *Drums, Rattles and Bells.* New York: Morrow, 1960.

_____. *Flutes, Whistles and Reeds.* New York: Morrow, 1962.

_____. *Horns.* New York: Morrow, 1964.

_____. *Singing Strings.* New York: Morrow, 1958.

Storms, Laura. *Careers with an Orchestra.* New York: Lerner Publishing, 1983.

Suggs, William W. *Meet the Orchestra.* New York: Macmillan, 1966.

Weil, Lisl. *Things that Go Bang.* New York: McGraw-Hill, 1969.

Instrument Making

Collier, James Lincoln. *Jug Bands and Handmade Music: A Creative Approach to Music Theory and the Instruments.* New York: Grosset & Dunlap, 1973.

Hawkinson, John. *Music and Instruments for Children to Make.* Chicago: Albert Whitman, 1969.

Mandell, Muriel. *Make Your Own Instruments.* New York: Sterling Publishing, 1957.

Walther, Tom. *Make Mine, Music!* Boston: Little, Brown, 1984.

Wilson, Robina Beckley. *Creative Drama and Musical Activities for Children.* Boston: Play, 1977.

Wiseman, Ann. *Making Musical Things.* New York: Charles Scribner's Sons, 1979.

Opera

Bulla, Clyde Robert. *The Ring and the Fire: Stories from Wagner's Nibelung Operas.* New York: Thomas Y. Crowell, 1962.

_____. *Stories of Gilbert and Sullivan Operas.* New York: Thomas Y. Crowell, 1968.

_____. *Stories of Favorite Operas.* New York: Thomas Y. Crowell, 1959.

Matthews, Thomas. *The Splendid Art: A History of the Opera.* New York: Crowell Collier, 1970.

Updike, John, and Warren Chappell, adapters. *The Magic Flute: Music by Wolfgang Amadeus Mozart.* New York: Knopf, 1964.

Music Production

Clemens, Virginia Phelps. *The Team behind Your Favorite Record.* Philadelphia: Westminster Press, 1980.

Gelly, David. *The Facts about a Rock Group: Featuring Wings.* New York: Harmony Books, 1977.

Powers, Bill. *Behind the Scenes in a Broadway Musical.* New York: Crown Pub., 1982.

Biography

Burch, Gladys. *Famous Composers for Young People.* New York: Dodd, Mead & Co., 1939.

Dunlop, Agnes Mary Robertson [Elizabeth Kyle, pseud.]. *Song of the Waterfall: The Story of Edvard and Nina Grieg.* London: Evans Bros., 1970.

Collier, James Lincoln. *Louis Armstrong.* New York: Macmillan, 1985.

Gutman, Bill. *Duke: The Musical Life of Duke Ellington.* New York: Random House, 1977.

Hamilton, Virginia. *Paul Robeson: The Life and Times of a Free Black Man.* New York: Harper & Row, 1974.

Mathis, Sharon Bell. *Ray Charles.* New York: Thomas Y. Crowell, 1973.

Montgomery, Elizabeth. *William C. Handy, Father of the Blues.* Champaign, Ill: Garrard Publishing, 1968.

Posell, Elsa Z. *American Composers.* Boston: Houghton Mifflin, 1963.

_____. *Russian Composers.* Boston: Houghton Mifflin, 1967.

Seroff, Victor Ilyitch. *Wolfgang Amadeus Mozart.* New York: Macmillan, 1965.

Sive, Helen R. *Music's Connecticut Yankee: An Introduction to the Life and Music of Charles Ives.* New York: Atheneum, 1977.

Terkel, Studs. *Giants of Jazz.* New York: Thomas Y. Crowell, 1957.

Tobias, Tobi. *Marian Anderson.* New York: Thomas Y. Crowell, 1972.

Wymer, Norman. *Gilbert and Sullivan.* New York: Dutton, 1963.

Folk Songs for Children

Berger, Donald Paul, compiler-arranger. *Folk Songs of Japanese Children.* Rutland, Vt.: Charles E. Tuttle, 1969.

Bertail, Inez. *Complete Nursery Song Book.* New York: Lothrop, Lee & Shepard, 1947.

Boni, Margaret Bradford. *Fireside Book of Folk Songs.* Illustrated by Alice and Martin Provensen. New York: Simon & Schuster, 1947.

Bryan, Ashley. *I'm Going to Sing: Black American Spirituals.* Book 2. New York: Atheneum, 1982.

_____. *Walk Together, Children: Black American Spirituals.* Book 1. New York: Atheneum, 1974.

Houston, James, ed. *Songs of the Dream People: Chants and Images from the Indians and Eskimos of North America.* Hartford: Connecticut Printers, 1972.

Knudsen, Lynn, ed. *Lullabies from Around the World.* Chicago: Follett, 1967.

Landeck, Beatrice. *Echoes of Africa in Folk Songs of the Americas.* New York: David McKay, 1968.

Langstaff, John M. *Sweetly Sings the Donkey: Animal Rounds for Children to Sing or Play on Recorders.* New York: Atheneum, 1976.

Mart, Jane, compiler. *Singing Bee! A Collection of Favorite Children's Songs.* Pictures by Anita Lobel. New York: Lothrop, Lee & Shepard, 1983.

Poston, Elizabeth, compiler-arranger. *The Children's Song Book.* London: Bodley Head, 1961. Folk songs from Great Britain and other countries in simple piano settings.

Rockwell, Anne, ed. *Savez-vous Planter les Choux? and Other French Songs.* Cleveland, Ohio: World, [1969].

Sackett, S. J. *Cowboys and the Songs They Sang.* New York: W. R. Scott, 1967.

Yurchenco, Henrietta. *A Fiesta of Folk Songs from Spain and Latin America.* New York: G. P. Putnam's Sons, 1967. Melodies only.

Folk Songs in a Picture-Story Setting

Ipcar, Dahlov. *The Cat Came Back.* New York: Knopf, 1971.

Leodhas, Sorche Nic, ed. *Kellyburn Braes.* Illustrated by Evaline Ness. New York: Holt, Rinehart & Winston, 1968.

Price, Christine, illus. *Widdecombe Fair: An Old English Folk Song.* New York: Frederick Warne, 1968.

Rounds, Glen. *Casey Jones, the Story of a Brave Engineer.* San Carlos, Calif.: Golden Gate Jr. Books, 1968.

Picture Stories and Music

Bolognese, Don. *A New Day.* New York: Delacorte, 1970.

Brown, Margaret Wise. *Indoor Noisy Book.* New York: Harper & Row, 1942.

_____. *Noisy Book.* New York: Harper & Row, 1939.

Carlson, Nancy. *Harriet's Recital.* Minneaplois: Carolrhoda Books, 1982.

Cathon, Laura E. *Tot Botot and His Little Flute.* New York: Macmillan, 1970.

Ets, Marie Hall. *In the Forest.* New York: Viking Press, 1944.

Freeman, Don. *Hattie, the Backstage Bat.* New York: Viking Press, 1970.

Giovanni, Nikki. *Spin a Soft Black Song.* New York: Farrar, Straus & Giroux, 1985.

Hurd, Thatcher. *Mama Don't Allow: Starring Miles and the Swamp Band.* New York: Harper & Row, 1984.

Isadora, Rachel. *Ben's Trumpet.* New York: Greenwillow Books, 1979.

Keats, Ezra Jack. *John Henry.* New York: Pantheon, 1965.

_____. *Whistle for Willie.* New York: Viking Press, 1964.

Kuskin, Karla. *The Philharmonic Gets Dressed.* New York: Harper & Row, 1982.

Lionni, Leo. *Geraldine, the Music Mouse.* New York: Pantheon, 1979.

Seeger, Pete. *The Foolish Frog.* New York: Macmillan, 1973.

Spier, Peter. *Crash! Bang! Boom!* New York: Doubleday, 1972.

_____. *Fox Went out on a Chilly Night.* New York: Macmillan, 1973.

Stecher, Miriam. *Max, the Music-maker.* New York: Lothrop, Lee, 1980.

Walter, Mildred Pitts. *Ty's One-Man Band.* Illustrated by Margot Tomes. New York: Four Winds Press, 1980.

Williams, Vera B. *Music, Music for Everyone.* New York: Greenwillow Books, 1984.

Fiction and Music

Alcott, Louisa May. *An Old-Fashioned Girl.* Boston: Little, Brown, 1897.

Alexander, Lloyd. *The Truthful Harp.* New York: Holt, Rinehart & Winston, 1967.

Bulla, Clyde Robert. *The Moon Singer*. New York: Thomas Y. Crowell, 1969.

Gray, Elizabeth Janet. *Adam of the Road*. New York: Viking Press, 1940.

Hentoff, Nat. *Jazz Country*. New York: Harper & Row, 1965.

Hunter, Kristin. *Soul Brothers and Sister Lou*. New York: Avon, 1975.

Kelly, Eric P. *The Trumpeter of Krakow*. New York: Macmillan, 1956.

Patersen, Katherine. *Come Sing, Jimmy Jo*. New York: Dutton, 1985.

DISCOGRAPHY

Introduction and Guide

This discography is intended to be a programming aid in itself. For this list of many kinds of sound materials and music, I have chosen works that seemed best to represent musical elements as I described them in the chapter, whether classical, contemporary, folk, or jazz. Although each one represented its period in some outstanding way, it is also a microcosm of a larger body of work contemporary to it and is meant to suggest further exploration. Those with no element suggested are not specifically representative.

The list has a broad geographical base and I have used works from many periods. But you may notice an American bias and this is intentional, for I would like to give our children some historical overview of their country's music. Also, I have purposefully omitted pop-rock items because their ephemeral quality gives them an uneasy and all-too-brief discographic relevance. I suggest you find out from the children what's "in" and invite them to bring in records and tapes from which you all can choose examples that illustrate elements and instruments.

Finally, I encourage each librarian to select whatever further musical works (or portions of works) seem especially appropriate to the workshop, including live performances by members of the library community.

Note: Many of the works listed below exist in a number of excellent recordings; consult the Schwann catalog for information regarding other recorded performances. Recordings available on tape are marked with the symbol TC; compact discs are indicated with the symbol CD. I was at the time of this writing unable to verify jazz and folk recordings, but many are available on tape.

melody	*Abiyoyo and Other Story Songs for Children*. Pete Seeger. Folkways 7525.
	Activity and Game Songs. Tom Glazer. 2-CMS 657-658.
	American Songbag. Carl Sandburg. 2-Caedmon 2025.
counterpoint	Bach, Johann Sebastian (1685-1750). *Two and Three Part Inventions*. Gould (piano). 3-Columbia D35-754.

counterpoint | Bach, Johann Sebastian (1685-1750). *Preludes and Fugues for Organ*. Newman. Columbia C-9022.

counterpoint/texture | Bach, Johann Sebastian (1685-1750). *Chorale Settings; Passacaglia and Fugue; Toccata and Fugue in d minor*. Biggs (organ). CBS MS-6261, MS-6748.

instruments/color | Bamboushay Steel Band. Folkways FS-3835.

counterpoint/rhythm | Bartók, Béla (1881-1945). *String Quartets 1-6*. Juilliard String Quartet. 3-CBS M-37857; TC T-37857.

instruments | Bartók, Béla (1881-1945). *Concerto for Orchestra*. Boulez/New York Philharmonic. CBS MY-37259; TC.

program | Beethoven, Ludwig van (1770-1827). *Symphony no. 6, "Pastorale."* Klemperer/Philadelphia Orchestra. AE-34426; TC 4AE-34426.

texture | Berio, Luciano (1925-). *Folk Songs*. Berberian (soprano). RCA LSC-3189.

instruments | Berlioz, Hector (1803-1869). *Symphonie fantastique,* op. 14. Ozawa/Toronto Symphony. Angel RL-32061.

harmony | Billings, William (1746-1800). *Hymns and Anthems*. Old Sturbridge Singers. Folkways 32377.

texture | Blakey, Art (1919-). *Art Blakey and the Jazz Messengers*. On Epic, Bluenote, Limelight, and others.

instruments | Britten, Benjamin (1913-1976). *Young Person's Guide to the Orchestra,* op. 34 (1946). Previn/London Symphony. Angel S-36962.

counterpoint | Byrd, William (1543-1623). *Mass in Four Parts*. Church of the Advent Choir. Afka 4676.

melody | *Chansons des troubadours*. Munich Studio for Early Music. Telefunken 641126; TC 4411126.

Chansons des trouveres. Munich Studio for Early Music. Telefunken 641275.

melody/instrument   Chopin, Frederic (1810-1849). *Collected Piano Music*. Rubinstein. 2-RCA ARL2-2359; TC ARK2-2359.

Children's Greatest Hits, vols. 1-2. Tom Glazer. CMS 689-691.

Coltrane, John (1926-). *Settin' the pace* (with Miles Davis). Prestige 7213.

Coltrane, John (1926-). *Coltrane Plays the Blues*. Atlantic 1382.

program   Copland, Aaron (1900-). *Appalachian Spring*. Bernstein/Los Angeles Philharmonic. DG 2532084; TC 423168-4.

melody   Copland, Aaron (1900-). *Quiet City for Trumpet and English Horn*. Foss/Buffalo Symphony. Turnabout 34398.

instruments   Couperin, Francois (1727-1789). *Pieces de clavecin*. Kipnis (harpsichord). 3-Columbia M3X-31521.

texture   Crumb, George (1929-). *Ancient Voices of Children* (1970). De Gaetani, Dash/Weisberg Ensemble. Nonesuch 71255.

instruments   *Dance Music of the Renaissance*. Ragossnig, Ulsamer/Collegium. CD DG ARC-415294-2.

melody   Davis, Miles (1926-). *Miles and Monk at Newport*. Columbia 8978.

harmony   Debussy, Claude (1862-1918). *La Mer*. Ansermet/Orchestra of the Suisse Romande. London 410281-4.

counterpoint   Des Prez, Josquin (c.1440-1521). *Motets; Instrumental Pieces*. Greenburg/N.Y. Pro Musica. MCA 2507.

color   Druckman, Jacob (1928-). *Electronic Music III, Animus I*. Turnabout TV 34177.

Early Early Childhood Songs. Ella Jenkins. Scholastic SC7630.

counterpoint   *English Madrigals* (Collection E2-68). Turnabout 34202.

Eno, Brian/Harold Budd (late 20th c.). *Ambient #2: The Plateaux of Mirror.* E.G. Records EGS202.

Folk Songs for Young Folks. Vol. 1: *Animals;* Vol. 2: *More Animals.* Alan Mills. Folkways Scholastic 7677, 7642.

Folk Songs for Young People. Pete Seeger. Folkways 7532.

melody   Foster, Stephen (1826-1862). *Songs.* de Gaetani, Guinn. Nonesuch 71268.

texture/instruments Gabrieli, Giovanni (c.1554/57-1612). *Canzoni for Brass Choirs.* Chicago, Cleveland, and Philadelphia Brass Ensembles. Columbia MP-38759; TC.

harmony   Gesualdo, Don Carlo (c.1560-1613). *Madrigals, Sacred Music.* CSP ARS-6318.

counterpoint   Gillespie, Dizzy. *Diz and Bird.* ROOST 2234.

Glass, Philip (1937-). *Glassworks.* Glass Ensemble. CBS FM-37265; CD MK-37265; TC FMT-37265.

color/instrumental *Gregorian Chant.* Benedictine Monks (Luxembourg). Philips Sequenza 6527073; TC 7311073.

Haydn, Franz Joseph (1732-1809). *Quartet in E Flat Major,* op. 33, no. 3 "Bird." Benthiem Quartet. Audio Fidelity 50080.

Haydn, Franz Joseph (1732-1809). *Symphony no. 73 in D Major,* "Hunt." Jones/Little Orchestra of London. Nonesuch 71096.

texture   Ibert, Jacques (1890-1962). *Music for 20 Saxophones.*

Ives, Charles (1874-1954). *Theatre Orchestra Set: In the Cage, In the Inn, At Night.* Farberman/Royal Philharmonic. Vanguard C-10013.

Ives, Charles (1874-1954). *Three Places in New England.* Davies/St. Paul Chamber Orchestra. Pro Arte PAD-140; CD CDB-140; TC PCD-140.

Lullabies and Other Children's Songs. Nancy Raven. Pacific Cascade LPC 7007.

Lully, Jean-Baptiste (1632-1687). *Alceste* (a masque). Malgoire/Grande Écurie and La Chambre du Roy. 3-CBS M3-34580.

MacDowell, Edward (1860-1908). *Sea Pieces*, op. 55. Fierro. Nonesuch 71411; TC.

harmony/instruments   Mahler, Gustav (1860-1911). *Das Lied von der Erde* (The song of the earth). Norman, Vickers, Davis/London Symphony. Philips 65142; CD 411474-2; TC 7337112.

Menotti, Gian Carlo (1911-). *Amahl and the Night Visitors*. King, Yaghijan, Grossman. RCA LSC-2762.

melody/texture   Monk, Meredith (1942-). *Dolmen Music*. ECM Records GmBH.

melody/rhythm   Monk, Thelonius (1920-1982). *Solo Monk*. Columbia 9149.

Monk, Thelonius (1920-1982). *Miles and Monk at Newport*. Columbia 8978.

Monk, Thelonius (1920-1982). *T.M. and Coleman Hawkins*. Riverside 12-242.

harmony   Monteverdi, Claudio (1567-1643). *Madrigals*. Deller Consort. Vanguard HM-10.

counterpoint   Morley, Thomas (1557/8-1602). *Madrigals*. Deller Consort. Vanguard HM-4; TC CHM-4.

melody/instruments   Mozart, Wolfgang Amadeus (1756-1791). *Concerto for Piano and Orchestra no. 12 in A Major*, K. 414. Serkin, Schneider/Marlboro Festival Orchestra. CBS M-31728.

Mozart, Wolfgang Amadeus (1756-1791). *Quintet in a minor for Clarinet and Strings*, K. 581. Peyer, Amadeus Quartet. DG 2530720.

Mozart, Wolfgang Amadeus (1756-1791). *Quintet in E flat Major for Horn and Strings*, K. 407. Huber, Endres Quartet. Turnabout 34035; TC CT-4035.

Mozart, Wolfgang Amadeus (1756-1791). *Symphony no. 40 in g minor,* K. 550. Szell/Cleveland Orchestra. 2-Columbia MG-30368.

Negro Folk Songs for Young People. Huddie Ledbetter (Leadbelly). Folkways 7533.

instruments/color

Mussorgsky, Modest (1839-1881). *Pictures at an Exhibition.* Schippers/New York Philharmonic. Odyssey 32160376; TC YT-60376.

New York 19. Documentary Sounds of New York City. Tony Schwartz. Folkways 5558.

harmony

Palestrina, Giovanni (c.1525-1594). *Choral Works.* Wagner Chorale. 3-Angel S-36013.

rhythm/melody

Parker, Charlie "The Bird" (1920-1955). *Diz n' Bird* (with Dizzy Gillespie). Roost 2234.

Parker, Charlie "The Bird" (1920-1955). *Jam Session nos. 1-2.* Verve 8049.

Peterson, Oscar (1925-). *Midnight Jazz at Carnegie Hall.* Verve 8189.

Peterson Field Guide to Bird Songs of Eastern and Central North America. Houghton (2).

Peterson Field Guide to Western Bird Songs. Houghton (3).

Coleman Hawkins and Confreres. Verve 6110.

Play Your Instrument and Make a Pretty Sound. Ella Jenkins. Folkways 7665.

program/instruments

Prokofiev, Sergei (1891-1953). *Peter and the Wolf.* Du Pre, Barenboim/English Chamber Orchestra. DG 2531275; TC 330125.

Prokofiev, Sergei (1891-1953). *Symphony no. 5,* op. 100. Szell/Cleveland Orchestra. Odyssey Y-35923.

harmony

Rameau, Jean-Philippe (1683-1764). *Harpsichord Music.* Pinnock (harpsichord). 3-Vanguard 71256, 71270, 71271.

instruments	Ravel, Maurice (1875-1937). *L'Enfant et les sortileges.* Wyner et al., Previn/London Symphony. Angel DS-37869; CD CDC-47169.
	Ravel, Maurice (1875-1937). *Complete Works for Piano Solo.* Gieseking (piano). Angel 3541.
	Ravel, Maurice (1875-1937). *Mother Goose Suite.* Ansermet/Orchestra of the Suisse Romande. London STS-15488.
instruments/texture	Reich, Steve (1936-). *Six Pianos (1973); Music for Mallet Instruments, Voices, and Organ* (1973). Reich Ensemble. 3-DG2535314; TC 3335314.
melody/counterpoint	Schubert, Franz (1797-1828). *Quartet no. 14 in d minor,* "Death and the Maiden." Amadeus Quartet. DG 2535314; TC 3335314.
	Schubert, Franz (1797-1828). *Die schöne Müllerin* (song cycle). Fischer-Dieskau, Moore. DG 2530544; CD 415186-2.
harmony	Schumann, Clara (1819-1896). *Trio in g minor for violin, cello, and piano,* op. 17. Beaux Arts Trio. 2-Philips 6700051.
instruments	Shankar, Ravi (1920-). *Raga Michara Pico.* Shankar (sitar), Khan (sarod) (recorded live at Carnegie Hall, 1982). Angel DS-37920.
program/harmony	Sibelius, Jean (1865-1957). *Swan of Tuonela.* Karajan/Berlin Philharmonic. DG 413755-1; CD 413755-2; TC 413755-4.
program	*Songs of My People.* Paul Robeson. RCA LM-3292.
instruments/rhythm	John Cage, Edgar Varese, Henry Cowell. *Sounds of New Music: The Story of Electronic Music.* Folkways RX 6160.
	Sounds and Ultra-Sounds of the Bottle-Nose Dolphin. The Dolphin. Folkways 6132.
	The Story of Jazz. Langston Hughes. Folkways 7312.
rhythm	Strauss, Johann (1825-1957). *Walzes.* Bernstein/New York Philharmonic. Columbia MS-7288.

harmony/instruments   Strauss, Richard (1864-1949). *Don Quixote.* Fournier (cello), Szell/Cleveland Orchestra. Odyssey Y-3224; TC YT-3224.

rhythm/program   Stravinsky, Igor (1882-1971). *Petrouchka* (complete ballet, 1911). Bernstein/New York Philharmonic. 2-Columbia MG-30269.

Stravinsky, Igor (1882-1971). *Le Sacre du printemps.* Ozawa/Boston Symphony. Philips 416246-1; TC 416246-4.

instruments   Tchaikovsky, Piotr Ilyich (1840-1893). *Nutcracker Suite.* Bernstein/New York Philharmonic. Columbia M-31806; TC MT-31806.

Tchaikovsky, Piotr Ilyich (1840-1893). *Serenade in C for Strings.* Munch/Boston Symphony. RCA AGL1-5218; TC.

Tchaikovsky, Piotr Ilyich (1840-1893). *Symphony no. 5 in e minor,* op. 64. Karajan/Berlin Philharmonic. DG 2530699; TC 3300699.

Travellin' with Ella Jenkins: A Bilingual Journey. Folkways FC 764.

rhythm/melody   Varèse, Edgar (1883-1965). *Integrales; Ionization; Hyperprism for Woodwinds, Brass, and Percussion.* Craft. 2-Columbia MG-31078.

melody   Villa Lobos, Heitor (1887-1954). *Bachianas Brasilieras no. 5 for soprano and 8 celli.* Villa-Lobos, Rose (solo cello). Columbia 71670-D.

program   Vivaldi, Antonio (1678-1759). *Four Seasons,* op. 8, nos. 1-4. Munchinger/Stuttgart Chamber Orchestra. London 417051-1; TC 417051-4.

instruments/harmony   Wagner, Richard (1813-1883). *Overtures and Preludes (Flying Dutchman, Meistersinger, Rienzi, Tristan).* Bernstein/New York Philharmonic. CBS M-31011; TC MT-31011.

FILMOGRAPHY

Blues de Balfa. 28 min. Color. Leo Diner Films.

An introduction to American Cajun music, the French-American music of Louisiana, *Blues de Balfa* is a moving evocation of the Balfa family. They are dedicated to playing and performing this regional blend of bluegrass, country violin, and folksinging special to this part of the world. Appropriate for young adults who can best appreciate the sense of the musician's life and work that seems to emerge from the film.

Chinese Musical Instruments. 23 min. Color. Taiwan Communication Division.

A teaching film that explores folk instruments and their function in Chinese civilization, both ancient and contemporary. Although it is somewhat too long and not very imaginative, it is thorough and would be useful to introduce children to music of an entirely different culture. In addition, many of the instruments shown are related to those that children themselves could make in a workshop. Best for older boys and girls or young adults.

Discovering the Music of Africa. 22 min. Color. BFA Educational Media.

Made by an African scholar, *Discovering the Music of Africa* is a careful teaching film, which shows important instruments of the culture, demonstrated by African musicians. The emphasis is on percussion--drums, rattles, and bells--with the function of the drum as a language within itself given a central place. Short dances are shown, which demonstrate in a clear way the important interrelation of music and dance in African culture.

Foolish Frog. 8 min. Color. Weston Woods.

Pete Seeger sings this delicious, swinging account of an entire rural community that winds up in a dance fest at the village store. When the barn joins in, the fun takes off.

Frog Went A-Courtin'. 12 min. Color. Films, Inc.

This musical folktale, sung by John Langstaff and superbly animated by Rojankovsky, tells the always compelling story of a frog's courtship of Miss Mousy. Children will enjoy the playful feeling and the absurd characters, but you may want to show only the first half--the second is a questionable effort in sing-along technique, certainly lost on preschoolers.

Jack and the Robbers. 14 1/2 min. Color. Pied Piper Productions.

Richard Chase, the famous collector of southern Appalachian folktales, narrates the story of *The Musicians of Bremen* as transplanted to this part of the world. Shot in a series of brightly colored animations, the film tells of homeless Jack, who adopts some animals on his travels, and shows how they come to his defense in unexpected and musical ways when robbers occupy the house they are staying in. It is told in a captivating and lively way, drawing the audience into the story.

Kuumba: Simon's New Sound. 8 min. Color. Nguzo Sago Films, Inc.

Kuumba means creativity in Swahili, and this animated and joyful celebration of African music shows Simon's search for the right instrument to express his own creativity. The film was shot at Port-of-Spain's annual carnival-festival. Wonderful masks and dances appear before us as we watch Simon experiment with making instruments out of everything he finds. He finally invents the steel drum, now a venerable expression of Trinidad's musical culture.

Luminauts. 9 min. Color. Christian Schiess.

An imaginative ride with the astronauts rendered in waves of abstract, light-fragmented images, Luminauts is supported by a percussive programmatic score that could serve to introduce some uses of contemporary electronic sound as well as the percussion section.

Navajo Rain Chant. 2 min. Color. Animation Workshop.

Abstractions of desert mesas and American Indian dwellings in brilliant color accompany a powerful male-voiced choral Navajo chanting that is designed to bring rain to the land--at the end it does! Children will grasp the fierce rhythmic excitement of the music, which echoes the intense, sharply etched desert landscape.

A Particular Man. 9 min. Color. William Lipper Film.

A thoughtfully made film that chronicles the life of an Italian violin maker and violinist, Mario Frusali. The clear rendering of his life and the way it interacts with the actual making of the instruments is very well done. Suitable for older boys and girls as an introduction to musicianship as well as instrument making.

The Pied Piper of Hamlin. 10 min. Color. BFA Productions.

The classic story of the avenging piper who rids a town of rats. When the townspeople refuse to pay him, he exacts a terrible revenge. The tale is told here in cartoon animation and rhymed verse. Although the verse is disappointing, Peter Ustinov's oleaginous guile manages to infuse the film with some measure of the original fascination.

Really Rosie. 26 min. Color. Weston.

This is a collage film, combining the television program "Really Rosie," with characters from the Nutshell Library and "The Sign on Rosie's Door" in an animated version. Rosie's swanky vitality as she heads up her neighborhood children's theatrical troupe is vividly rendered by the songs and singing of Carole King.

Steffan the Violinmaker. 25 min. Color. Coronet.

A sympathetic look at music making from the point of view of sixteen-year-old Steffan, a young member of a German violin-making family and apprentice to the trade. The making of an instrument is traced from wood carving to finished product at the school for violinmakers, while the camera lingers on the natural beauty of forests and rivers enjoyed by Steffan and his friends in their off-school time. Although the film is somewhat long-winded, it is a sensitive portrayal of this important craft.

Sunshine's on the Way. 30 min. Color. Learning Corp. of America.

Bobba June Strong, a teenaged trombonist, works at the local nursing home. When her idol T. T. Jackson, the famous jazz trombonist, moves in, Bobba June, in an effort to cheer him up, organizes the Sugar Hill Nursing Home Jazz Band, and they get a chance to perform in Hollywood. The story reflects an optimistic, sympathetic view of youth and the elderly, and how music can bond as well as inspire.

Ty's Home-made Band. 20 min. Color. Phoenix.

Mildred Walter's book becomes a lively film starring Taj Majal as a modern-day minstrel who invades a small southern town with his acting, music, and comedy act. He soon draws Ty and his friends into his home-made band, and they decide to stage a live performance. On the big day they nimbly play jug, comb, paper, washboard, and thimbles to the amazement of families and friends in the schoolyard. Although the film perfectly illustrates introducing music to children at their own level, it seem a pity that only boys are included in the act--a definite drawback to the film's effectiveness.

WORKSHOPS

Music: The Elements of Play

Introduction: For a children's librarian or teacher who likes and listens to music, this workshop should be a good one. Those who like the idea but would prefer working with a professional could ask a local teacher or university student to collaborate. In this case the teacher and librarian should confer on the chapter itself and on the materials to be used to illustrate.

Ages: 7-13.

Number of Children: 10-12.

Time: One-and-a-half to two hours to introduce the elements of music (one session).

Space: A room separate from the library or the use of library space at off-hours; comfortable chairs or cushions; pin-up wall space.

Materials: A recorder or tape player; illustrative records or tapes; guitar or Autoharp, if possible; books and pictures appropriate to music; perhaps some orchestra instruments to display, if these are available; crayons or felt-tip pens and paper; watercolors; fabric swatches illustrative of the various types of textures as described.

After the children have been welcomed and are comfortable, ask them what music is for them. Talk a little about it to introduce your idea of what it is. Play a little of the bird song record and let children experience the world of our ancestors, their own beginnings. Introduce the elements of music to them, using a record like Prokofiev's *Peter and the Wolf,* which they may know and which clearly and simply illustrates melody, rhythm, and so on. This leads easily in to a discussion of the elements, one at a time.

Melody: What is it? Whistle or hum a melody and ask the children to sing some examples of music they know. Then pass out crayons or felt-tip pens and suggest that, as they listen to some pieces, they let their fingers draw the melody out on paper, free-form style, letting it go where it wants. Try playing some short examples, melodies that have a strong shape and a listenable quality, like the main theme of *Peter and the Wolf,* a folk song of Pete

Seeger's, some country music, Copland's *Quiet City* theme, Meredith Monk, or a good strong show tune. Can they see the difference in the pictures? Invite volunteers to show some melody sketches and hold them up. How did the themes differ? What colors did they pick for different themes? What moods did they reflect? Hold onto the pictures to use later and move on.

Rhythm: Define it for them, and demonstrate by clapping out the difference between triple and duple rhythm and then letting them clap it back to you. Play a small amount of country music singing, William Billings's *Hymns and Anthems*, or four-square Lutheran chorales and then some Strauss waltzes or other dance music in triple time to illustrate. Invite the children to clap out the rhythms with you as they emerge, stopping the record from time to time to go over it. Try demonstrating the rhythm yourself and see if one or two of the children will join you in doing the beat. Then review the pieces you chose very briefly in terms of fast and slow. Ask one or two of the children to walk or run to illustrate tempo, clapping along to help them establish it.

Counterpoint: Pass out fresh paper. Say briefly what counterpoint is and hold up their melody line drawings one over the other to show how the melodies look juxtaposed. Suggest they use different colors to draw different voices, and then, playing pieces that are very clear in their counterpoint, such as Johann Sebastian Bach's *Two- and Three-Part Inventions,* Thomas Morley's *Madrigals*, or John Coltrane's *Settin' the Pace,* ask them to draw the interweaving sounds. They can draw--one at a time as you play a piece over-- soprano, tenor, and bass, using a different color for each one. When they have a picture with interwoven lines, show them and pin these up next to the pictures of melody.

Harmony: Using a very large white sheet (shelf paper or the like), draw treble and bass staves and lines on it. With a guitar, Autoharp, or keyboard instrument, play a chord for the children. Paint in the notes of the chord, using a different watercolor for each one; then hold it up and let the colors run freely in together. Do this with several chords, using major and minor, consonant and dissonant, and employing different colors for each one. When all the colors have run, pin them up by one another to show the children your "harmonies" and to illustrate the difference from melody and counterpoint. Play a few, highly harmonic examples: a few measures of Berlioz's *Symphonie fantastique,* the Grateful Dead, or Monteverdi's choral music should suggest the richness of the possibilities. Then ask one child at a time to come up front and "be" a note; say the color of each one's shirt or dress and ask them to cluster tightly together. Now the remainder of the group can see a giant "chord," a live difference between single notes, melody, and harmonic "cluster."

Texture: Bring out your material samples. The idea of texture in music is derived from textiles, so choose some examples ahead of time to match up: for instance, *heavy:* Mahler; *light:* Mozart; *loose:* Grateful Dead; *tight:* madrigals; *thin:* Gregorian chant; *thick:* Rachmaninoff; *smooth:* jazz; *rough:* electronic; *soft:* blues; *hard:* dissonant music.

Play each example a very short time and pass around the sample appropriate to each one as it is being played.

Instruments: This can be the most fun of all the elements of music for some of the children, as many play instruments themselves. You may want to ask them ahead of time to bring in their instruments to demonstrate. Begin with Benjamin Britten's *Young Person's Guide to the Orchestra,* an excellent teaching piece, as the repetition and verbal introductions allow children to grasp the sense of the music while they are also beginning to identify each instrument and section of the orchestra. Let the children who have brought in an instrument show how it looks and sounds, and ask the others to decide "color" of the instrument by choosing a color for each and then labelling it. If there is time, play brief selections from a few records that demonstrate the uses of instruments together--for instance, Edgar Varèse's *Integrales,* Mozart's *Clarinet Quintet,* Gabrieli's *Canzoni for Brass,* or a rich orchestral work like Igor Stravinsky's *Le Sacre du printemps,* all excellent examples of instrumental "color."

This completes the exploration of music's elements, but in closing it might be revealing to invite the children to talk about their own "element," their audience role in the workshop, what they experienced and learned, and how the workshop affected their understanding of music. If possible, arrange to exhibit some of the pictures of music the children made in the library, together with books and records, if there is space.

Records from the Discography for Use in This Workshop

Bach, Johann Sebastian. *Two and Three-Part Inventions*. Gould (piano). 3-Columbia D35-754.

Bamboushay Steel Band. Folkways FS-3835.

Berlioz, Hector. *Symphonie fantastique,* op. 14. Ozawa/Toronto Symphony. Angel RL-32061.

Billings, William. *Hymns and Anthems*. Old Sturbridge Singers. Folkways 32377.

Britten, Benjamin. *Young Person's Guide to the Orchestra,* op. 34. Previn/London Symphony. Angel S-36962.

Coltrane, John. *Settin' the Pace* (with Miles Davis). Prestige 7213.

Davis, Miles. *Miles and Monk at Newport.* Columbia 8978.

Debussy, Claude. *La Mer.* Ansermet/Orchestra of the Suisse Romande. London 410281-4.

Druckman, Jacob. *Electronic Music III.* Turnabout TV-34177.

Folk Songs for Young People. Pete Seeger. Folkways 7532.

Gabrieli, Giovanni. *Canzoni for Brass Choirs.* Chicago, Cleveland, and Philadelphia Brass Ensembles. Columbia MP-38759; TC.

Gregorian Chant. Benedictine Monks (Luxembourg). Philips Sequenza 6527073; TC 7311073.

Ives, Charles. *Three Places in New England.* Davies/St. Paul Chamber Orchestra. Pro Arte PAD-140; CD CDD-140; TC PCD-140.

Monk, Meredith. *Dolmen Music.* ECM Records GmbH.

Mozart, Wolfgang Amadeus. *Quintet in a minor for Clarinet and Strings,* K.581. Peyer, Amadeus Quartet. DG 2530720.

Peterson Field Guide to Western Bird Songs. Houghton (3).

Prokofiev, Sergei. *Peter and the Wolf.* Du Pre, Barenboim/English Chamber Orchestra. DG 2531275; TC 330125.

Rameau, Jean-Philippe. *Harpsichord Music.* Pinnock (harpsichord). 3-Vanguard 71256, 71270, 71271.

Strauss, Johann. *Waltzes.* Bernstein/New York Philharmonic. Columbia MS-7288.

Strauss, Richard. *Don Quixote.* Fournier (cello), Szell/Cleveland Orchestra. Odyssey Y-32224; TC YT-32224.

Stravinsky, Igor. *Le Sacre du printemps.* Ozawa/Boston Symphony. Philips 416246-1; TC 416246-4.

How to Make Your Own Instruments

This is a good workshop for a craft-minded librarian with or without a local musician.

Ages: 6-13

Number of Children: 5-10

Space: A room that can hold good-sized bare tables for working materials and work space.

Materials: Hacksaw, contact cement or silicone sealer, PVC cement, white glue, 120 grit sandpaper, scissors, hand drill, masking tape, string, screwdriver, 1/2-inch thinwall PVC (hard) plastic pipe, corks (or chunks of wood dowels or poster paper or cardboard from tablet backing), soda straws, pieces of 3/4-inch plywood about 5 x 5 inches, Popsicle sticks, carpet tubes about 3 inches in diameter.

Display: Put up pictures of the instruments copied from this book and backed. Books on instrument making and on music and musical instruments can be displayed.

In structuring the workshop select the instruments that are appealing to you, seem most appropriate to your children, and can be made in the amount of time you want to spend. Setting up the materials and experimenting with instrument making ahead of time is a good idea. It will give you an idea of how much time is necessary.

Move from making one instrument to the next, being sure to show appropriate illustrations and picture displays. Leave time for children to test-play their new instruments before moving on. When all the instruments are made, set up a little orchestra and let the children improvise for a while in ensemble. If possible, put up a few of the instruments on display for a week or so.

If you have access to it, showing the video *Ty's One-man Band*, which features homemade instruments, would provide an incentive and give the children a lively context for their efforts.

Pan Pipes

Materials: 1/2-inch thinwall PVC plastic pipe. This comes in 10-foot lengths and costs a little over a dollar for 10 feet. Stoppers can be corks, chunks of wood, dowels of stiff paper like poster paper or the cardboard from the backs of tablets. Good glues to use include silicone sealer, contact cement, or PVC cement if you are working in a ventilated area.

Procedure: Cut the PVC pipe to various lengths with a hacksaw and plug one end of each piece of the tube. The seal must be airtight. If you use cardboard pieces, glue them on with contact cement or silicone sealer, and tape with masking tape until the sealer dries. Fasten the tubes side to side with the open ends along a straight line. Tubes can be glued to each other with PVC cement or to a piece of cardboard with silicone sealer or contact cement.

To Play: Blow across the open ends of the tubes so the stream of air coming from your lips hits the opposite edge of the tube. Blow at different velocities until the tube sounds.

Afterthoughts: I like to sand with 120 grit or finer sandpaper the open ends of the tubes where my lips will touch them. To raise the pitch of any of your tubes to a higher pitch cut the tube shorter. To lower the pitch select a longer tube.

Soda Straw Oboe

Materials: Soda straws (plastic or paper), scissors.

Procedure: Flatten approximately 1/2 inch of one end of the straw. Cut a point with the point centered at the end of the flat area with two angles of approximately 45 degrees. You may cut or poke finger holes along the length of the straw to vary the pitch. But no more holes than you have fingers! You may also vary the pitch by fastening the straw to the end of a longer tube with masking tape.

To Play: Place the pointed flattened end of the straw into your mouth. Seal your lips firmly around the shaft of the tube. BLOW HARD!

Afterthoughts: Some students may have difficulty getting a sound. Try reflattening the tip or blowing harder. A great demonstration of the relationship between pitch and length is to blow the oboe as you cut pieces from it; the shorter the straw gets, the higher the pitch. Watch out for your nose! With a little practice you can play a near perfect scale.

Carpet-Tube Bongos

Materials: Carpet tubes approximately 3 inches in diameter cut to lengths of 8 inches to 12 inches, heavy cardboard disks (tablet-back weight) cut to the size of the tube, white or carpenter's glue, masking tape, string.

Procedure: Glue a cardboard disk to the end of a chunk of carpet tube and tape on with masking tape. Glue two or more tubes together side to side and bind with string. The longer the tube the lower the pitch.

To Play: Hold drums between your knees and tap the disk-covered ends of the tubes with your fingers.

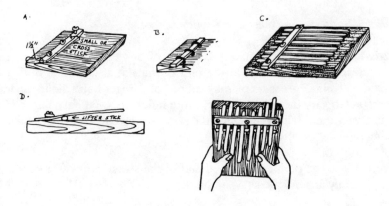

Thumb Piano

Materials: Pieces of plywood approximately 5 x 5 inches, three #6 (1 inch) panhead wood screws per piano, at least two five-inch pieces of 3/16- to 1/4-inch dowel or facsimile, a drill to drill holes for the screws, and Popsicle sticks (approximately 8 per piano), one section of 3/8-inch dowel 4 1/2 inches long.

Procedure: Using three screws attach a small stick to the board about 1 1/2-inches from one side. Or you can drill holes through the board and lace the small stick to it with strong string, leather, or wire if you want. Arrange the Popsicle sticks parallel to each other with one end under the cross stick. Tighten the screws so the cross stick almost touches the Popsicle sticks. Slip a thin stick under the Popsicle sticks at their long ends. Push the stick as far toward the cross stick as it will go.

To Play: Hold the plywood square with both hands, thumbs to the top, doweled end of the thumb piano away from you. Pluck the ends of the sticks with your thumbs.

Afterthoughts: I like to coat the tips of the sticks with fingernail polish to make them smooth. The polish dries fast, is easy for kids to handle, and adds color. I usually tune my thumb pianos with the low notes toward the center and alternate the rising pitch from side to side.

Workshop by Tom Walther, from *Make Mine Music*.
© 1981 by Yolla Bolla Press. A Brown School Book.
Reprinted by permission.
Adapted by Lea Burroughs

Poetry

T hen already I know the storms and am stirred
  like the sea
And spread myself out and fall back into myself
  and fling myself out and am all alone in
  the great storm.

--Rainer Maria Rilke

Long before children are ready to take on the complex difficult journeys of the adult, they are ready to feel them, to experience them in poems. To be a child hearing a poem is to be a child on a journey of the mind--the mind's window framing the pictures, the mind's ear ringing with sounds--with the memory recording the shapes and colors and rhythms for all time.

Beginning very early with Mother Goose, rhythms and rhymes and music and colors can work this magic for children. By the time they're two, A. A. Milne's *When We Were Very Young*, Richard Lewis's *In a Spring*

Garden, Harry Behn's *Cricket Songs* work to expand the first experience. And the growing child continues to enjoy them more deeply, perhaps, at three or four. By five, children appreciate Edward Lear, *A Child's Garden of Verses,* poems by that famous author Anon., silly poems, and poems by other children from all over the world.

Reading aloud, first at home and then in the children's room, is the key. As the middle years unfold, with this substantial grounding in the sound, children feel friendly to poetry, and every kind of poetry in the world can open up for them. And they do like all kinds: exciting story poems, lyric poems, brief and intense; humorous verse, tongue twisters, and riddles and gigglers of every variety.

In the children's room, right at hand lie dozens of books of poetry and a wealth of wonderful poems. Exploring a few will give you an idea of what's there and reveal in passing some of the elements of poetry, the craft of it. This is important, because although children do not need to know the technical side of poetry, their attention deepens if a poem is strong and well made--it frees the expression and clarifies the meaning. A crafted poem stays with the memory, deep in the mind.

Structure

Dramatic structure is important in, for instance, the narrative poem if it is to have strength; if it is loose and sloppy or sentimental, the poem is flabby and dull. But look at "The Highwayman" of Alfred Noyes:

The Highwayman

Part One

The wind was a torrent of darkness among the gusty trees,
The moon was a ghostly galleon tossed upon cloudy seas,
The road was a ribbon of moonlight over the purple moor,
And the highwayman came riding--
　　　　　Riding--riding--
The highwayman came riding, up to the old inn-door.

He'd a French cocked-hat on his forehead, a bunch of lace at his chin,
A coat of the claret velvet, and breeches of brown doeskin:
They fitted with never a wrinkle; his boots were up to the thigh!
And he rode with a jewelled twinkle,
　　　　　His pistol butts a-twinkle,
His rapier hilt a-twinkle, under the jewelled sky.

136

Over the cobbles he clattered and clashed in the dark inn-yard,
And he tapped with his whip on the shutters, but it was all locked and barred:
He whistled a tune to the window, and who should be waiting there
But the landlord's black-eyed daughter,
    Bess, the landlord's daughter,
Plaiting a dark red love-knot into her long black hair.

And dark in the dark old inn-yard a stable-wicket creaked
Where Tim, the ostler, listened; his face was white and peaked,
His eyes were hollows of madness, his hair like moldy hay;
But he loved the landlord's daughter,
    The landlord's red-lipped daughter:
Dumb as a dog he listened, and he heard the robber say--

"One kiss, my bonny sweetheart, I'm after a prize tonight,
But I shall be back with the yellow gold before the morning light.
Yet if they press me sharply, and harry me through the day,
Then look for me by moonlight
    Watch for me by moonlight:
I'll come to thee by moonlight, though Hell should bar the way."

He rose upright in the stirrups, he scarce could reach her hand;
But she loosed her hair i'the casement! His face burnt like a brand
As the black cascade of perfume came tumbling over his breast;
And he kissed its waves in the moonlight,
    (Oh, sweet black waves in the moonlight)
Then he tugged at his reins in the moonlight, and galloped away to the West.

Part Two

He did not come in the dawning; he did not come at noon;
And out of the tawny sunset, before the rise o'the moon,
When the road was a gypsy's ribbon, looping the purple moor,
A red-coat troop came marching--
    Marching--marching--
King George's men came marching, up to the old inn-door.

They said no word to the landlord, they drank his ale instead;
But they gagged his daughter and bound her to the foot of her narrow bed.
Two of them knelt at her casement, with muskets at the side!
There was death at every window;
    And Hell at one dark window;
For Bess could see, through her casement, the road that *he* would ride.

They had tied her up to attention, with many a sniggering jest:
They had bound a musket beside her, with the barrel beneath her breast!
"Now keep good watch!" and they kissed her.
                She heard the dead man say --
Look for me by moonlight;
                Watch for me by moonlight;
I'll come to thee by moonlight, though Hell should bar the way!

She twisted her hands behind her; but all the knots held good!
She writhed her hands till her fingers were wet with sweat or blood!
They stretched and strained in the darkness, and the hours crawled by like
                years;
Till, now, on the stroke of midnight,
                Cold, on the stroke of midnight,
The tip of one finger touched it! The trigger at least was hers!

The tip of one finger touched it; she strove no more for the rest!
Up, she stood up to attention, with the barrel beneath her breast,
She would not risk their hearing: she would not strive again;
For the road lay bare in the moonlight;
                Blank and bare in the moonlight;
And the blood of her veins in the moonlight throbbed to her Love's refrain.

Tlot-tlot, tlot-tlot! Had they heard it? The horse-hoofs ringing clear?
Tlot-tlot, tlot-tlot, in the distance? Were they deaf that they did not hear?
Down the ribbon of moonlight, over the brow of the hill,
The highwayman came riding,
                Riding, riding!
The redcoats looked to their priming! She stood up straight and still!

Tlot-tlot, in the frosty silence! Tlot-tlot in the echoing night!
Nearer he came and nearer! Her face was like a light!
Her eyes grew wide for the moment; she drew one last deep breath,
Then her finger moved in the moonlight,
                Her musket shattered the moonlight,
Shattered her breast in the moonlight and warned him--with her death.

He turned; he spurred him westward; he did not know who stood
Bowed with her head o'er the musket, drenched with her own red blood!
Not till the dawn he heard it, and slowly blanched to hear
How Bess, the landlord's daughter,
                The landlord's black-eyed daughter,
Had watched for her love in the moonlight; and died in the darkness there.

Back, he spurred like a madman, shrieking a curse to the sky,
With the white road smoking behind him, and his rapier brandished high
Blood-red were his spurs i'the golden noon; wine-red was his velvet coat;
When they shot him down on the highway,
        Down like a dog on the highway.
And he lay in his blood on the highway, with the bunch of lace at his throat.

      * * * * * * * * * * * * * * * *

And still of a winter's night, they say, when the wind is in the trees
When the moon is a ghostly galleon tossed upon cloudy seas,
When the road is a ribbon of moonlight over the purple moor,
A highwayman comes riding--
        Riding--riding--
A highwayman comes riding, up to the old inn-door.

Over the cobbles he clatters and clangs in the dark inn-yard;
And he taps with his whip on the shutters, but all is locked and barred:
He whistles a tune to the window, and who should be waiting there
But the landlord's black-eyed daughter,
        Bess, the landlord's daughter,
Plaiting a dark red love-knot into her long black hair.

    Here the tale is told in an all-out thrust; it rides like the highwayman, hardly varying in tone, building up intensity line by line. But there is an undertone, a sympathy for the gorgeous gallantry of the highwayman and the brave sacrifice of Bess. Children hear the vigorous quality and the exciting story, carried in the apparent simplicity of the tale by a strong dramatic structure. Noyes builds the action through repetitive stanzas, using rhyming, rhythmic schemes, and poetic repetitions of phrase to suggest atmosphere. The story is told in a clean way that moves fast, revealing the plot without the waste of a word. The way children know this is they aren't bored.

    In contrast this little story from Mother Goose is told softly, in a tiny space:

        Saw ye ought of my love a-coming
        from the market?
        A pack of meal upon her back,
        A babby in her basket,
        Saw ye ought of my love a-coming
        from the market?

            --Anon.

Here the tale is only suggested; the dramatic structure cleverly forces us to fill in the events and the emotions. The adult asks if he has been cuckolded, if he has lost his love. But the child appreciates the image and the homely facts. Mother Goose, as is so often true, is understandable on two levels.

But in this lightning-bug poem of Archy's the structure is all in the actual telling of the story by the speaker:

the flattered lightning bug

a lightning bug got
in here the other night a
regular hick from
the real country he was
awful proud of himself you
city insects may think
you are some punkins
but i don't see any
of you flashing in the dark
like we do in
the country all right go
to it says i mehitable the
cat and that green
spider who lives in your locker
and two or three cockroach
friends of mine and a
friendly rat all gathered
around him and urged him on
and he lightened and
lightened and lightened you
don't see anything like this
in town often he says go to it
we told him it's a
real treat to us and
we nicknamed him broadway
which pleased him
this is the life
he said all i
need is a harbor
under me to be a
statue of liberty and
he got so vain of
himself i had to take

him down a peg you've
made lightning for two hours
little bug i told him
but i don't hear
any claps of thunder
yet there are some men
like that when he wore
himself out mehitable
the cat ate him
      archy

        --Don Marquis

Don Marquis's nonstop style of talk provides the structure here, pell-mell continuity, funny and sly, giving old archy's wry-tongued tale unity. And children enjoy his writing (at night) on the ancient typewriter whose capitals are too high for him to reach.

Another story poem, successful in a different way, is Edward Lear's *The Owl and the Pussy-Cat:*

The Owl and the Pussy-Cat went to sea
    In a beautiful pea-green boat:
They took some honey, and plenty of money
    Wrapped up in a five-pound note.
The Owl looked up to the stars above,
    And sang to a small guitar,
"O lovely Pussy, O Pussy, my love,
    What a beautiful Pussy you are,
        You are,
        You are!
    What a beautiful Pussy you are!"

Pussy said to the Owl, "You elegant fowl,
    How charmingly sweet you sing!
Oh! let us be married; too long we have tarried
    But what shall we do for a ring?"
They sailed away, for a year and a day,
    To the land where the bong-tree grows;
And there in the wood a Piggy-wig stood,
    With a ring at the end of his nose,
        His nose,
        His nose,
    With a ring at the end of his nose.

"Dear Pig, are you willing to sell for one shilling
      Your ring?" Said the Piggy, "I will."
So they took it away, and were married next day
      By the turkey who lives on the hill.
They dined on mince and slices of quince,
      Which they ate with a runcible spoon;
And hand in hand, on the edge of the sand,
      They danced by the light of the moon,
         The moon,
         The moon,
      They danced by the light of the moon.

This poem is traditional in structure: a beginning, a middle, and an end, carefully inlaid with an intricate set of rhyme schemes, internal rhyme, and lively rhythms to ride it out.

So narrative can adapt in myriad ways to reveal the intimate drama at the center; and children can enjoy the story while absorbing a deeper poetic meaning on a different level altogether.

Tone

Tone is an elusive but important part of poetry, showing how the speaker feels about what he is writing. A striking example of this is Lewis Carroll's *Jabberwocky:*

      'Twas brillig, and the slithy toves
         Did gyre and gimble in the wabe:
      All mimsy were the borogoves,
         And the mome raths outgrabe.

What could better set a tone of irony and life's bewildering twists and turns? It then proceeds, but only apparently more coherently:

      "Beware the Jabberwock, my son!
         The jaws that bite, the claws that catch!
      Beware the Jubjub bird, and shun
         The frumious Bandersnatch!"

      He took his vorpal sword in hand:
         Long time the manxome foe he sought--
      So rested he by the Tumtum tree
         And stood awhile in thought.

And as in uffish thought he stood,
    The Jabberwock, with eyes of flame,
Came whiffling through the tulgey wood,
    And burbled as it came!

One, two! One, two! And through and through
    The vorpal blade went snicker-snack!
He left it dead, and with its head
    He went galumphing back.

"And hast thou slain the Jabberwock?
    Come to my arms, my beamish boy!
O frabjous day! Callooh! Callay!"
    He chortled in his joy.

'Twas brillig, and the slithy toves
    Did gyre and gimble in the wabe;
All mimsy were the borogoves,
    And the mome raths outgrabe.

      --Lewis Carroll

Carroll is mocking that worship of violence at the heart of dueling, a practice beloved of the Europe of an earlier period. He doubles the mockery by telling the story in his elegant gibberish. But children are fascinated just with the sound--they don't need to know the reasons to linger in the music.

Contrast Carroll's tone with the *Last Song of Sitting Bull,* an American Indian poem:

a warrior
I have been.
Now
It is all over.
A hard time
I have.

      --Teton Sioux

In a few words, the despair, the fatigue, and the feeling of ending are irrevocably established in our minds in an iron tone.

Thus, although it is not always so clear as in these two examples, tone is there and children feel it.

Imagery

In lyric poetry, every aspect of poetics takes its place, of course, but central to the lyric is imagery, the picture that constitutes the heart of the poem. The richness of meanings that lie here is what makes us remember it and can give back the picture years later.

Children's response to imagery is interesting: to even quite extravagant examples, they respond quietly, internalizing dreamily and then utilizing them later in their lives in ways we can't see. They may be polite or just passive, reserving their listening energy for a deeper inner response.

Imagery has many parts: simile and metaphor, irony and hyperbole, and a host of othersfigures of speech that come naturally to poets:

> I walk to school
> beside my friend.
> Our gray-blue uniforms
> as neat as the petals of a flower.

> --Noelene Qualthrough

Noelene, an eleven-year-old Australian girl, uses her simile (saying one thing is like another) so well that the flower petal uniforms seem to bloom before our eyes.

Simile can extend itself powerfully, too, molding and developing a poem, as Rilke does in the poem at the head of this chapter:

> Then already I know the storms and am stirred
> like the sea
> And spread myself out and fall back into myself
> and fling myself out and am all alone in
> the great storm.

And here the simile grows stronger line by line, building a central image.

Normally, this is a more natural function for the metaphor, where the poet dispenses with "like" and "as," simply stating that one thing is another:

> No sky at all;
> no earth at all--and still
> the snowflakes fall.

The Japanese poet, Hasin, makes loneliness envelop and surround us, the snow taking light and joy away with it.

144

Extending out from a powerful central metaphor is a good way to give a lyric a strong shape, too, as Thomas McGrath does in *The Landscape inside Me:*

> Now I go riding through my morning self
> Between West Elbow and Little East Elbow,
> Between Hotspur Heart and the Islands of Langerhans,
> On the Rock Island Line of my central nervous system.
>
> And I note the landscape which inhabits me--
> How excellent in the morning to be populated by trees!
> And all the hydrants are manned by dogs
> And every dog is a landscape full of fleas,
>
> And every flea is an index to the mountains!
> I am well pleased with myself that I've kept the mountains.
> What I can't understand is why I've kept the smog.
> But since it inhabits me, why should I deny it?
>
> Especially, why deny it on a morning like this
> When I've a large unidentified star in my left
> Elbow and in my head a windy palette of birds,
> And a lively line-storm crossing my pancreas?

His own body provides the basis for a whole world of feeling, and tiny metaphors ("what I can't understand is why I've kept the smog") enrich the landscape he's showing us. Children laugh with him, feeling a kinship to this wacky index.

Mother Goose poems are full of clever, sometimes spectacular use of imagery. Here's a metaphor for daffodils:

> Daffy-down-dilly has come to town
> In a yellow petticoat and a green gown.

Even a very little child can see an intense, vivid picture of the flower. Simple and clear, too, is *The Song of the Thunders:*

> Sometimes
> I go about pitying myself
> While I am carried by the wind
> across the sky.
>
> --Chippewa (North American)

Children know that feeling of helplessness, of being driven along, and then, too, they know their "thunders," their secret strength.

In fact, though imagery is so sophisticated, children grasp it easily; irony, for instance, seems a far cry from the child's world, but there is a winning example in Kenneth Grahame's *Wind in the Willows:*

The Song of Mr. Toad

The world has held great Heroes,
    As history-books have showed;
But never a name to go down to fame
    Compared with that of Toad!

The clever men at Oxford
    Know all that there is to be knowed.
But they none of them know one half as much
    As intelligent Mr. Toad!

The animals sat in the Ark and cried,
    Their tears in torrents flowed.
Who was it said, "There's land ahead"?
    Encouraging Mr. Toad!

The very outrageousness of the imaginings show Toad at his most foolish and endearing, as Grahame laces his ironic lines with hyperbole, cleverly overstating his case for affect.

The twin figures of speech, metonymy and synecdoche aren't very common now, but Walter De la Mare uses synecdoche, that is, the interchangeability of parts for whole and whole for parts, in *Miss T.* to give us a delicious picture of her:

It's a very odd thing--
    As odd as can be--
That whatever Miss T. eats
    Turns into Miss T.,
Porridge and apples,
    Mince, muffins and mutton,
Jam, junket, jumbles--
    Not a rap, not a button
It matters; the moment
    They're out of her plate,
Though shared by Miss Butcher
    And sour Mr. Bate;
Tiny and cheerful

And neat as can be,
Whatever Miss T. eats
Turns into Miss T.

What child can resist this intertwining of favorite food fantasies?
Allusion, directly appealing to some natural phenomenon or quality as
if it were a person, is used sensitively by Lew Sarett in *The Four Little Foxes*.

Speak gently, Spring, and make no sudden sound;
For in my windy valley, yesterday I found
New-born foxes squirming on the ground--
Speak gently.

Sarett's calling out to spring is direct and fresh, it draws us right in.

Rhythm

Rhythm! Among the poetic elements, rhythm is the part of poetry most
natural to children, being a verbal transposition of varying stresses in motion,
so close to dance and to music. Rhythm's divider system, meter, seems less
important to study in terms of children's poetry. Not only has informal stress
come to supplant the formal, measured verse of an earlier time, but poems
for children have mostly tended to freshness and informality anyway--think of
nineteenth-century poets such as Kipling and Carroll. Kipling's *The Way
through the Woods* particularly captures these qualities:

They shut the road through the woods
Seventy years ago.
Weather and rain have undone it again,
And now you would never know
There was once a path through the woods
Before they planted the trees,
It is underneath the coppice and heath,
And the thin anemones.
Only the keeper sees
That, where the ring-dove broods,
And the badgers roll at ease,
There was once a road through the woods.

Yet, if you enter the woods
Of a summer evening late,
When the night-air cools on the trout-ring'd pools
Where the otter whistles his mate,
(They fear not men in the woods

Because they see so few)
You will hear the beat of a horse's feet
And the swish of a skirt in the dew,
Steadily cantering through
The misty solitudes,
As though they perfectly knew
The old lost road through the woods . . .
But there is no road through the woods.

With its intense yet unhurried rhythmic building, the poem captures the horse galloping up fast, then slowing; and exciting emotional structure is built of a nostalgic memory with this disciplined, forceful rhythmic scheme.

Conversely, children's poetry is at its worst when, in a mistaken effort toward simplicity, the poet resorts to a kind of rhythmic doggerel, simplistic and repetitive.

The Elf and the Dormouse

Under a toadstool crept a wee Elf,
Out of the rain to shelter himself.

Under the toadstool, sound asleep,
Set a big dormouse all in a heap

Trembled the wee elf, frightened and yet
Fearing to fly away lest he get wet.
                    -etc., etc.

            --Oliver Herford

Here the dogged insistence on symmetrical repetition cripples the poem. Contrast Mother Goose:

Hark, hark! the dogs do bark!
The beggars are coming to town:
Some in jags, and some in rags,
And some in velvet gown.

Impossible not to give in to the heavily accented swing-rhythm literally pushing the picture along.

Blake does it also in *The Tyger,* building a powerful rhythmic pattern to a terrifically exciting pitch:

Tyger! Tyger! burning bright
In the forests of the night,
What immortal hand or eye
Could frame thy fearful symmetry?

In what distant deeps or skies
Burnt the fire of thine eyes?
On what wings dare he aspire?
What the hand dare seize the fire?

And what shoulder, & what art,
Could twist the sinews of thy heart?
And when thy heart began to beat,
What dread hand? & what dread feet?

What the hammer? What the chain?
In what furnace was thy brain?
What the anvil? what dread grasp?
Dare its deadly terrors clasp?

When the stars threw down their spears,
And water'd heaven with their tears,
Did He smile his work to see?
Did He who made the Lamb make thee?

Tyger! Tyger! burning bright
In the forests of the night,
What immortal hand or eye,
Dare frame thy fearful symmetry?

A different approach entirely is William Carlos Williams's use of rhythm in *Poem:*

As the cat
climbed over
the top of

the jamcloset
first the right
forefoot

carefully
then the hind
stepped down

into the pit of
the empty
flowerpot.

The off-beat series of stresses is very informal; the exact, dainty, asymmetrical purpose of a cat's movement is caught, yet with no predefined structure and with easy simplicity--certainly a twentieth-century poem.

Rhyme

Rhyme can be important, too, if it's used as a tool and not a crutch; Emily Dickinson frequently does it to heighten awareness, as in *A Narrow Fellow in the Grass.*

A narrow Fellow in the grass
Occasionally rides--
You may have met Him--did you not?
His notice sudden is--

The Grass divides as with a Comb,
A spotted shaft is seen--
And then it closes at your feet
And opens further on--

* * * * * * *

Several of Nature's People
I know, and they know me--
I feel for them a transport
Of cordiality--

But never met this Fellow
Attended, or alone
Without a tighter breathing
And Zero at the Bone--

"Seen" and "on" are startling like the snake, whereas "alone" and "bone" make a smooth, undulating rhyme that slides him forward.

Blake's rhymes are strong and straightforward:

The Sick Rose

O Rose, thou art sick:
The invisible worm,
That flies in the night,
In the howling storm,

Has found out thy bed
Of crimson joy;
And his dark secret love
Does thy life destroy.

"Worm" and "storm" are dissonant," "joy" and "destroy" liquid, thus joining meaning and sound. When it is read aloud, the rhymes sound exciting and strange.

Far from the dark fantasy are the lovely, gentle verses of Robert Louis Stevenson in *A Child's Garden of Verses:*

Windy Nights

Whenever the moon and stars are set,
    Whenever the wind is high,
All night long in the dark and wet
    A man goes riding by.
Late in the night, when the fires are out
Why does he gallop and gallop about?

Whenever the trees are crying aloud,
    And ships are tossed at sea,
By, on the highway, low and loud,
    By at the gallop goes he.
By at the gallop he goes, and then
By he comes back at the gallop again.

The swaying rhythms and tight rhyme scheme work together to create intensity and excitement about the mysterious rider.

Internal rhyme can have a powerful effect, as in this poem from *The Inner City Mother Goose,* by Eve Merriam:

Fire! Fire! said Mrs. Dwyer;
Where? Where? said Mrs. Dare;

In that part of town, said Mrs. Gown;
Any damage? said Mrs. Gamage;
Only to them, said Mrs. Hem;
So no worry at all, said Mrs. Hall.

The verse or sound texture of poems is what makes them sing when read aloud. William Blake's *The Fly* is a good example:

Little Fly,
Thy summer's play
My thoughtless hand
Has brushed away.

Am not I
A fly like thee?
Or art not thou
A man like me?

For I dance,
And drink, and sing,
Till some blind hand
Shall brush my wing.

If thought is life
And strength and breath,
And the want
Of thought is death,

Then am I
A happy fly
If I live
Or if I die.

The pulse of the poem buzzes along, swaying a little in the air, exactly like a fly; internal rhyme ("drink" and "sing"; "strength" and "breath") and the use of alliteration, lightly sprinkled throughout, add to the buzzing sound.

Onomatopoeia

Onomatopoeia, making words sound like the thing described, is especially dear to children, as they like making words that sound like what they are doing:

Poetry

Splish! Splosh!

I feel a
    drop of rain

And it goes:
SPLISH! SPLOSH!
    on my head
    And sometimes it goes:
SPLASH! BANG! CRASH!
    on my coconut.

           --Stefan Martol, age 7
           New Zealand

Theme

Finally, there is the question of theme, the statement about life the poet is making. Noyes's *The Highwayman* is about courage and independence and in it the theme presents itself with the story. But when theme becomes sermon, as in many early children's verses, it becomes unwelcome. It is an aspect of the craft that is at its best when least stated:

The Pasture

I'm going out to clean the pasture spring;
I'll only stop to take the leaves away
(And wait to watch the water clear, I may):
I shan't be gone long.--You come too.

I'm going out to fetch the little calf
That's standing by the mother. It's so young
It totters when she licks it with her tongue.
I shan't be gone long.--You come too.

           --Robert Frost

The poet's invitation, warm and direct, is to the child, but really it is to all of us to share nature between the generations, to pass it on. Not a trace of lecture comes in to spoil the gentle message.

153

Thus, lyric poetry, with its rhythm, rhyme, and imagery, its subtle themes, is the heart of poetic experience for children, but for delight and refreshment, the fizz in the soda, nothing surpasses nonsense and humor poems.

Humorous Poems

A great deal of this kind of verse is anonymous and is of the folk tradition-- ideas, jokes, and fancies passed down from person to person, and written down not too long ago. Some is by children, themselves, in the form of jump- rope jingles, street games, and the like; some by well-known authors and poets like Lewis Carroll, Edward Lear, and Hilaire Belloc.

Humorous poetry carries in it all of poetry's elements, but the poet's direct, original thinking seems to sparkle in the rhymes and metrical patterns.

Take *Polly, Dolly, Kate and Molly:*

> Polly, Dolly, Kate and Molly,
> All are filled with pride and folly.
> > Polly tattles,
> > Dolly wriggles,
> > Kate rattles,
> > Molly giggles;
> Whoever knew such constant rattling,
> Wriggling, giggling, noise and tattling.
>
> > > --Anon.

Or *Eletelephony* of Laura Richards--a sharp example of internal rhyming:

> Once there was an elephant,
> Who tried to use the telephant--
> No! No! I mean an elephone
> Who tried to use the telephone--
> (Dear me! I am not certain quite
> That even now I've got it right.)
>
> Howe'er it was, he got his trunk
> Entangled in the telephunk;
> The more he tried to get it free,
> The louder buzzed the telephee--

154

> (I fear I'd better drop the song
> Of elephop and telephong!)

The rhyme and meter in this old game rhyme are subtle and sure:

> Intery, mintery, cutery, corn
> Apple seed and apple thorn,
> Wire, briar, limber lock,
> Three geese in a flock,
> One flew east and one flew west,
> One flew over the cuckoo's nest,
> O-U-T spells out!
>
> --Anon.

And finally, Edward Lear, who at his best is a kind of factory of good rhymes:

> I raised a great hullabaloo
> When I found a large mouse in my stew,
> Said the waiter, "Don't shout
> And wave it about,
> Or the rest will be wanting one, too!"

Under its disguise of lightness, then, humorous poetry can carry a technical virtuosity, equal to the other forms of poetry. But whether it be lyric, narrative, or humorous, the elements of craft are essential to build a strong structure to the poem and to free it so that it can achieve its fullest power and clarity.

Bringing these poems to the children's rooms, and reading them aloud as a special event bring poetry to life in their minds and make it attractive to them. Many of the poems in this chapter are to be found on the shelves of the children's room, whose poetry section is a wellspring of possibility, the poems just waiting to be used. But there is a possible snag between the shelf and the living experience. Some librarians may feel a certain shyness about using poetry that gives them pause, a fear that children will laugh or be bored. I think this is the fear of revealing one's self, one's own intimate feelings. But actually, when one tries reading a poem to one's self, the response may be surprising. Children may be relieved to find that others feel as they do and that poems such as these are exciting when they are read with warmth and pleasure. Then they can forget their own self-consciousness and respond straightforwardly, with interest.

It is sometimes easiest to begin using them informally and spontaneously, sharing a new or interesting poem, or a funny one, with children who come in often. Using poetry in the preschool story hour is a good way to institute the regular reading of poems, and one can slip them into odd situations like a school visit, an out-of-doors storytelling, or a parent-toddler hour. Or one can give a little older child a book of poems along with fiction to read. Sometimes parents like to take a poetry collection home to read aloud, too. A good visual device is to hand-print some favorite poems and post them around the library with a companion book exhibit. Records or tapes of poetry read aloud are especially useful for a sick child or a child already interested in a certain poet. Otherwise, the disembodied voice may seem too remote to be interesting. The trick is to make a habit of using poetry in an ordinary way on a daily basis, and soon the books will be going out as more than material for class assignments.

For in-depth working with poetry, the library workshop is a good place. One possibility is a reading-aloud workshop to introduce poetry to children. This is easy to structure and present and a great deal of fun. Children from five to twelve can be invited to come on a special day and share their favorite poem, or one they have written themselves. The children's librarian can also read a wide variety of poems from the literature. Long or short, serious or funny, poems can lead children into an amazing world of colors, sights, sounds and new ideas.

For others--among them the kind of child who can't easily listen to anything--poetry assumes an importance relative to their own making of it. Chanting, singing, sounding out or saying words, telling riddles, and making rhymes release their creativity and open them up to poetry. Actually, this very difficulty in listening can be a sign of talent; detecting it and helping it develop become a rewarding experience for the librarian. And the library itself is in an ideal position to provide a rich ground for this adventure.

By arranging a series of times for children to come to the library for the fun of experimenting, of playing with words, the children's librarian can be part of their poetry making, part of the process of helping them recognize opportunity. For writing poetry is based on opening oneself to experience, on entering a voyage of discovery by being willing moment by moment to look carefully at what one is feeling, trying to catch it in the simplest, most direct way possible. It's a kind of divine fishing trip.

In the workshop, the children's librarian is the guide on this voyage. The crucial aspect of that guidance is the creation of a safe place for expression, a place where real feelings (not just pretty ones) are acceptable, where children feel they can open up secret places and share their ideas. Getting to know them a little ahead helps with this, especially at first; then reading a poem aloud and accepting their real feelings about it helps, too.

156

Finally, actually listening to and working on a poem builds security and leads toward a solid, creative relationship between librarian and child.

In this interior journey, as William Stafford says, the "essential is some kind of lead and then a willingness to allow the development." To get things under way there are dozens of "starters," such as the collaborative poem on a set subject (my body, a great animal, the fair, the endless story, and so forth), a neighborhood walk, a group of mysterious realia on the shelves, friendships, words-from-a-bowl, and many others. As children get into their writing (and they always do), many things help encourage development: being available to a child, sitting by his or her side on the floor, listening; then questioning ("how did you feel up in the air?" "where are you going?" "what color are you?") can catch a child up and keep the poem in motion. A wonderful technique for a shy boy or girl is to accept dictation, writing down the words right there with the child, allowing the intimate voice to be heard and helping it emerge.

This is the center of the poetry-writing process, and its richness. Taking time, letting children learn at their own speed, paying attention to their readiness to tune in or not help the process along. Above all, trusting oneself and one's own intuition is the firmest guide to opening up the poet and encouraging poems.

Another important point is listening for spontaneous criticism from the children themselves. This can be a way in to the sensitive area of helping them tailor their poems and give them a finish. It comes late in the process and is best when suggested by the child, not by the voice of critical authority, which tends to distance and freeze creativity. If it fails to happen spontaneously, then one way to get it started is by letting the children choose and edit the poems they will use for a workshop book, the publication that so often suggests itself from these sessions. As they work over the poems and discuss them together, a natural, unanxious critical voice can emerge. Catching this helps them shape and clarify their poems, the last stage of the creative process.

Actually, working with children in poetry writing is quite a traditional activity, but this way of teaching, the being alone on a trip into a new country, is a comparatively new way of helping a child find his or her own poetry. In earlier times there was more emphasis upon set form and memorization. Such rigid presentation often turned earlier generations against the enjoyment of poetry later in life. By contemporary teaching methods, the actual working process should come first because it is this intimate process that sets the inner life of the child in motion; then later, as adjunct to poetry understanding, memorization can play a part. Learning a few poems by heart from time to time can strengthen a child's sense of form and the music of poetry and can become valuable on several levels.

Many books have been written in the last decades chronicling and analyzing contemporary approaches to bringing children and poetry together, and a list of some of them is to be found at the end of the chapter. Certainly they will help a children's librarian who wants to lead a poetry workshop series. For those who do not, however, a new body of resource has emerged in the last years, "Poets in the Schools." These groups are often loosely affiliated with local universities; grant-funded, they are available for leading (or co-leading) library workshops. They are enthusiastic and supportive groups.

For anthologies and good books of individual poetry, including those containing the poems used in this chapter, several lists are given below, followed by a close description of two workshops. Current periodicals, such as *Cricket* and *Stone Soup*, include poems for children and some, such as *Highlights*, publish poems by children.

Whether children come to poetry through books and hearing it read aloud at home or at the library, or through the intense experience of making up their own, the value of their journey into the inner self is vital and far-reaching. For some, a new growth, self-esteem, joy, and confidence are the gifts they take with them from the secret garden that is the library. And for the children's librarian--may each of your imaginary gardens resound with the songs of live toads!

Illustration from *The Randolph Caldecott Treasury*. All rights reserved. Used by arrangement with Viking Penguin Inc./Frederick Warne & Co., Inc.

BIBLIOGRAPHY

Classified Bibliography

Sources of Quoted Poems

Sources are given in abbreviated form. Complete information will be found in the lists that follow.

"Then Already I Know the Storms" (Rainer Maria Rilke), *A Tune beyond Us* (Livingston), 82.

"The Highwayman" (Alfred Noyes), *The Highwayman* (single volume).

"Saw Ye Ought of My Love" (Mother Goose), *The Real Mother Goose* (Wright) 75.

"the flattered lightning bug" (Don Marquis), *The Poet's Tales: A New Book of Story Poems* (Cole), 134.

"The Owl and the Pussy-Cat" (Edward Lear), *The Complete Nonsense Book,* 125.

"Jabberwocky" (Lewis Carroll), *The Golden Treasury of Poetry* (Untermeyer), 208.

"Last Song of Sitting Bull" (Teton Sioux), *Out of the Earth I Sing* (Lewis), 121.

"No Sky at All" (Hasin), *A Tune beyond Us* (Livingston), 201.

"The Landscape inside Me" (Thomas McGrath), *I Sing the Song of Myself* (Kherdian), 72.

"Daffy-down Dilly" (Mother Goose), *The Real Mother Goose* (Wright), 47.

"Song of the Thunders" (Chippewa), *Out of the Earth I Sing* (Lewis), 77.

"The Song of Mr. Toad" (Kenneth Grahame), *The Wind in the Willows.*

"Miss T." (Walter De La Mare), *Peacock Pie,* 25.

"The Four Little Foxes" (Lew Sarrett), *Reflections on a Gift of Watermelon Pickle* (Dunning), 98.

"The Way through the Woods" (Rudyard Kipling), *A Poetry Sampler* (Hall), 154.

"The Elf and the Dormouse" (Oliver Herford), *Time for Poetry: A Representative Collection of Poetry for Children*, 153.

"Hark, Hark! The Dogs Do Bark" (Mother Goose), *The Real Mother Goose* (Wright), 175.

"The Tyger" (William Blake), *The Golden Treasury of Poetry* (Untermeyer), 36.

"Poem" (William Carlos Williams), *Reflections on a Gift of Watermelon Pickle* (Dunning).

"A Narrow Fellow in the Grass" (Emily Dickinson), *A Flock of Words* (MacKay), 210.

"The Sick Rose" (William Blake), *Songs of Innocence and Experience.*

"Windy Nights" (Robert Louis Stevenson), *A Child's Garden of Verse,* 20.

"Fire! Fire! Said Mrs. Dwyer" (Mother Goose), *Inner City Mother Goose* (Merriam), 29.

"The Fly" (William Blake), *The Golden Treasury of Poetry* (Untermeyer), 81.

"SPLISH! SPLOSH!" (Stefan Martol), *The Unicef Book of Children's Poems* (Kaufman), 49.

"The Pasture" (Robert Frost) *You Come Too,* 14.

"Polly, Dolly, Kate and Molly" (Anonymous), *Beastly Boys and Ghastly Girls* (Cole), 33.

"Eletelephony" (Laura Richards), *Piping Down the Valleys Wide* (Larrick), 73.

"Intery, Mintery, Cutery, Corn" (Anonymous), *Oxford Nursery Rhyme Book* (Opie), 111.

"I Raised a Great Hullabaloo" (Edward Lear), *Laughable Limericks* (Brewton), 81.

Anthologies

Adoff, Arnold. *All the Colors of the Race.* New York: Lothrop, Lee & Shepard, 1982.

_____. *Black Out Loud: An Anthology of Modern Poems by Black Americans.* New York: Macmillan, 1970.

_____. *City in All Directions: An Anthology of Modern Poetry.* New York: Macmillan, 1969.

Allen, Samuel, ed. *Poems from Africa.* New York: Crowell, 1973.

Behn, Harry, ed. and trans. *Cricket Songs: Japanese Haiku.* New York: Harcourt, Brace & World, 1964.

_____. *More Cricket Songs.* New York: Harcourt, Brace & World, 1971.

Benedetti, Mario. *Unstill Life: An Introduction to Spanish Poetry of Latin America.* New York: Harcourt, Brace & World, 1969.

Bierhorst, John, ed. *In the Trail of the Wind: American Indian Poems and Ritual Orations.* New York: Farrar, Straus & Giroux, 1972.

Bogan, Louise, and William Smith, comps. *The Golden Journey: Poems for Young People.* New York: Contemporary Books, 1976. Dual translation.

Bontemps, Arna. *Golden Slippers: An Anthology of Negro Poetry for Young People.* New York: Harper & Row, 1941.

_____. *Hold Fast to Dreams.* New York: Follett Publishing, 1969.

Coffey, Dairine, ed. *The Dark Tower: Nineteenth Century Narrative Poems.* New York: Atheneum, 1967.

Cole, William, ed. *The Birds and the Beasts Were There.* Cleveland: World Publishing, 1963.

_____. *A Book of Love Poems.* New York: World Publishing, 1957.

_____. *Story Poems, Old and New.* New York: World Publishing, 1957.

De La Mare, Walter. *Come Hither: A Collection of Rhymes and Poems for the Young of All Ages.* New York: Knopf, 1957.

_____. *Tom Tiddler's Ground.* New York: Knopf, 1962.

Doob, Leonard W., ed. *A Crocodile Has Me by the Leg.* New York: Walter, 1966.

Dunning, Stephen, Edward Lueders, and Hugo Smith. *Reflections on a Gift of Watermelon Pickle. . . .* Glenview, Ill.: Scott, Foresman, 1966.

Gerez, Toni de. *2-Rabbit, 7-Wind: Poems from Ancient Mexico Retold from Nahuatl Texts.* New York: Viking Press, 1971.

Goodrich, Aline Amon. *The Earth Is Sore: A Collection of Writings by Native Americans.* New York: Atheneum, 1981.

Hall, Donald, ed. *A Poetry Sampler.* New York: Watts, 1962.

_____. *Oxford Book of Children's Verse in America.* New York: Oxford University Press, 1985.

Houston, James, ed. *Songs of the Dream People: Chants and Images from the Indians and Eskimos of North America.* New York: Atheneum, 1972.

Howard, Coralee, comp. *Lyric Poems.* Woodcuts by Mel Fowler. New York: Franklin Watts, 1968.

Janeczko, Paul B. *Pocket Poems.* New York: Bradbury Press, 1985.

_____. Strings: *A Gathering of Family Poems.* New York: Bradbury Press, 1984.

Kherdian, David, ed. *I Sing the Song of Myself: A Collection of Autobiographical Poems.* New York: Greenwillow Books, 1978.

_____. *Poems Here and Now.* Woodcuts by Nonny Hogrogian. New York: Greenwillow Books, 1976.

Larrick, Nancy, ed. *Bring Me All of Your Dreams: Poems of Dreams and Dreamers.* New York: Dell, 1968, 1984.

Lewis, Richard, ed. *I Breathe a New Song: Poems of the Eskimo.* Illustrated by Oonark. New York: Simon & Schuster, 1971.

_____. *In a Spring Garden: Japanese Haiku.* Translated by Richard Lewis. Illustrated by Ezra Jack Keats. New York: Dial Press, 1964.

_____. *Moment of Wonder: A Collection of Chinese and Japanese Poetry.* New York: Dial Press, 1964.

_____. *Of This World: A Poet's Life in Poetry.* New York: Dial Press, 1969. Translation of Issa from the Japanese.

_____. *Out of the Earth I Sing: Poetry and Songs of Primitive Peoples of the World.* New York: W. W. Norton, 1968.

Livingston, Myra Cohn, ed. *A Tune Beyond Us: A Collection of Poetry from around the World in Dual Translation.* New York: Harcourt, Brace & World, 1968.

_____. *Why Am I Grown So Cold? Poems of the Unknowable.* New York: Atheneum, 1982.

MacKay, David, ed. *A Flock of Words.* New York: Harcourt, Brace & World, 1970.

Mezey, Robert. *Poems from the Hebrew.* New York: Thomas Y. Crowell, 1973.

Michels, Barbara, and Bettye White. *Apples on a Stick.* New York: Putnam Publishing, 1983. Contemporary street rhymes of black children.

Morrison, Lillian. *Touch Blue: Signs and Spells, Love Charms and Chants, Auguries and Old Beliefs in Rhyme.* New York: Thomas Y. Crowell, 1958.

Parker, Elinor. *Four Seasons, Five Senses: A Collection of Nineteenth Century Poetry.* New York: Charles Scribner's Sons, 1974.

Peck, Richard, ed. *Sounds and Silences: Poetry for Now.* New York: Delacorte Press, 1970.

Plotz, Helen, ed. *As I Walked out One Evening: A Book of Ballads.* New York: Greenwillow Books, 1976.

_____. *The Gift Outright: America to Her Poets.* New York: Greenwillow Books, 1977.

_____. *Imagination's Other Place: Poems of Science and Mathematics.* New York: Thomas Y. Crowell, 1955.

Reed, Gwendolyn. *Out of the Ark: An Anthology of Animal Verse.* New York: Atheneum, 1968.

Smith, William Jay, comp. *A Green Place: Modern Poems.* New York: Delacorte Press, 1982.

_____. *Poems from France.* Drawings by Roger Duvoisin. New York: Thomas Crowell, 1967.

Stresch, Corinne. *Grandparents' Houses: Poems about Grandparents.* Illustrated by Lillian Hoban. New York: Greenwillow Books, 1984.

Untermeyer, Louis, comp. *The Golden Treasury of Poetry.* New York: Golden Press, 1959.

Weiss, Renee K., comp. *A Paper Zoo: A Collection of Animal Poems by Modern American Poets.* Pictures by Ellen Raskin. New York: Macmillan, 1968.

Yeadon, David. *When the Earth Was Young: Songs of the American Indian.* Garden City, N.Y.: Doubleday, 1978.

Mother Goose Poems

Brooke, Leslie. *Ring o' Roses: A Nursery Rhyme Picture Book.* New York: Frederick Warne, n.d.

Caldecott, Randolph. *Sing a Song of Sixpence.* New York: Frederick Warne, n.d.

_____. *The Three Jovial Huntsmen.* New York: Frederick Warne, n.d.

Chorao, Kay. *Baby's Lap Book.* New York: Dutton, 1977.

de Angeli, Marguerite. *Book of Nursery and Mother Goose Rhymes.* Garden City, N.Y.: Doubleday, 1954.

de Paola, Tomie. *Mother Goose Story Streamers.* New York: Putnam Publishing, 1985.

Greenaway, Kate. *Mother Goose: or the Old Nursery Rhymes.* London: Frederick Warne, 1882.

Hyndman, Robert U. [Robert Whyndham, pseud.], ed. *Chinese Mother Goose Rhymes.* Cleveland: World Publishing, 1968.

Lines, Kathleen, ed. *Lavender's Blue: A Book of Nursery Rhymes.* Illustrations by Harold Jones. New York: Franklin Watts, 1954.

Mulherin, Jennifer, ed. *Popular Nursery Rhymes.* New York: Grosset & Dunlap, 1983.

Opie, Iona, and Peter Opie, eds. *Oxford Nursery Rhyme Book.* Illustrated by Joan Hassal. New York: Oxford University Press, 1955.

Provensen, Alice and Martin Provensen. *The Mother Goose Book.* New York: Random House, 1976.

Tudor, Tasha. *Mother Goose.* New York: David McKay, 1944.

Wildsmith, Brian. *Mother Goose.* New York: Oxford University Press, 1982.

Wright, Blanche Fisher. *The Real Mother Goose.* New York: Random House, 1916.

Poetry by Individual Poets

Blake, William. *William Blake, an Introduction.* Edited by Anne Malcolmson. Illustrations by Blake from his paintings and engravings. New York: Harcourt, Brace & World, [1967].

Chaucer, Geoffrey. *A Taste of Chaucer: Selections from the Canterbury Tales.* Chosen and edited by Anne Malcolmson. New York: Harcourt, Brace & World, [1964].

De la Mare, Walter. *Peacock Pie.* Illustrated by Barbara Cooney. New York: Knopf, [1961].

_____. *Rhymes and Verse: Collected Poems for Children.* New York: Henry Holt, 1947.

Dickinson, Emily. *Poems of Emily Dickinson.* Selected by Helen Plotz. New York: Thomas Y. Crowell, 1964.

Eliot, T. S. *Old Possum's Book of Practical Cats.* New York: Harcourt, Brace, Jovanovich, 1928.

Field, Eugene. *Wynken, Blynken & Nod.* New York: Hastings House, 1964.

Frost, Robert. *Stopping by Woods on a Snowy Evening.* Illustrated by Susan Jeffers. New York: E. P. Dutton, 1978.

_____. *You Come Too.* New York: Henry Holt & Co., 1959.

Gasztold, Carmen B. de. *Prayers from the Ark.* Translated from the French and with a foreword and epilogue by Rumer Godden. New York: Viking Press, [1962].

Grahame, Kenneth. *The Wind in the Willows.* Illustrated by Ernest H. Shepard. New York: Charles Scribner's Sons, 1960.

_____. *The Wind in the Willows.* Illustrated by John Burningham. New York: Viking Press, 1983.

_____. *The Wind in the Willows.* Illustrated by Michael Hague. New York: Holt, Rinehart & Winston, 1980.

Hughes, Langston. *The Dreamkeeper and Other Poems.* New York: Knopf, 1932.

Jarrell, Randall. *The Bat-poet.* Illustrated by Maurice Sendak. New York: Macmillan, 1964.

Johnson, James Weldon. *God's Trombones.* New York: Viking Press, 1927 [1969].

Kipling, Rudyard. *Just-so Stories.* New York: Doubleday, 1972.

_____. *A Selection of Stories and Poems.* 2 vols. Edited by John Beecraft. New York: Doubleday, 1956.

Masefield, John. *Salt-water Poems and Ballads.* New York: Macmillan, 1960.

Millay, Edna St. Vincent. *Poems Selected for Young People.* New York: Harper & Row, 1979.

Poe, Edgar Allan. *Poems of Edgar Allan Poe.* Selected by Dwight Macdonald. New York: Thomas Y. Crowell, 1964.

Roethke, Theodore. *I Am, Says the Lamb.* Garden City, N.Y.: Doubleday, 1961.

Rossetti, Christina. *Sing-song, a Nursery Rhyme Book.* Illustrated by Arthur Hughes. Boston: Roberts Bros., 1872.

_____. *Doves and Pomegranates.* New York: Macmillan, 1969.

Sandburg, Carl. *Early Moon.* New York: Harcourt Brace Jovanovich, 1930.

_____. *Rainbows Are Made.* Selected by Lee Bennett Hopkins. Illustrated with woodcuts by Fritz Eichenberg. New York: Harcourt Brace Jovanovich, 1982.

_____. *Wind Song.* New York: Harcourt Brace Jovanovich, 1960.

Stevens, James. *A Singing Wind: Selected Poems.* Edited by Quail Hawkins. New York: Macmillan, [1968].

Stevenson, Robert Louis. *A Child's Garden of Verses.* New York: Henry Z. Walck, 1947.

Swenson, May. *Poems to Solve.* New York: Charles Scribner's Sons, 1966.

_____. *More Poems to Solve.* New York: Charles Scribner's Sons, 1971.

Tagore, Sir Rabindranath. *Moon, for What Do You Wait?* Edited by Richard Lewis. Illustrated by Ashley Bryan. New York: Atheneum, 1967.

Whitman, Walt. *Leaves of Grass.* Selected by Lawrence Clark Powell. New York: Thomas Y. Crowell, 1964.

Yeats, William B. *Running to Paradise.* New York: Macmillan, [1967].

Poetry for Children by Individual Poets

Adoff, Arnold. *Birds.* Drawings by Troy Howell. New York: J. B. Lippincott, 1983.

_____. *Eats.* New York: William Morrow, 1979.

_____. *Mn DA La.* New York: Harper & Row, 1971.

Behn, Harry. *All Kinds of Time.* New York: Harcourt, Brace & World, [1950].

Brooks, Gwendolyn. *Bronzeville Boys and Girls.* New York: Harper, 1959.

Chute, Marchette. *Rhymes about Us.* New York: E. P. Dutton, 1974.

Clifton, Lucille. *Some of the Days of Everett Anderson.* New York: Holt, Rinehart & Winston, 1970.

Coatsworth, Elizabeth. *Down Half the World.* New York: Macmillan, 1968.

Field, Rachel. *Poems.* New York: Macmillan, 1965.

_____. *Taxis and Toadstools.* Garden City, N.Y.: Doubleday, Page, 1926.

Giovanni, Nikki. *Vacation Time: Poems for Children.* New York: Morrow, 1980.

Greenfield, Eloise. *Honey, I Love, and Other Love Poems.* New York: Harper & Row, 1978.

Jordan, June. *Who Look at Me.* New York: Thomas Y. Crowell, 1969.

Krauss, Ruth. *The Cantilever Rainbow.* Woodcuts by Antonio Frasconi. New York: Pantheon, 1965.

McCord, David. *All Day Long.* Boston: Little, Brown, 1965-66.

_____. *Away and Ago.* Drawings by Leslie Morrill. Boston: Little, Brown, 1975.

Merriam, Eve. *Out Loud.* New York: Atheneum, 1973.

_____. *There Is No Rhyme for Silver.* New York: Atheneum, 1964.

Prelutsky, Jack. *The Headless Horseman Rides Tonight.* Illustrated by Arnold Lobel. New York: Greenwillow Press, 1980.

_____. *Nightmares: Poems to Trouble Your Sleep.* New York: Greenwillow Press, 1976.

Updike, John. *A Child's Calendar.* New York: Alfred Knopf, 1965.

Worth, Valerie. *More Small Poems.* Illustrated by Natalie Babbitt. New York: Farrar, Straus & Giroux, 1972.

Zolotov, Charlotte. *River Winding.* New York: Abelard-Schuman, 1970.

Books of Narrative Poetry

Bishop, Elizabeth. *The Ballad of the Burglar of Babylon.* Woodcuts by Ann Grifalcone. New York: Farrar, Straus & Giroux, 1968.

Browning, Robert. *The Pied Piper.* Illustrated by Kate Greenaway. London: Frederick Warne, 1889.

Coffey, Dairine, ed. *The Dark Tower: Nineteenth Century Narrative Poems.* New York: Atheneum, 1967.

Cole, William, ed. *The Poet's Tales: A New Book of Story Poems.* New York: World Publishing, 1971.

_____. *Story Poems Old and New.* New York: World Publishing, 1957.

Forgberg, Ati. *On a Grass-green Horn: Old Scotch and English Ballads.* New York: Atheneum, 1965.

Lindsay, Nicholas V. *Johnny Appleseed and Other Poems.* New York: Macmillan, 1926.

Longfellow, Henry Wadsworth. *The Song of Hiawatha.* Illustrated by Paul Galdone. London: J. M. Dent, 1960.

_____. *Paul Revere's Ride.* New York: Thomas Y. Crowell, 1963.

Manning-Saunders, Ruth. *A Bundle of Ballads.* Philadelphia: J. B. Lippincott, 1959.

Noyes, Alfred. *The Highwayman.* Illustrated by Charles Mikolaycak. New York: Lothrop, Lee & Shepard, 1983.

Rounds, Glen. *Casey Jones, the Story of a Brave Engineer.* San Carlos, Calif.: Golden Gate Jr. Books, 1968.

Service, Robert. *The Spell of the Yukon.* New York: Dodd, Mead, 1907.

Thayer, Ernest Lawrence. *Casey at the Bat.* New York: Coward, McCann, [1888], 1978.

Humorous Poetry for Children

Armour, Richard. *On Your Marks: A Package of Punctuation.* New York: McGraw-Hill, [1969].

Belloc, Hilaire. *The Bad Child's Book of Beasts.* New York: Knopf, 1965.

Brewton, Sara. *My Tongue's Tangled and Other Ridiculous Situations.* New York: Thomas Y. Crowell, 1973.

Brewton, Sara, and John Brewton, comps. *Laughable Limericks.* New York: Thomas Y. Crowell, 1965.

Ciardi, John. *The Man Who Sang the Sillies.* Illustrated by Edward Gorey. Philadelphia: J.B. Lippincott, 1961.

_____. *You Know Who.* Philadelphia: J.B. Lippincott, 1964.

Cole, William, comp. *Beastly Boys and Ghastly Girls.* New York: World Publishing, 1964.

_____. *I Went to the Animal Fair.* New York: World Publishing, 1958.

_____. *O, What Nonsense!* New York: Viking Press, 1970.

Dodgson, Charles L. *The Humorous Verse of Lewis Carroll, the Rev. C. Lutwidge Dodgson.* Illustrated by John Tenniel and others. New York: Dover, 1933, 1960.

_____. *The Hunting of the Snark: An Agony in Eight Fits.* New York: Pantheon, 1966.

Emrich, Donan. *The Nonsense Book of Riddles, Rhymes, Tongue Twisters, Puzzles and Jokes from American Folklore.* New York: Four Winds Press, 1973.

Kennedy, X. J. *The Phantom Ice-cream Man.* Illustrated by David McPhail. New York: Atheneum, 1979.

Lear, Edward. *The Complete Nonsense Book.* Edited by Lady Strachey. New York: Dodd, Mead, 1964.

_____. *How Pleasant to Know Mr. Lear: Edward Lear's Selected Works.* With an introduction and notes by Myra Cohn Livingstone. New York: Holiday House, 1982.

_____. *Nonsense Songs.* Illustrated by Leslie Brooke. London: Frederick Warne, n.d.

Morrison, Lillian. *Best Wishes, Amen.* Illustrated by Loretta Lustig. New York: Thomas Y. Crowell, 1974.

_____. *Remember Me When This You See: A Collection of Autograph Verses.* Illustrated by Marjorie Bauernschmidt. New York: Thomas Y. Crowell, 1961.

_____. *Yours till Niagara Falls.* Illustrated by Maurice Kaplan. New York: Thomas Y. Crowell, 1950.

Nash, Ogden. *Custard & Co.* Selected and illustrated by Quentin Blake. Boston: Little, Brown, 1980.

_____. *The Moon Is Shining Bright as Day: An Anthology of Good-Humored Verse.* Philadelphia: J. B. Lippincott, 1953.

Prelutsky, Jack. *The Random House Book of Poetry.* Illustrated by Arnold Lobel. New York: Random House, 1983.

Richards, Laura E. M. *Tirra Lirra: Rhymes Old and New.* Foreword by Mary Hill Arbuthnot. Boston: Little, Brown, 1955.

Schwarz, Alvin. *A Twister of Twists, a Tangler of Tongues.* Philadelphia: J. B. Lippincott, 1972.

Silverstein, Shel. *Light in the Attic.* New York: Harper & Row, 1981.

_____. *Where the Sidewalk Ends.* New York: Harper & Row, 1974.

Smith, William Jay. *Mr. Smith and Other Nonsense.* Illustrated by Don Bolognese. New York: Delacorte Press, 1968.

Tashjian, Virginia. *Juba This and Juba That: Story Hour Stretches for Large or Small Groups.* Boston: Little, Brown, 1967.

Withers, Carl. *I Saw a Rocket Walk a Mile: Nonsense Tales, Chants and Songs from Many Lands.* New York: Holt, Rinehart & Winston, 1965.

_____. *A Rocket in My Pocket: The Rhymes and Chants of Young Americans.* New York: Holt, Rinehart & Winston, 1948.

Programming

Working with Children: How to Write Poetry

Arnstein, Flora. *Children Write Poetry: A Creative Approach.* New York: Dover Publishing Co., 1951, 1967.

Behn, Harry. *Chrysalis: Concerning Children and Poetry.* New York: Harcourt, Brace & World, 1968.

Gensler, Kenneth, and Nina Nyhar. *The Poetry Connection.* New York: Teachers and Writers Collaborative, n.d.

Hughes, Ted. *Poetry in the Making.* New York: Faber & Faber, 1967.

Koch, Kenneth. *Wishes, Lies and Dreams: Teaching Children to Write Poetry.* New York: Vintage Books, 1970.

Larrick, Nancy, ed. *Somebody Turned a Tap in These Kids.* New York: Delacorte Press, 1971.

Lopate, Philip. *Being with Children.* New York: Bantam Books, 1975.

_____. *Journal of a Living Experiment.* New York: Teachers and Writers Collaborative, 1979.

McKim, Elizabeth. *Beyond Words: Writing Poems with Children.* Green Harbour, Mass.: Wampeter Press, 1983.

Mearns, Hughes. *Creative Power: The Education of Youth in the Creative Arts.* New York: Dover, 1958.

Stafford, William. *Writing the Australian Crawl.* Ann Arbor: University of Michigan Press, 1978.

This Poem Knows You. California Poets-in-the-Schools Statewide Anthology, 1984. Many artists-in-the-schools and poets-in-the-schools programs publish yearly or occasional collections of children's work and poets' commentary. This one includes generous essays for teachers on ways and means of bringing poetry writing into the schools.

Zavatsky, Bill, and Ron Padgett. *Whole Words Catalogues--2.* New York: McGraw-Hill, in association with Teachers and Writers Collaborative, 1977.

Working with Children: How to Understand Poetry

Behn, Harry. *Chrysalis: Concerning Children and Poetry.* New York: Harcourt, Brace & World, 1968.

Chukovsky, Kornei. *From Two to Five.* Edited and translated by Miriam Morton. Berkeley: University of California Press, 1963.

Hughes, Ted. *Poetry Is.* Garden City, N.Y.: Doubleday, 1969.

Janeczko, Paul. *Poetspeak: In Their Work, about Their Work.* Scarsdale, N.Y.: Bradbury Press, 1963.

Kennedy, X. J., and Dorothy M. Kennedy. *Knock at a Star: A Child's Introduction to Poetry.* Boston: Little, Brown, 1982.

Koch, Kenneth. *Rose, Where Did You Get That Red?* New York: Random House, 1973.

Koch, Kenneth, and Kate Farrell. *Sleeping on the Wing: An Anthology of Modern Poetry with Essays on Reading and Writing.* New York: Random House, 1981.

_____. *Talking to the Sun: An Anthology of Poetry for Young People.* New York: Holt, Rinehart, Winston and the Metropolitan Museum of Art, 1985.

Untermeyer, Louis. *The Paths of Poetry: Twenty-five Poets and Their Poems.* Illustrated by Ellen Raskin. New York: Delacorte Press, 1966.

Collections of Poetry by Children

Jordan, June, and Terri Bush, comps. *The Voice of the Children.* New York: Holt, Rinehart & Winston, 1970.

Joseph, Stephen M. *The Me Nobody Knows: Children's Voices from the Ghetto.* New York: Avon Books, 1969.

Kaufman, William I., comp. *Unicef Book of Children's Poems.* Harrisburg, Pa.: Stackpole Books, 1970.

Koch, Kenneth. *Wishes, Lies and Dreams.* New York: Vintage Books, 1970.

Larrick, Nancy. *I Heard a Scream in the Street: Poems by Young People in the City.* New York: M. Evans, 1970.

Lewis, Richard. *Miracles: Poems by Children of the English-Speaking World.* New York: Simon & Schuster, 1966.

Morton, Miriam. *The Moon Is Like a Silver Sickle: A Celebration of Poetry by Russian Children.* New York: Simon & Schuster, 1972.

A-Z Bibliography

Adoff, Arnold. *All the Colors of the Race.* New York: Lothrop, Lee & Shapard, 1982.

_____. *Birds.* Drawings by Troy Howell. New York: J. B. Lippincott, 1983.

_____. *Black Out Loud: An Anthology of Modern Poems by Black Americans.* New York: Macmillan, 1970.

_____. *City in All Directions: An Anthology of Modern Poetry.* New York: Macmillan, 1969.

_____. *Eats.* New York: William Morrow, 1979.

_____. *Mn DA La.* New York: Harper & Row, 1971.

Allen, Samuel, ed. *Poems from Africa.* New York: Thomas Y. Crowell, 1973.

Amstein, Flora. *Children Write Poetry: A Creative Approach.* New York: Dover, 1951, 1967.

Armour, Richard. *On Your Marks: A Package of Punctuation.* New York: McGraw-Hill, 1969.

Behn, Harry. *All Kinds of Time.* Illustrated by Harry Behn. New York: Harcourt, Brace and World, 1950.

_____. *Chrysalis: Concerning Children and Poetry.* New York: Harcourt, Brace & World, 1968.

_____. *More Cricket Songs.* New York: Harcourt, Brace & World, 1971.

_____. trans. *Cricket Songs: Japanese Haiku.* New York: Harcourt, Brace & World, 1964.

Belloc, Hilaire. *The Bad Child's Book of Beasts.* New York: Knopf, 1965.

Benedetti, Mario. *Unstill Life: An Introduction to Spanish Poetry of Latin America.* In dual translation. New York: Harcourt, Brace & World, 1969.

Bierhorst, John, ed. *In the Trail of the Wind: American Indian Poems and Ritual Orations.* New York: Farrar, Straus and Giroux, 1972.

Bishop, Elizabeth. *The Ballad of the Burglar of Babylon.* Woodcuts by Ann Grifalcone. New York: Farrar, Straus & Giroux, 1968.

Blake, William. *William Blake, an Introduction.* Edited by Anne Malcolmson With illustrations by Blake from his paintings and engravings. New York: Harcourt, Brace & World, 1967.

Bogan, Louise, and William Smith, comps. *The Golden Journey: Poems for Young People.* New York: Contemporary Books, 1976.

Bontemps, Arna. *Golden Slippers: An Anthology of Negro Poetry for Young People.* New York: Harper & Row, 1941.

_____. *Hold Fast to Dreams.* New York: Follett Publishing, 1969.

Brewton, Sara, and John Brewton, comps. *Laughable Limericks.* New York: Thomas Y. Crowell, 1965.

_____. *My Tongue's Tangled and Other Ridiculous Situations.* New York: Thomas Y. Crowell, 1973.

Brooke, Leslie. *Ring O'Roses: A Nursery Rhyme Picture Book.* Illustrated by Leslie Brooke. New York: Frederick Warne, n.d.

Brooks, Gwendolyn. *Bronzeville Boys and Girls.* New York: Harper, 1959.

Browning, Robert. *The Pied Piper.* Illustrated by Kate Greenaway. London: Frederick Warne, 1889.

Caldecott, Randolph. *Sing a Song for Sixpence.* New York: Frederick Warne, n.d.

_____. *The Three Jovial Huntsmen.* New York: Frederick Warne, n.d.

Chaucer, Geoffrey. *A Taste of Chaucer: Selections from the Canterbury Tales.* Chosen and edited by Anne Malcomson. New York: Harcourt, Brace & World, [1964].

Chorao, Kay. *Baby's Lap Book.* New York: Dutton, 1977.

Chukovsky, Kornei. *From Two to Five.* Edited and translated by Miriam Morton. Berkeley, Calif.: University of California Press, 1963.

Chute, Marchette. *Rhymes about Us.* New York: E. P. Dutton & Co., 1974.

Ciardi, John. *The Man Who Sang the Sillies.* Illustrated by Edward Gorey. Philadelphia: J.B. Lippincott & Co., 1961.

_____. *You Know Who.* Philadelphia: J. B. Lippincott & Co., 1964.

Clifton, Lucille. *Some of the Days of Everett Anderson.* New York: Holt, Rinehart, Winston, 1970.

Coatsworth, Elizabeth. *Down Half the World.* New York: Macmillan, 1968.

Coffey, Dairine, ed. *The Dark Tower: Nineteenth Century Narrative Poems.* New York: Atheneum, 1967.

Cole, William. *Beastly Boys and Ghostly Girls.* New York: World Publishing, 1964.

____. *I Went to the Animal Fair.* New York: World Publishing, 1958.

____. *O, What Nonsense!* New York: Viking Press, 1970.

____. *The Poet's Tales: A New Book of Story Poems.* New York: World Publishing, 1971.

____, ed. *The Birds and the Beasts Were There.* New York: World Publishing, 1963.

____, ed. *A Book of Love Poems.* New York: Viking Press, 1965.

____, ed. *Story Poems Old and New.* New York: World Publishing, 1957.

de Angeli, Marguerite. *Book of Nursery and Mother Goose Rhymes.* Garden City, N.Y.: Doubleday, 1954.

De la Mare, Walter. *Come Hither: A Collection of Rhymes and Poems for the Young of All Ages. New York: Knopf, 1957.*

____. *Peacock Pie.* Illustrated by Barbara Cooney. New York: Knopf, [1961].

____. *Rhymes and Verse: Collected Poems for Children.* New York: Holt, 1947.

____. *Tom Tiddler's Ground.* New York: Knopf, 1962.

de Paola, Tomie. *Mother Goose Story Streamers.* New York: Putnam Publishing, 1984.

Dickinson, Emily. *Poems of Emily Dickinson.* Selected by Helen Plotz. New York: Thomas Y. Crowell, 1964.

Dodgson, Charles L. *The Humorous Verse of Lewis Carroll.* Illustrated by John Tenniel and others. New York: Dover, 1933, 1960.

____. *The Hunting of the Snark: An Agony in Eight Fits.* New York: Pantheon, 1966.

Doob, Leonard W., ed. *A Crocodile Has Me by the Leg.* New York: Walter, 1966. African poems.

Dunning, Stephen. *Reflections on a Gift of Watermelon Pickle. . . .* Glenview, Ill.: Scott, Foresman, 1966. A collection of modern verse by Stephen Dunning, Edward Lueders, and Hugh Smith.

Eliot, T. S. *Old Possum's Book of Practical Cats*. New York: Harcourt Brace Jovanovich, 1982.

Emrich, Donan. *The Nonsense Book of Riddles, Rhymes, Tongue Twisters, Puzzles and Jokes from American Folklore*. New York: Four Winds Press, 1973.

Field, Eugene. *Wynken, Blynken & Nod*. New York: Hastings House, 1964.

Field, Rachel. *Poems*. New York: Macmillan, 1965.

_____. *Taxis and Toadstools*. Garden City, N.Y.: Doubleday, Page, 1926.

Forberg, Ati. *On a Grass-Green Horn: Old Scotch and English Ballads*. New York: Atheneum, 1965.

Frost, Robert. *Stopping by Woods on a Snowy Evening*. Illustrated by Susan Jeffers. New York: E. P. Dutton, 1978.

_____. *You Come Too*. New York: Henry Holt, 1959.

Gasztold, Carmen B. de. *Prayers from the Ark*. Translated from the French and with a foreword and epilogue by Rumer Godden. New York: Viking Press, 1962.

Gensler, Kenneth, and Nina Nyhar. *The Poetry Connection*. New York: Teachers and Writers Collaborative, n.d.

Gerez, Toni de. *2-Rabbit, 7-Wind: Poems from Ancient Mexico Retold from Nahuatl Texts*. New York: Viking Press, 1971.

Giovanni, Nikki. *Vacation Time: Poems for Children*. New York: Morrow, 1980.

Goodrich, Aline Amon. *The Earth Is Sore: A Collection of Writings by Native Americans*. New York: Atheneum, 1981.

Grahame, Kenneth. *The Wind in the Willows*. Illustrated by Ernest H. Shepard. New York: Charles Scribner's Sons, 1933, 1961.

_____. *The Wind in the Willows*. Illustrated by Michael Hague. New York: Holt, Rinehart & Winston, 1980.

_____. *The Wind in the Willows*. Illustrated by John Burningham. New York: Viking Press, 1983.

Greenaway, Kate. *Mother Goose; or the Old Nursery Rhymes*. London: Frederick Warne, 1882.

Greenfield, Eloise. *Honey, I Love, and Other Love Poems*. New York: Harper & Row, 1978.

Hall, Donald, ed. *Oxford Book of Children's Verse in America.* New York: Oxford University Press, 1985.

_____. *A Poetry Sampler.* New York: Watts, [1962].

Houston, James. *Songs of the Dream People: Chants and Images from the Indians and Eskimos of North America.* New York: Atheneum, 1972.

Howard, Coralee, comp. *Lyric Poems.* Woodcuts by Mel Fowler. New York: Franklin Watts, 1968.

Hughes, Langston. *The Dreamkeeper and Other Poems.* New York: Knopf, 1932.

Hughes, Ted. *Poetry in the Making.* New York: Faber & Faber, 1967.

_____. *Poetry Is.* Garden City, N.Y.: Doubleday, 1967.

Hyndman, Robert V. [Robert Whyndham, pseud.], ed. *Chinese Mother Goose Rhymes.* Cleveland: World Publishing, 1968.

Janeczko, Paul. *Pocket Poems.* New York: Bradbury Press, 1985

_____. *Poetspeak: In Their Words, about Their Work.* Scarsdale, N.Y.: Bradbury Press, 1983.

_____. *Strings: A Gathering of Family Poems.* Scarsdale, N.Y.: Bradbury Press, 1984.

Jarrell, Randall. *The Bat-Poet.* Illustrated by Maurice Sendak. New York: Macmillan, 1964.

Johnson, James Weldon. *God's Trombones.* New York: Viking Press, 1927 1969.

Jordan, June, and Terri Bush. *The Voice of the Children.* New York: Holt, Rinehart & Winston, 1970.

_____. *Who Look at Me.* New York: Thomas Y. Crowell, 1969.

Joseph, Stephen M. *The Me Nobody Knows: Children's Voices from the Ghetto.* New York: Avon Books, 1969.

Kaufman, William I., comp. *Unicef Book of Children's Poems.* Harrisburg, Pa.: Stackpole Books, 1970.

Kennedy, X. J. *The Phantom Ice-Cream Man.* Illustrated by David McPhail. New York: Atheneum, 1979.

Kennedy, X. J., and Dorothy M. Kennedy. *Knock at a Star: A Child's Introduction to Poetry.* Boston: Little, Brown, 1982.

Kherdian, David, ed. *I Sing the Song of Myself: A Collection of Autobiographical Poems.* New York: Greenwillow Books, 1978.

_____. *Poems Here and Now.* Woodcuts by Nonny Hogrogian. New York: Greenwillow Books, 1976.

Kipling, Rudyard. *Just-so Stories.* New York: Doubleday, 1972.

_____. *A Selection of Stories and Poems.* 2 vols. Edited by John Beecraft. New York: Doubleday, 1956.

Koch, Kenneth. *Rose, Where Did You Get that Red?* New York: Random House, 1973.

Koch, Kenneth, and Kate Farrell. *Sleeping on the Wing: An Anthology of Modern Poetry with Essays on Reading and Writing.* New York: Random House, 1981.

_____. *Talking to the Sun: An Illustrated Anthology of Poetry for Young People.* New York: Holt, Rinehart, Winston and the Metropolitan Museum of Art, 1985.

_____. *Wishes, Lies and Dreams: Teaching Children to Write Poetry.* New York: Vintage Books, 1970.

Krauss, Ruth. *The Cantilever Rainbow.* Woodcuts by Antonio Frasconi. New York: Pantheon Books, [1965].

Larrick, Nancy. *Bring Me All of Your Dreams: Poems of Dreams and Dreamers.* New York: M. Evans, 1980.

_____. *I Heard a Scream in the Street: Poems by Young People in the City.* New York: M. Evans, 1970.

_____. *Piper, Pipe that Song Again.* New York: Random House, 1965.

_____. *Somebody Turned a Tap in These Kids.* New York: Delacorte Press, 1971.

_____, ed. *Piping Down the Valleys Wild.* Illustrated by Ellen Raskin. New York: Dell, 1968, 1984.

Lear, Edward. *The Complete Nonsense Book.* Edited by Lady Strachey. New York, Dodd, Mead, 1882, 1964.

_____. *How Pleasant to Know Mr.* Lear: Edward Lear's selected works. Introduction and notes by Myra Cohn Livingstone. New York: Holiday House, 1982.

_____. *Nonsense Songs.* Illustrated by Leslie Brooke. London: Frederick Warne, n.d.

Lewis, Richard. *I Breathe a New Song: Poems of the Eskimo.* Illus by Oonark. New York: Simon & Schuster, 1971.

_____. *In a Spring Garden: Japanese Haiku.* Translated by Richard Lewis. Illustrated by Ezra Jack Keats. New York: Dial Press, 1964.

_____. *Miracles: Poems by Children of the English-speaking World.* New York: Simon & Schuster, 1966.

_____. *Moment of Wonder: A Collection of Chinese and Japanese Poetry.* New York: Dial Press, 1864.

_____. *Of This World: A Poet's Life in Poetry.* New York: Dial Press, 1969.Translation of Issa from the Japanese.

_____. *Out of the Earth I Sing.* New York: W. W. Norton, 1968. Poetry and songs of primitive peoples.

Lindsay, Nicholas V. *Johnny Appleseed and Other Poems.* New York: Macmillan, 1926.

Lines, Kathleen, comp. *Lavender's Blue: A Book of Nursery Rhymes.* Illustrated by Harold Jones. New York: Franklin Watts, 1954.

Livingston, Myra Cohn. *A Tune beyond Us: A Collection of Poetry from Around the World in Dual Translation.* New York: Harcourt, Brace & World, 1968.

_____. *Why Am I Grown So Cold? Poems of the Unknowable.* New York: Atheneum, 1982.

Longfellow, Henry Wadsworth. *Paul Revere's Ride.* New York: Thomas Y. Crowell, 1963.

_____. *The Song of Hiawatha.* Illustrated by Paul Galdone. London: J. M. Dent, 1960.

Lopate, Philip. *Being with Children.* New York: Bantam Books, 1975.

_____. *Journal of a Living Experiment.* New York: Teachers and Writers Collaborative, 1979.

MacKay, David, ed. *A Flock of Words.* New York: Harcourt, Brace & World, 1970.

McCord, David. *All Day Long.* Boston: Little, Brown, 1965-66.

_____. *Away and Ago.* Drawings by Leslie Morrill. Boston: Little, Brown, 1975.

McKim, Elizabeth. *Beyond Words: Writing Poems with Children.* Green Harbour, Mass.: Wampeter Press, 1983.

Masefield, John. *Salt-Water Poems and Ballads.* New York: Macmillan, 1960.

Mearns, Hughes. *Creative Power: The Education of Youth in the Creative Arts.* New York: Dover, 1958.

_____. *Creative Youth.* New York: Doubleday, 1926.

Merriam, Eve. *The Inner City Mother Goose.* New York: Simon & Schuster, 1969.

_____. *Out Loud.* New York: Atheneum, 1973.

_____. *There Is No Rhyme for Silver.* New York: Atheneum, 1964.

Mezey, Robert. *Poems from the Hebrew.* New York: Thomas Y. Crowell, 1973.

Michels, Barbara, and Bettye White. *Apples on a Stick.* New York: Putnam Publishing, 1983. Contemporary street rhymes of black children.

Millay, Edna St. Vincent. *Poems Selected for Young People.* Illustrated by Ronald Keller. New York: Harper & Row, 1979.

Morrison, Lillian. *Best Wishes, Amen.* Illustrated by Loretta Lustig. New York: Thomas Y. Crowell, 1974.

_____. *Touch Blue: Signs and Spells, Love Charms and Chants, Augeries and Old Beliefs in Rhyme.* New York: Thomas Y. Crowell, 1958.

_____. *Yours Till Niagara Falls.* Illustrated by Arnold Lobell. New York: Random House, 1983.

_____, comp. *Remember Me When This You See: A Collection of Autograph Verses.* Illustrated by Marjorie Bauernschmidt. New York: Thomas Y. Crowell, 1961.

Morton, Miriam. *The Moon Is like a Silver Sickle: A Celebration of Poetry by Russian Children.* New York: Simon & Schuster, 1972.

Mulherin, Jennifer, ed. *Popular Nursery Rhymes.* New York: Grosset & Dunlap, 1983.

Nash, Ogden. *Custard & Co.* Selected and illus. by Quentin Blake. Boston: Little, Brown, 1980.

_____. *The Moon Is Shining Bright as Day: An Anthology of Good-Humored Verse.* Philadelphia: J. B. Lippincott, 1953.

Noyes, Alfred. *The Highwayman.* Illustrated by Charles Mikolaycak. New York: Lothrop, Lee & Shepard, 1983.

Opie, Iona, and Peter Opie. *Oxford Nursery Rhyme Book.* Illustrated by Joan Hassal. New York: Oxford University Press, 1955.

Parker, Elinor. *Four Seasons, Five Senses: A Collection of Nineteenth Century Poetry.* New York: Charles Scribner's Sons, 1974.

Peck, Richard, ed. *Sounds and Silences: Poetry for Now.* New York: Delacorte Press, 1970.

Plotz, Helen. *As I Walked out One Evening: A Book of Ballads.* New York: Greenwillow Books, 1976.

_____. *The Gift Outright: America to Her Poets.* New York: Greenwillow Books, 1977.

_____, comp. *Imagination's Other Place: Poems of Science and Mathematics.* New York: Thomas Y. Crowell, 1955.

Poe, Edgar Allan. *Poems of Edgar Allan Poe.* Selected by Dwight Macdonald. New York: Thomas Y. Crowell, 1964.

Prehutsky, Jack. *The Headless Horseman Rides Tonight.* Illustrated by Arnold Lobel. New York: Greenwillow Books, 1980.

_____. *Nightmares: Poems to Trouble Your Sleep.* New York: Greenwillow, 1976.

_____. *The Random House Book of Poetry.* Illustrated by Arnold Lobel. New York: Random House, 1983.

Provenson, Alice, and Martin Provenson. *The Mother Goose Book.* New York: Random House, 1976.

Reed, Gwedolyn. *Out of the Ark: An Anthology of Animal Verse.* New York: Atheneum, 1968.

Richards, Laura E. H. *Tirra Lirra, Rhymes Old and New.* Foreword by Mary Hill Arbuthnot. Boston: Little, Brown, 1955.

Roethke, Theodore. *I Am Says the Lamb.* Garden City, N.Y.: Doubleday, 1961.

Rossetti, Christina. *Doves and Pomegranates.* New York: Macmillan, 1969.

_____. *Sing-Song, a Nursery Rhyme Book.* Illustrated by Arthur Hughes. Boston: Roberts Bros., 1872.

Rounds, Glen, comp. and illus. *Casey Jones, the Story of a Brave Engineer.* San Carlos, Calif.: Golden Gate Jr. Books, 1968.

Sandburg, Carl. *Early Moon.* New York: Harcourt Brace Jovanovich, 1930.

_____. *Rainbows Are Made.* Selected by Lee Bennett Hopkins. Woodcuts by Fritz Eichenberg. New York: Harcourt Brace Jovanovich, 1982.

_____. *Windsong.* New York: Harcourt Brace Jovanovich, 1960.

Schwartz, Alvin. *A Twister of Twists, a Tangler of Tongues.* Philadelphia: J. B. Lippincott, 1972.

Service, Robert. *The Spell of the Yukon.* New York: Dodd, Mead, 1907.

Silverstein, Shel. *Light in the Attic.* New York: Harper & Row, 1981.

_____. *Where the Sidewalk Ends.* New York: Harper & Row, 1974.

Smith, William Jay, comp. *A Green Place: Modern Poems.* Illustrated by Jacques Huizdovsky. New York: Delacorte Press, 1982.

_____. *Mr. Smith and Other Nonsense.* Pictures by Don Bolognese. New York: Delacorte Press, 1968.

_____. *Poems from France.* Drawings by Roger Duvoisin. New York: Thomas Y. Crowell, 1967.

Stafford, William. *Writing the Australian Crawl.* Ann Arbor: University of Michigan Press, 1978.

Stevens, James. *A Singing Wind: Selected Poems.* Edited by Quail Hawkins. New York: Macmillan, 1968.

Stevenson, Robert Louis. *A Child's Garden of Verses.* New York: Henry Z. Walck, 1947.

Stresch, Corinne. *Grandparents' Houses: Poems about Grandparents.* Illustrated by Lillian Hoban. New York: Greenwillow Books, 1984.

Swenson, May. *Poems to Solve.* New York: Charles Scribner's Sons, 1971.

_____. *More Poems to Solve.* New York: Charles Scribner's Sons, 1971.

Tagore, Sir Rabindranath. *Moon, for What Do You Wait?* Edited by Richard Lewis. Illustrated by Ashley Bryan. New York: Atheneum, 1967.

Tashjihan, Virginia. *Juba This and Juba That: Using Poetry and Rhymes in Story Hour.* Boston: Little, Brown, 1967.

Thayer, Ernest Lawrence. *Casey at the Bat.* New York: Coward, McCann, 1888, 1978.

This Poem Knows You. California Poets in the Schools Statewide Anthology, 1984. Many artist-in-the-schools and poets-in-the-schools programs publish yearly or occasional collections of children's work and poet's commentaries. This one includes generous essays for teachers on ways and means of bringing poetry writing into the schools.

Time for Poetry: A Representative Collection of Poetry for Children. Glenview, Ill., 1968.

Tudor, Tasha. *Mother Goose.* New York: McKay, 1944.

Untermeyer, Louis. *The Golden Treasury of Poetry.* New York: Golden Press, 1959.

_____. *The Paths of Poetry: Twenty-five Poets and Their Poems.* New York: Delacorte Press, 1966.

Updike, John. *A Child's Calendar.* New York: Knopf, 1965.

Weiss, Renee J., comp. *A Paper Zoo: A Collection of Animal Poems by Modern American Poets.* Illustrated by Ellen Raskin. New York: Macmillan, 1968.

Whitman, Walt. *Leaves of Grass.* Selected by Lawrence Clark Powell. New York: Thomas Y. Crowell Co., 1964.

Wildsmith, Brian. *Mother Goose.* New York: Oxford University Press, 1982.

Withers, Carl. *I Saw a Rocket Walk a Mile: Nonsense Tales, Chants and Songs from Many Lands.* New York: Holt, Rinehart & Winston, 1965.

_____. *A Rocket in My Pocket: The Rhymes and Chants of Young Americans.* New York: Holt, Rinehart & Winston, 1948.

Worth, Valerie. *More Small Poems.* Illustrated by Natalie Babbitt. New York: Farrar, Straus & Giroux, 1976.

_____. *Small Poems.* Illustrated by Natalie Babbitt. New York: Farrar, Straus & Giroux, 1972.

Wright, Blanche Fisher. *The Real Mother Goose.* New York: Rand, 1916.

Yeadon, David. *When the Earth Was Young: Songs of the American Indian.* Garden City, N.Y.: Doubleday, 1978.

Yeats, William B. *Running to Paradise.* New York: Macmillan, [1967].

Zavatsky, Bill, and Ron Padgett. *Whole Words Catalogues--2.* New York: McGraw-Hill, in association with Teachers and Writers Collaborative, 1977.

Zolotov, Charlotte. *River Winding.* New York: Abelard-Schuman, 1970.

FILMOGRAPHY

Frederick. 6 min. Color. Conn. Films.

Only Frederick, a little mouse, knows what his contribution to the winter storage preparations will be, and when the snow falls, he reveals it: poems and stories to give color, cheer, and joy to his winter-bound community. Leo Lionni's picture book is gently and attractively animated, uniquely presenting the poet's way to little children.

In a Spring Garden. 6 min. Color. Weston Woods.

Colored illustrations flow by to Japanese instrumental accompaniment, as various haiku are spoken. The mildly commercial illustrations of Leo Lionni, so appropriate to Frederick, seem a little out of place here, but the haikus' beauty survives in spite of this and a rather mannered narration.

The Pied Piper of Hamlin. 10 min. Color. (Great Britain).

In this poetic version of the famous story by Robert Browning, the art work is magnificent, but the literary quality and sophisticated narration make it most appropriate for older boys and girls.

Robert Frost. 45 min. b/w. Holt, 1966.

This film accompanies Robert Frost on tour in the East and at home in a kind of poetic travelogue in which he explores his philosophy of poets and poetry and gives some lively readings of his own work. ("The Pasture" is included.) For older boys and girls.

DISCOGRAPHY

An Anthology of Negro Poetry for Young People. Arna Bontemps. Folkways 7114.

A Child's Garden of Verses. Read by Judith Anderson. Caedmon TC-1077; TC.

Chinese Folk Tales, Legends, Proverbs, and Rhymes. Told by Anne Pellowski. CMS 594; TC.

Discovering Rhythm and Rhyme in Poetry. Read by Julie Harris and David Wayne. Caedmon TC-1156; TC.

Dream Keeper. Langston Hughes reads from his poetry. 10" Folkways 7774.

Edward Lear's Nonsense Stories and Poems. Read by Claire Bloom. Caedmon TC-1279; TC.

Favorite American Poems. Read by Ed Begley. Caedmon TC-1207.

Gathering of Great Poetry for Children, vols 1-4. Read by Julie Harris, Cyril Ritchard, and David Wayne. Caedmon TC-1235-38.

God's Trombones (James Weldon Johnson). Read by Bryce Bond. Folkways 9788.

It's a "Children's World." An introduction to stories, folk tales, legends and songs from around the world. CMS 071; TC.

Miracles (Richard Lewis). Children's poetry read by Julie Harris and Roddy McDowell. Caedmon TC-1227.

Mother Goose. Read by Cyril Ritchard, Celeste Holm, and Boris Karloff. Caedmon TC-1091; TC.

Nursery Rhymes, Games and Folk Songs. Sung by Cisco Houston. Folkways FC-7006.

Parents Keep Out! Ogden Nash reads his own poetry. Caedmon TC-1282.

Paso a Paso (Step by Step). Nursery rhymes, riddles, short poems and stories read in Spanish by Octavio Corvalan. Scholastic 7824.

The Pickety Fence and Other Poems. David McCord reads from his books. Pathways POS-1047.

The Pied Piper (Robert Browning). Boris Karloff reads Browning and Lewis Carroll's "Hunting of the Snark." Caedmon TC-1075; TC.

Poems and Letters of Emily Dickinson. Read by Julie Harris. Caedmon TC-1119.

Poems for Children (Carl Sandburg). The poet reads his work. Caedmon TC-1124; TC.

Poems of A. A. Milne: When We Were Very Young and Now We Are Six. Read by Judith Anderson. Caedmon TC-1356; TC.

Poetry of Edna St. Vincent Millay. Read by Judith Anderson. Caedmon 1024.

The Raven, The Bells, and Other Poems by Edgar Allan Poe. Read by Judith Anderson. Spoken Arts 1023.

Reflections on a Gift of Watermelon Pickle. Modern poetry for middle ages read by the compilers of the collection. Scholastic R-1007.

Robert Frost Reads "The Road not Taken" and Other Poems. Caedmon TC-1060.

Treasury of Lewis Carroll. Read by Christopher Casson. SAC 7014.

William Jay Smith Reads His Poems for Children, vols. 1-2. CMS 628/631.

Wynken, Blynken and Nod and Other Poems (Eugene Field). Read by Julie Harris. Caedmon TC-1298; TC.

You Read to Me, I'll Read to You. John Ciardi reads his own poems. Spoken Arts 835.

WORKSHOPS

Note for Special Children:
For visually impaired children these workshops can be accessible through a variety of ways. Children can be helped to grasp some of the workshop starter ideas with concrete shapes that they hold in their hands: plants, animal figures, dolls, realia of all kinds, foods to taste and touch. These can be used for poetry illustration, for reading aloud, and for the writing workshop. Talking with children about their own experiences may encourage them to open up. Giving the children the opportunity to read poems in Braille or large print and then letting them read these aloud to the group is very effective. Memory is a fine tool, also. And last, the electronic media can be excellent communication devices. For example, prerecorded tapes or a record can warm up the group. Best of all, let the children record and listen to their own poems or their own readings. It's magic.

Poetry Writing

Introduction: This is a workshop in six sessions for a small group of children. Leaders may want to use only three sessions or expand to the full six, depending on time and interest. Although there is a theme for each session, the development of the workshop is through discussion, active creation, and what happens on the spot.

Ages: 6-12. The children can be divided into a younger group (6-9) and an older one (10-12).

Time: Roughly an hour.

Environment: Find, if possible, a quiet room within the library, or the children's room at closed hours, in which you are all free to work and talk. Comfortable, informal seating is important. A table and chairs, chairs in a circle, or just pillows on the floor--whichever suits the space and sets a pleasant tone is the best arrangement. Post favorite, hand-printed poems on the walls. Each week, new poems and illustrative material can be posted, according to the theme of that week. Suggestions are given below.

Materials: Paper and pencils for every session; a tape recorder (optional); a bowl full of paper scraps on which are written starter ideas for poems; paper for drawing, felt-tip pens and crayons. Have available a record or tape player, drums, whistles, and noisemakers.

1. Beginning

After the children assemble, ask them to introduce themselves. Then, with their eyes closed, lead them on a trip--to a lake, to a neighborhood store, or down the block in the neighborhood--anywhere, telling the story of what happens there and letting them imagine it with you. When they open their eyes, suggest that they write a few words, a line or two, about what they saw--anything that comes to mind. Each can pick a favorite line from what they have written, and you can put these on a pad, under the title of the trip. This will be their first collaborative poem. Read it aloud.

But is it a poem? What is a poem really? Discuss this, and talk with them about poetry. You can choose a favorite poem and read it aloud. Is this a more "real" poem than theirs? Why? Or why not? Their answers will give you a list of poetry elements for them to think about later. Read their choice of elements back in your own words. Now suggest that a child pick a poem from those posted on the walls and read it aloud. Then work with the group to decide on some of poetry's elements from it.

If there is time, ask someone to pick a starter idea from the bowl, and do another collaborative poem on this subject. Put up the poems for them to see. Before they go, ask them to be alert for any poems that may come to them during the week and to write them down. Suggest taking an idea from the starter bowl.

2. Music and Poetry

Before the children come in, start a record or tape of music like Claude Debussy, Brian Eno's environmental music, jazz or African, or Charles Ives's patriotic music. Any evocative or programmatic music is good that is rich in mood and rhythm and that may intrigue, annoy, or inspire.

As they come in, have them form a circle and pass out paper and pencils. After they have listened to the music a little while, ask them to write a word or line that it suggests to them. Using the drum, emphasize the rhythm a little so they can work this into the fabric of the poem, suiting word-rhythm to music-rhythm, helping to give them a sense of beat.

Now get a "word-train" going: ask a volunteer to say a chosen word and, going around the circle, have each child add a rhyme or word association to it. Go around several times. Keep your drum going lightly until the energy for invention begins to slow. Write these rhymes on a large sheet to pin up or on a blackboard and suggest that they use these as a word-file to develop their own words and lines.

Now move around quietly, getting an idea of who is doing what and helping as you can to bring the poem out, suggesting or taking dictation, staying with a child when it seems appropriate. When they are finished ask for volunteers to read aloud some of them.

For home play suggest they take a drum or coffee can at home and invent a set of sounds on their own. What is the word that is like the sound? What words shape themselves to the beat? Nonsense words (as Dr. Seuss uses them) or odd syllables can intersperse with real words for this game.

At the close each child can pick a starter idea from the bowl to use for a home poem during the week.

3. Giant Animals

After children assemble, ask who has found that a poem came to them during the week. Read it aloud, or let the child read it. Then someone can pick a starter idea from the bowl--one like "Giant Animals," which follows--and use it as the basic material for this workshop.

Distribute drawing paper and felt-tip pens. Do any children have a giant animal friend? Who is it? What does it look like? Suggest they paint a picture of it on their paper. This will generate a barrage of questions and conversation, after which some interesting beings will come into the room.

As a child finishes the picture, sit nearby, and let him or her dictate a few lines for a poem about the giant animal. As this happens, tune in, trying to catch a fragment that is especially alive or a rich metaphor or a group of words with a strong rhythmic quality, praising when it's apt, writing down the ideas as they come. When there is a sense of completion, the child can paint the poem in color right on the picture and sign it. When all the children have finished, request a volunteer to read and to show the giant animal's picture.

Put the picture/poems around the space you've chosen during the week. Ask them to bring a special family photo for next week also.

Giant Animals: Poems for around the Walls

These poems came out of a workshop I did with the artist Debra Disman. The workshop was scheduled for after school, 3:15 to 4:45 P.M., and the children were aged six through twelve.

Robin Redbreast

I fly around,
I feel lonely up high,
I sing in the breeze
      and fly on the wind
      to see spring begin.

    --Kemba

A Bird

I'd like to fly,
I'd like to sing,
in a tree
in a house
     up
     high

    --Monique

Victor's Animal

It's an animal like a hot dog--
It's gonna scare someone yellow
     red green
     and some others.

    --Victor

Cat

I am a cat.
I feel very proud.
I don't make noise.
I live in a house.
I like to climb.
I like to wash myself.
I am yellow.

--Alexandra

Cat

I am a flying cat. I live in the air.
There are clouds in the air.
I have a friend whose name is fairy.
I am going to fly down to earth to play in
       the playground.

--David

Black Tiger

I roam through the hot, sweaty jungles
      in deep, dark Africa;

I swim through lakes of summer
I even swim through the harshest of rivers
      to keep myself free

--Lela

Puppet

I am a puppet
I have a yo-yo
I scream all night.
I am seven years old

I have silver eyes

--Ricky

Rabbit

Rabbit live in hillside;
a rabbit feels like kiss
a rabbit likes swing.

--Alexandra

Butterfly

I am a butterfly
I fly high in the sky
It is a wonderful sight.

--Kathy

A Rabbit

I am a rabbit
I live in the hole
I feel warm, I can hop.

--Elana

4. Family

This is family day. As the children come in, have them pin up their photos around the wall. After they're assembled, ask them to think about their family. What is it like to be a child in their family? Which family members are important to them? Why? Ask them to write about some special incident or story, or the feeling that the family gives them, or a special person within the family whom they think of right away. If anyone does not want to do that, he or she can pick a photograph from the wall to write about.

When you have helped by suggesting, accepting dictation, and asking questions, do some reading aloud with them, mixing up their poems with poems from a book like *Strings,* which specializes in poems about the family or some of the poems in the list that follows. Then suggest that each child give a sense of his or her family, in one special line and have this be the workshop's collaborative, extended family poem. At the close, post it with the photos and animal and music poems from the earlier workshops. Offer the starter bowl again.

Stephen Spender, "Rough," *Lyric Poems,* p. 59.

T. S. Eliot, "Cousin Nancy," *A Poetry Sampler,* p. 68.

Anne Sexton, "Mothers," *Strings,* p. 43.

Roy Scheele, "A Kitchen Memory," *Strings*, p. 66.

X. J. Kennedy, "In the Motel," *Strings*, p. 96.

Frank Steele, "Shaggy Dog Story," *Strings*, p. 24.

Anon., "Diddle, Diddle Dumpling," *The Real Mother Goose,* p. 37.

5. Neighborhood Walk

Today you will be out of the library. Meet the children at the door and, after you have distributed pencils and paper, set out around the neighborhood with them to explore and speculate.

What is the neighborhood like for them? Stop at special places and when a particular child spots something important, stop, and touch and smell, noticing colors and textures of buildings, sky, fences, feelings, cats, cars, and sidewalk. What does this mean to them? What words and lines come to their minds? Does it come now, or is the poem waiting for a quiet time before it emerges?

After you return to the library, sit quietly and let the walk replay itself in your minds, letting the poem about it take shape as part of remembering. Do you write, too? If so, share your poem with them--this is a good time to do it. Or if you prefer, read a poem or poems from the list that follows. At the close, ask how it felt to do this, what it was like to write poems about the walk. What did they like or not like?

Pin up poems and any photos of the library neighborhood you have available. Next week there will be a surprise for the last session. Ask them to bring all their poems.

City Poems

Carl Sandburg, "Even Numbers," *Early Moon,* p. 38.

Michael Benson (age 11), "Scrapyard," *Miracles,* p. 71.

Anon., "Oranges and Lemons," *Popular Nursery Rhymes,* p. 55.

Barbara, "No One," *I Heard a Scream in the Street,* p. 68.

Lawrence Ferlinghetti, "Fortune," *On City Streets,* p. 83.

William Carlos Williams, "Young Woman at a Window," *On City Streets,* p. 56.

"Wee Willie Winkle," *Popular Nursery Rhymes,* p. 73.

Country Poems

Theodore Roethke, "Root Cellar," *Lyric Poems,* p. 43.

Edwin Arlington Robinson, "The Dark Hills," *A Poetry Sampler,* p. 84.

Robert Frost, "Stopping by woods on a snowy evening," *A Poetry Sampler,* p. 90.

Robert Frost, "The Pasture," *You Come Too,* p. 14.

6. Judgment Day

Today it is important to have a table and chairs, as the children will be deciding which of the poems should be chosen for a workshop book that will be made from their work.

Have them sit around the table and sort their own poems, choosing their favorites. When they are finished, they can read them one at a time, and their own natural criticism will start to surface as well as that of others. Here is where the leader can help, asking questions, pinning down and highlighting apt comments, generally clarifying the process.

Establish a set number of poems from each child and collect the chosen ones at the close. Format, illustrations, number of copies, and so on, can be a group decision. Certainly one copy should be on exhibit. Plan to move it into the main area of the library for everyone to see.

At the end of the session invite feedback on the workshop--what children liked and what they didn't. Point out to them that this is not the end of their poetry writing, that they can continue to write, and invite them to share their poems with you when they come in to choose books or to visit.

A few starter ideas for the bowl: Specific poetry examples for these follow, which can be copied and posted, or distributed, or read aloud, or not used at all.

body
dreams
animals
colors
foods
streets
weather
comparisons
chants
me
heroes and heroines
lies
people I hate, or "I hate---"
sky/space
crazy rhymes
Dr. Seuss words

Body

Thomas McGrath, "The Landscape Inside Me," *I Sing the Song of Myself,* p. 72.

Chippewa, "The Noise of Passing Feet on the Prairie," *Out of the Earth I Sing,* p. 8.

Langston Hughes, "Subway Rush Hour," *On City Streets,* p. 63.

Karai Senryu, "The Chicken Wants," *A Flock of Words,* p. 93.

Gelett Burgess, "Table Manners," *Beastly Boys and Ghastly Girls,* p. 45.

Dreams

There seem to be few poems about dreams. Children can use their own as a way of storytelling in brief, a poem-dream story.

Animals

Christian Morgenstern, "Night Song of the Fish," *A Flock of Words,* p. 56.

Eve Merriam, "Lullaby," *Out Loud,* pp. 10-11.

Lew Sarett, "Four Little Foxes," *Reflections on a Gift of Watermelon Pickle,* p. 98.

Robert Louis Stevenson, "The Cow," *A Child's Garden of Verses,* p. 46.

Elizabeth Bishop, "The Fish," *The Golden Treasury of Poetry,* p. 128.

William Blake, "The Tyger," *The Golden Treasury of Poetry*, p. 36.

Navajo, "The Squirrel in His Shirt Stands There," *Out of the Earth I Sing,* p. 53.

Emily Dickinson, "A Narrow Fellow in the Grass," *Poems of Emily Dickinson,* p. 56.

William Carlos Williams, "Poem," *The Birds and the Beasts Were There,* p. 125.

Colors

Eve Merriam, "City Traffic," *On City Streets,* p. 20.

Issa, "A Red Morning Sky," *In a Spring Garden.*

S. Kershaw (age 10), "I Saw a Green Beetle," *Miracles,* p. 129.

Walter De la Mare, "Silver," *The Golden Treasury of Poetry,* p. 262.

Gerard Manley Hopkins, "Pied Beauty," *The Golden Treasury of Poetry,* p. 246.

Alexander Pushkin, "Grapes," *Lyric Poems,* p. 27.

Robert Francis, "Blue Winter," *Lyric Poems,* p. 34.

Foods

William Carlos Williams, "This Is Just to Say," *Knock at a Star,* p. 85.

Shel Silverstein, "Sarah Cynthia Sylvia Stout," *Beastly Boys and Ghastly Girls,* p. 73.

Dylan Thomas, from "Conversations about Christmas . . . The Useless Presents," *A Tune beyond Us,* p. 38.

Anon., "Apples on a Stick," *Apples on a Stick,* p. 11.

Arnold Adoff, "Chocolate," *Eats,* p. 5.

Streets

Lawrence Ferlinghetti, "Fortune," *On City Streets,* p. 83.

T. S. Eliot, "Prelude," *On City Streets,* p. 130.

Timothy Langley (age 11), "The Concrete Mixer," *Miracles,* p. 69.

Rachel Field, "Taxis," *Taxis and Toadstools,* p. 21.

Shelley McCoy, "Faces," *I Heard a Scream in the Street,* p. 16.

Weather

Eve Merriam, "Windshield Wiper," *Out Loud,* p. 3.

A child, "The Rain Has Come," *Unicef Book of Children's Poems*, p. 15.

Carl Sandburg, "Fog," *Early Moon,* p. 73.

Robert Louis Stevenson, "Windy Nights," *A Child's Garden of Verses*, p. 20.

Hassen, "No Sky at All," *A Tune beyond Us,* p. 201.

Comparisons

Carl Sandburg, "Doors," *Wind Song,* p. 48.

Anon., "Comparisons," *The Golden Treasury of Poetry,* p. 24.

Adam Koehn (sixth grade), "Divorce," *This Poem Knows You,* p. 68.

Brian Mueller (seventh grade), "Kissing," *This Poem Knows You,* p. 69.

Many children, favorites chosen, *Wishes, Lies and Dreams.*

Emily Dickinson, "I'm Nobody, Who Are You?" *Piping Down the Valleys Wild,* p. 221.

Chants

Anselm Hollo, "'Troll Chanting,' *from Out of the Kalevala,"* *Why Am I Grown So Cold?* p. 24.

Anon., "In the Dark, Dark World" and others, chanted, from Lillian Morrison collections, *Best Wishes, Amen,* p. 127.

Anon., *Apples on a Stick.*

Anon., "This Is the House that Jack Built," *Popular Nursery Rhymes,* p. 131.

Me

Lucille Clifton, "Friday Mom Is Home--Payday," *Some of the Days of Everett Anderson.*

A. A. Milne, "Solitude," *Now We Are Six,* p. 3.

Emily Dickinson, "I'm Nobody, Who Are You?" *Piping Down the Valleys Wild,* p. 221.

Sun Yun Feng, "Riding at Daybreak," *A Flock of Words,* p. 129.

Heroes and Heroines

Ernest Lawrence Thayer, *Casey at the Bat.*

Anon., *Casey Jones.*

E. E. Cummings, "Portrait," *Lyric Poems,* p. 91.

Stephen Vincent Benet, "Daniel Boone: 1735-1820," *Lyric Poems,* p. 89.

Anon., "Bobby Shaftoe," *The Real Mother Goose,* p. 12.

Lies

Many children, *Wishes, Lies and Dreams.*

Anon., "What Are Little Boys Made Of?" *Popular Nursery Rhymes*, p. 97.

Anon., "I Had a Little Nut Tree," *Popular Nursery Rhymes,* p. 54.

People I Hate, or I Hate _____

Anon., "I Do Not Like Thee, Doctor Fell," *The Real Mother Goose,* p. 60.

Heinrich Hoffmann, "Slovenly Peter," *Beastly Boys and Ghastly Girls,* p. 55.

Lewis Carroll, "You Are Old, Father William," *The Golden Treasury of Poetry,* p. 206.

Edward Lear, "There Was an Old Person of Bromley," *The Complete Nonsense Book,* p. 298.

Sky/Space

Federico García Lorca, "Half Moon," *A Tune beyond Us,* p. 205.

Ewe (Africa), "The Sky," *Out of the Earth I Sing,* p. 109.

Issa, "The Full Moon," *Of This World: A Poet's Life in Poetry,* p. 39.

Crazy Rhymes

Laura Richards, "Eletelophony," *Piping down the Valleys Wild,* p. 73.

Shel Silverstein, "Nothing to Do?" *Beastly Boys and Ghastly Girls,* p. 15.

Lewis Carroll, "Jabberwocky," *The Golden Treasury of Poetry,* p. 208.

Edward Lear, "Nonsense Botany," *The Complete Nonsense Book,* pp. 194-219.

Alfred Adoff, *Mn DA la.*

Anon., "Peter Piper," *Popular Nursery Rhymes,* p. 137.

Dr. Suess Words: Some Books with Good Ones

Fox in Socks (New York: Random House, 1965).

Green Eggs and Ham (New York: Beginner Books, 1960).

Scrambled Eggs Super (New York: Random House, 1953).

Reading Aloud: Exploring Poetry

Introduction: An expandable series of workshops, presented here in four parts. This is an informal workshop designed to introduce children to poetry of many times, kinds, and places. Themes are used to give some shape and definition.

Ages: 5-12. Younger or older groups can be accommodated by choosing appropriate poems.

Number of Children: 6-12.

Time: One hour.

Space: A well-lit, comfortable corner or a separate story room is best for reading aloud.

Materials: With the exception of a film and projector, no materials or supplies are needed; this workshop emphasizes listening and the imagination.

1. Animals

When the children come in, it's a good time to have introductions and also to find out what they think about poetry, what they have heard, and what they like and don't like. At first, the children's librarian can read and invite comments. Later, having children read some of the poems is a good idea, and comments will come of themselves. Here are some ideas for poems that can be found in the bibliographical sections of this chapter. Include, also, your own favorites.

Robert Frost, "The Pasture," *You Come Too.*

Kenneth Grahame, "Duck's Ditty," *The Wind in the Willows.*

T. S. Eliot, "Macavity, the Mystery Cat," *Old Possum's Book of Practical Cats.*

Theodore Roethke, "The Bat," *Sounds and Silence.*

American Indian, "Lizard," Cricket," "Squirrel, "Antelope," "Hummingbird," "Duck," *Out of the Earth I Sing.*

Yoruba tribe, "The Viper," *African Poetry.*

Issa, "The Frog," *In a Spring Garden.*

Carmen de Gasztold, "Prayer of the Mouse," *Piping down the Valleys Wild.*

T. S. Eliot, "Rum-tum Tigger," *Old Possum's Book of Practical Cats.*

Costa Rican child, "The Hummingbird," *Unicef Book of Children's Poems.*

William Blake, "The Fly," *The Golden Treasury of Poetry.*

William Blake, "The Tyger," *The Golden Treasury of Poetry.*

Emily Dickinson, "The Hummingbird," *The Golden Treasury of Poetry.*

Rosalie Moore, "Catalog," *Flock of Words.*

John Gittings, "A Cat," *Miracles.*

Anonymous, "The Icebound Swans," *Out of the Earth I Sing.*

2. Story Poems

Today is story day. This is a vigorous theme, especially suited to a volunteer reader or two. Let the children respond to the poems with ideas and feelings, and let yourself respond with some points of poetic value you may want to share. At the close, suggest the children bring in a favorite "people" poem for next week, or one they have written themselves about their own feelings.

William Rose Benét, "He Fell among Thieves," *Story Poems.*

Don Marquis, "the flattered lightning bug," *Story Poems.*

Edna St. Vincent Millay, "Ballad of the Harp Weaver," *Story Poems.*

"Get up and bar the door," *Story Poems.*

Edward Lear, "The Owl and the Pussy-Cat," *The Poetry Sampler.*

Rudyard Kipling, "The Way through the Woods," *The Poetry Sampler.*

James Stephens, "Turn of the Road," *A Tune beyond Us.*

Walter De la Mare, "The Listeners."

3. People--Including Me

For this workshop, a film is a natural. Read a few poems, including any that were brought in by the children. Then show *Frederick* or *Story of a Writer*, films that emphasize the human relationship of poet, work, and culture. For the next workshop, "The World," children may want to bring poems for the country of their background to share.

Nikki Giovanni, "Knoxville, Tennessee," *Black Out Loud.*

Robert Herrick, "Delight in Disorder," *The Poetry Sampler.*

Geoffrey Chaucer, "Ten of Chaucer's People," *The Poetry Sampler.*

Walt Whitman, "Miracles," *Flock of Words.*

Langston Hughes, "Mother to Son," *On City Streets.*

William Carlos Williams, "Young Woman at a Window," *On City Streets.*

Lawrence Ferlinghetti, "November 20," *Sounds and Silences.*

Lucille Clifton, "This Morning," *I Sing the Song of Myself.*

García Lorca, "Ballad of the Little Square," *A Tune beyond Us.*

Emily Dickinson, "The Soul Selects," *Paths of Poetry.*

Winnebago, "O Throughout the World," *Out of the Earth I Sing.*

Iroquois, "Darkness Song," *Out of the Earth I Sing.*

Chippewa, "Farewell to the Warriors," *Out of the Earth I Sing.*

William Butler Yeats, "The Old Men Admiring Themselves in the Water," *A Tune beyond Us.*

4. The World

On this last day, you throw open the poetry windows on the world's landscape. This is especially well reflected in the many beautifully translated, exciting works of poetry published for children in the last decade or so. Here are a few poems from them. In addition, the children's own selections can be read and perhaps you will want to add some. At the close, invite then to come in often and share poems they find or make up.

Chippewa (American Indian) "Song of the Thunders," *Out of the Earth I Sing.*

Eskimo, untitled, *Out of the Earth I Sing.*

Teton Sioux, "Last Song of Sitting Bull," *Out of the Earth I Sing.*

Ewe (African), "The Sky," *Out of the Earth I Sing.*

Sedelius Scottus (Latin), "Easter Sunday," *A Tune beyond Us.*

T. S. Eliot (English), "Journey of the Magi," *A Poetry Sampler.*

Li Shang-yin (Chinese), "Midnight in the Garden," *Moments of Wonder.*

Anon. (Anglo-Saxon), from *Beowulf, A Flock of Words.*

García Lorca (Spanish), "Ballad of the Little Square," *A Tune beyond Us.*

Issa (Japanese), "The snow thaws . . ." (haiku), *A Flock of Words.*

Haiku of the librarian's choosing, *Of the World: A Poet's Life in Poetry.*

Yevgeny Yevtushenko (Russian), from "Lima Junction," *A Tune beyond Us.*

Nicanor Parra (Chilean), "Ode to Some Pigeons," *Unstill Life.*

William Blake (English), "Infant Sorrow," *Songs of Innocence and Experience.*

Carl Sandburg (American), "Even Numbers," *Early Moon.*

Tagore (Indian), "The Rainy Day," *A Flock of Words.*

Jean-Nicolas-Arthur Rimbaud (French), from "Phrases," *A Tune beyond Us.*

Children's poems, selections of the librarian from *Miracles* or *The Unicef Book of Children's Poems.*

This put Mr. Frog in a terrible fright;
    Heigho, says ROWLEY!
He took up his hat, and he wished them
    good night.
    With a rowley-powley, gammon and spinach,
    Heigho, says ANTHONY ROWLEY!

Story

A Story! A Story!" When Nyame, the sky god, lost his bargain with Anansi and emptied out his great golden pot of stories to the world, children were right there waiting to pick them up. Here, in a million forms and from every country of the world, children receive that unique blend of excitement, learning, fun, and beauty that is the story.

Each one has its own quality, its own shape and texture. There are silly stories, drolls, fables, and tall tales. Powerful fairy tales project the deep images of the unconscious of kings and princesses and sun and wind. Creation tales bring animals and plants and elements into being and tell us how and why things have happened; legends of saints and adventurers give us lives to think about beyond our own. The great epics bring the world of the distant past to life, introducing heroism and taking us on adventures set against a vast, strange landscape.

Humanity has always had stories, and each has its own story that reaches in a long chain of development far into the past. In that distant beginning people needed to communicate about themselves as well as survive; in fact, communication was in itself a survival skill. This early communication could take an anecdotal form, which expanded into tales. Sitting about the fire people told these tales to occupy their minds and make the dark evenings cheerful. Stories were fun, providing entertainment for old and young alike, and hidden in the fun was a vein of teaching, too--of rituals and modes of behavior the group needed to absorb. Their inner statements enriched and centered the stories: proverbs suggested right behavior, hero tales gave a model for adventure and courage in action, tales of the fool sharpened the understanding as well as the sense of humor.

Thus, stories took their shape from the needs of people at the time. At the beginning, in the time of the rising of nations to power, the group and its bard gathered together at night by the campfire. Here, throwing its great shadow over the early millennia, the epic grew, chanted and carried down by the poet-singers of prehistory. The epic told the story of the hero's role in the national struggle, carrying with it a quality of familiarity but dignity, a dignity we find in litany and solemn rite. Epics formed in many parts of the world. The very earliest we know of, *Gilgamesh*, was told in Sumeria about 3000 B.C. A Mesopotamian king engages Enkido, the beast-man, in battle. He wins the struggle and they fuse, almost mystically, to become the cobuilders of the kingdom. The archetypes of our sophisticated and primitive sides invest the story with enduring strength and dignity.

Succeeding *Gilgamesh*, with root-tales forming in Phoenicia in the fourteenth century B.C., were the *Iliad* and the *Odyssey* of Homer, composed, possibly by several writer-poets, about 800 B.C. The *Iliad* is a tale of war, whose center is the story of Achilles and his adventures in the storming of Troy to retrieve Helen, the beautiful wife of Menelaus, who has been stolen by Paris. The tale recounts his slow maturing through the struggle as he achieves his full manhood. The *Odyssey* takes place after the fall of Troy and traces the adventures of Odysseus (Ulysses) in his nine years of wanderings to return home to his beloved wife, Penelope, and son, Telemachus. Odysseus lashes himself to the mast of his raft to ride out a storm at sea; he slays the great Cyclops by putting out the beast's single eye with a pole he has forged himself; he escapes from Circe, the enchantress, who would change him and his men into pigs. All these magical adventures carry with them a deep tenderness and empathy enriching the quick action. Later Virgil, writing in Italy in the first century B.C., retold the *Odyssey*, calling the story the *Aeneid* and using a more elegiac, literary tone.

Overlapping the centuries before and after was the Hebraic-Christian epic told in the Bible. The story of the wandering tribes of Israel, their creation by God, their struggles to survive hundreds of years of famine, war, and exile, carries within it philosophy and poetry. Its many hero tales include the stories of Noah escaping the flood by building an ark and filling it with animals; of Joseph and his coat of many colors, his victimization by jealous brothers, and his later growth to power; of the courageous young David, the shepherd, slaying the giant Goliath with his slingshot. But it is the New Testament that, within the story of the founding of a church, recounts a super-hero tale of Jesus Christ, the low-born prophet who, enduring jealousy and persecution, transforms humanity with his vision.

In India, the mystical epic of Rama, the *Ramayana,* also cojncerns a religion, Hinduism. It tells of Rama, the hero's exile and wanderings in the wilderness, the terrible loss of his beautiful wife, Sita, and her pursuit by the protean son of the wind god, the monkey Hanuman. Their story has become the basis for the Hindu god and goddess, Rama and Sita, and makes for a mysterious, magical tale.

During the first post-Christian centuries, epics arose in various parts of the world, reflecting the rise of nationalism. The German tribes wandered through Northern Europe, fighting battles and settling here and there, and composing the story of the monster-killing hero, Beowulf. At the same time, on the other side of the world, the elegant, sophisticated *Katari-be,* the national epic of Japan, was forming. Centuries later a Finnish scholar, Dr. Elias Lonnrut, worked to integrate the group of surviving poem-stories he had gathered over the years in Finland. He named this epic the *Kalevala.* These magical, sensitive stories of Vainamoinen, the poet-singer who sang up the earth, his friends, and their adventures, convey the awesomeness of the great snows, the woods, and the sweep of northern lands. But the vitality of these stories eventually waned as church doctrine replaced ancient tribal beliefs. With the rise of Christianity in Finland, as with Buddhism in Japan centuries earlier, religious awareness and introspection came to dominate both the substance and the source of the epic.

In Europe, a group of epic poems called *chansons de geste* evolved that reflected the age of chivalry, an upsurge in the return to Christian values after the Dark Ages. The most famous, *The Song of Roland,* tells the story of Roland's battles in the wars of Charlemagne, his friendship with Oliver, and his complicity in their deaths through his pride, his refusal to ask for help.

The group of stories about King Arthur and his knights represents the other major epic infused with Christian values. It has a good story of its own: Arthur was a rough pagan king who probably lived in Wales in the sixth century, and he was first written about by Geoffrey of Monmouth in 1135. But as the tales were told over and over--the stories of the buried sword, Excalibur, which only the boy Arthur could extract, the gathering of his knights and the wizard, Merlin, around him, the love story of Lancelot and Guinevere--they became infused with Christian meaning. They found their perfect voice three hundred years later when Thomas Malory wrote *Morte d'Arthur*, which has become a classic tragedy of search and sacrifice.

With the winning of national identity throughout the world, however, the epic voice faded, and great individual works of literature like Dante's

Divine Comedy and Milton's *Paradise Lost* replaced them. But still, for children, the magic of Hanuman's exploits, the struggles of Odysseus to sail between Scylla, the eight-headed monster, and Charybdis, the terrible whirlpool, and the picture of the boy, David, destroying the giant Goliath with his slingshot, remain as exciting, easily understood models of the heroic and a call to adventure.

More contemporary in form, more personal, the hero tale honors the man or woman of noble character who has served humanity in action. It has survived into the twentieth century in the stories about Wonder Woman and Superman, the cardboard pop heroes, half myth, half cartoon, whose remote ancestors were Jason, Theseus, and Hercules. The hero's rigorous journey, as he meets difficulties and strives to overcome them, is similar to our own struggle to mature. As we follow the tale, this is objectified and clarified; we see how it can be done. For children the hero tale tells something of how to live, how to risk, yet it never preaches.

Hero tales show an interesting pattern. The hero, born in mysterious circumstances, is abandoned by his parents. Despite early attempts to kill him, he survives, nurtured in secret or by animals, and grows through an anonymous childhood. After a series of adventures in his youth, he returns to the scene of his birth and triumphantly vanquishes his father, the king. Although he lives to rule wisely, he loses favor in the end and meets with a strange death. Echoes of this sequence can be found in the lives of heroes as disparate as the Italian artist Leonardo da Vinci, our own Huck Finn and Malcolm X, and, above all, in the life of Jesus. The struggle to survive, the overcoming of difficulty and the achievement of stature and power, and the final overthrow--this sequence is the essence of the hero tale and the child's romance.

Of course, they are not all exactly the same in form as this, yet nearly all share the pattern to some degree. Jason, the Greek hero, for example, is brought up by the kindly centaur, Chiron, half man and half horse, and becomes the leader of the Argonauts, a group who sails to capture the Golden Fleece, stolen symbol of magical properties and supernatural wisdom. After many adventures, and with the help of the witch Medea, Jason wins back the fleece. But when he deserts Medea to marry another, he brings tragedy to his family: Medea, in a rage, kills their two sons.

While children concentrate on the excitement of the adventure themselves, they are being treated to a set of home-truths about living, and absorbing the look and feel of courage.

Throughout the history of the tale, the heroes are linked, almost always, to their culture's mythology, as gods and goddesses advise them and help or hinder their progress. For our ancestors, myths were stories that composed religious systems, explaining creation, the elements, and human nature, through the personas of gods and goddesses. They projected the human

208

need for order into a framework all could clearly see, and, as such, they formed parables for social behavior. The gods combined the supernatural and the human in an absorbing round of incident and exploit.

The Greeks' gods and goddesses watched over them, sometimes helping and sometimes not, sometimes vengeful, sometimes kind. When Pallas Athene, goddess of wisdom, is offended by the challenge of Arachne in weaving, she turns her into a spider--yet it is Athene who guides Odysseus's hand to escape the whirlpool on his long voyage home.

And when Diana, moon goddess of the hunt, is seen naked by Actaeon, she changes him into a stag. Yet she is so moved by the beauty of the young Endymion, she guards him in his eternal sleep and keeps his flocks of sheep from harm. So too the descendants of the Titans, sons of earth and heaven, carry on their intricate affairs in the liveliest style, half magical and half human. Their clear, simply structured stories make excellent telling for children.

To the north, the severe, cold lands of southern Scandinavia and the Teutons were the setting for a darker mythic world: Thor, god of war, carries his great hammer to bring the thunder of storm and of war to humanity; trickster Loki, the fire god of mischief, changes shape to play his tricks; Odin, the wise, the Wanderer, with his black patch over one eye, his great cloak and staff, goes in eternal search for truth. Their adventures among the dwarfs and giants and dragons of the North reflect ferocity and sensuality. The Norse myths quiver with primitive excitement.

Of course, to the south, the Romans followed the lead of the Greeks, creating a similar god-family, but naming its members differently. The Romans, however, failed to infuse their images with the same intense strength, light, and color.

In India, elaborate, many-headed deities shape intricate tales of creation, reincarnation, and worldly experience. In China, the three great religions of Confucianism, Buddhism, and Taoism merged to give the nation its rich, diverse storytelling. Here the gods are human, but their function is immortal: a god of thunders, a god of examinations, a god of literature.

Each culture, as it has sought to explain our beginnings and how things work, has employed personification in its myths and, by so doing, has given us a heritage of stories to tell. In North America, the creation myths of Native Americans from the Atlantic to the Pacific explain everything from fire to rainbows. Natural wonders and fundamental struggles are acted through by animal-formed gods and goddesses of each local landscape: Coyote, Raven-Who-Put-Things-Right, Old Man, and Hare, the magic transformer. The saltiness of the myths is revealed in the half-divine, half-human quality of these folk figures, sometimes wise, sometimes tricky, as they conjure up the landscape and set it in motion.

Across the centuries, as companions to myths and hero tales, legends grew up in every country around famous men and women. A legend is the narrative of a life, often one that is historically important, traditionally embroidered a little to show more brightly than life's plain stuff. Often these have been tales of the religious saints, like Francis, who was the son of a wealthy Italian merchant in the twelfth century. Materialistic and profligate in his youth, he suffered two years' imprisonment in time of war and slowly, painfully rethought his life's meaning to become, at last, the gentle saint of pure vision whom we know as a lover of animals and founder of the Franciscan Order of Christian monks. Little legends bloomed like flowers around him. Once, for instance, he stopped to talk to the birds. They flew in to listen quietly as he talked of God's goodness and then rose up singing the praises of God as he finished.

In England the tale of Dick Whittington has fascinated children for generations. A poor boy sets out with only his cat, his brains, and his courage; through hard work and shrewdness he becomes wealthy and famous, "thrice Lord Mayor of London." The country's legends come in all shapes and sizes. Consider the legend that has grown up around Findhorn Garden. This British community attributes the enormous size of its vegetables and its sumptuous flower gardens to daily conversations with the divas, or small gods, that inhabit each plant.

In America legends sometimes have taken a grotesque and humorous turn with Paul Bunyan and Casey Jones, Old Stormalong and the Tall Tales. But the legends of the great Indian chiefs, such as Sitting Bull, are inspirational. In hard times Sitting Bull appeals in a dream to the White Buffalo Maiden for help, and has a vision of a "Sand Dog." Soon after, a strange animal-creature arrives in the village and, tamed and befriended by Sitting Bull, becomes Horse, the great warrior and faithful friend of human beings.

Other American legends have grown up around our national heroes: George Washington--remember his legendary cherry tree?--Wild Bill Hickock, and in our own time, the young John F. Kennedy and the heroine of Memphis, Rosa Parks. As for the media, the exploits of stars from Tallulah Bankhead to Mick Jagger have kept the nation's tongue wagging in fine style.

The hapless, sweet tales of Johnny Appleseed deserve a special place in American legend, encompassing as they do his peculiar character combination of benevolence and personal eccentricity. Spreading seeds for trees from New England to the Midwest, this strange man with his long hair and raggedy clothes brought us the apple and a wonderful story to tell. Such legends are important to children, standing for their national history in a personal way and giving it some bravado and humor.

Yet when we look into Nyame's pot, it is the folktale that seems to represent the essence of the story. A folktale is a story handed down by word of mouth; of all the thousands told around the world, there are a few jewels called fairy tales, or in German, *Marchen*. These are complex tales that, strictly speaking, include a hero or heroine and an element of magic embodied in fairies, elves, wizards, dragons, or other fey figures. More deeply, the fairy tale has evolved into a tale invested with diverse and profound meaning, clean and clear of form, polished by repeated tellings, and developed by writers and storytellers until it has emerged as a brief, compact work of art. Like a pool, it reflects reality on the surface, then penetrates level after level of truth below.

Mostly the great tales grew up in the European countries of Germany, France, England, Scandinavia, and Russia, some finding their way from India. In crude, primitive form, tales such as "The Three Bears" and "Puss in Boots" can be found very early, in the third and fourth centuries as the reflection of tribal rituals. The time of their maturation was long and unhurried. Even when in the ninth century, *The Book of Sinbad,* a simple version of *The Arabian Nights,* appeared or, in Kashmir in the year 1000, a clear rendition of "The Princess and the Pea" was recorded, they had already ripened for centuries.

It was not, however, practically speaking, until 1634 that the Neapolitan collection *Lo conto di li conti,* the *Tale of Tales,* appeared, bringing us "Cinderella," "Sleeping Beauty," "Beauty and the Beast," "Toads and Diamonds," "Snow White," and "Puss in Boots." Then a flurry of gifted French writers contributed to them. In 1697 Charles Perrault wrote down his straightforward, finely crafted versions in *Contes du temps passé.* Only two years later the enchanting writings of Mme. d'Aulnoy, *Contes de fées,* were published, including the "Yellow Dwarf," and in the mid-eighteenth century the tales were brought to England and translated and published by Mme. Le Prince de Beaumont, a French governess living there.

Now all was ready for the great folklorists Jakob and Wilhelm Grimm, whose lifelong passion for the folktale gave us their foundation work, *Household Stories*. First published in Berlin in 1812, it included fairy tales (and some other kinds of folktales as well) from many parts of Europe and Scandinavia. It remains today, rewritten, retold, and reillustrated countless times, as rich, accessible, and fascinating as it was at publication. From that powerful beginning have come dozens of collections of fairy tales all over the world, responding to the renewed hunger of each new generation for their power, instruction, and delight.

Their call is to self-realization, to an understanding of an impasse in growth, the great homely truths of life, and rites of passage. When she recognizes the gardener as her true love in "The Twelve Dancing Princesses," embraces the toad in "The Frog Prince," or cherishes the beast in "Beauty and the Beast," the heroine is leaving behind her childhood of self-absorption and dreams and becoming aware for the first time of a grown-up life and a different joy.

Over and over, the tales show the kind of transformation that begins with a difficult situation that must be resolved by risk and imagination and, often, discouraging years of hard work and discipline. Think of the heroine of "East of the Sun and West of the Moon," who must journey through skies and centuries, and always alone, before she can find her love. Thus, the tales encourage fortitude, realism, courage, and imagination. Scheherazade, as she faces her nightly task of inventing tales in the *Arabian Nights,* must accept and express her own creativity. Only then can she be freed and in turn free the king to his own wisest self by the power and compassion of her tales.

Then in "Baba Yaga," as Arthur Ransome shows us in *Old Peter's Russian Tales,* the lesson the heroine learns as she befriends the world around her is that one will reap what one has sown: literally, in this tale, for the comb the girl saves becomes the dense forest that saves her from the witch in her flight, the dog she is kind to bites the witch and stops her, and the plant she ties back grows to twice its size to keep the witch at her gate. And the lessons Jack learns in "Jack and the Beanstalk" are responsibility, risk, courage, and resourcefulness. Forced to face the consequences of his folly in selling the family cow for a few beans, he must climb up his beanstalk and face the ogre, conquering his fear and using his originality before he wins the magic goose that lays the golden egg of success.

The tales end after a certain conflict has been resolved with the traditional and symbolic "and they lived happily ever after," their way of expressing the end of one stage of the journey. In addition, there is a collective lesson. If we band together, as does, say, our "Fool of the World and the Flying Ship," we will overthrow a mighty and unjust authority, no matter how humble our talents or backgrounds. Thus do tales provide their layer upon layer of symbolic truths, while at the surface seeking to provide only an escape; they are the trompe l'oeil of literature.

The folktale, the told story, lends itself gracefully to a hundred forms, of which the fairy tale is only one example. Its history is as amorphous as the wind, blowing about, never gone for long, but never staying either. Yet its oral transmission has been the very thing that has kept the tradition vital. A story has had to be entertaining to survive. Moving from village to village and place to place, people brought the good ones with them, like unofficial troubadours bringing in the news. As they spread from tale tellers to tribe to family members, stories changed and localized, sometimes leaping right over borders and taking on a new cultural or linguistic style.

In form, however, the told story, like all literature and drama, consists of a beginning, a middle, and an end; although the form is so short it must have the strength of a steel skeleton. Characters, clear and archetypal in kind, are introduced at once, sharp in outline. The chain of incidents that form the plot moves fast and rhythmically through initial conflict, building through incident to climax in successive, often repetitive sections, and thence to resolution, all in the time it takes to whistle a tune.

Within with this tight, formal construction can come an infinite variety of detail: fabulous settings, as opulent as "Beauty and the Beast" or as homely as "The Gingerbread Boy"; tellings that take the shape of humorous incidents, as in "The Musicians of Bremen," or of a sequence of pure dialogue, as in "Talk." Mood, setting, length, theme, time, tone, and region--all may differ, and it is these qualities of difference that establish the character of the folktale.

The great themes and varieties within the body of tales, retold and enriched by countless storytellers, are pan-national. They appear in India as well as South America. They reflect, mirrorlike, the growths, vagaries, and moods that are shared by us all. Yet cultural idiosyncrasies stand out strongly. As we increasingly explore and respect different cultures, regional quality--the tone and spice of the folktale--fulfills our need to differentiate, in order to understand the world around us as well as ourselves. Although tales of cleverness like "Brave Little Tailor" from Grimm, and tales of the fool like our friend of the flying ship, and tales of luck, of ghosts, and of creation crop up everywhere, sharing universal themes, the quality of the tales, their style and color, emerges in the original voice of a given country.

Persian tales, for instance, are discursive, richly embroidered; their detail and texture give a tapestry quality to the Sinbadian versions of the Odyssey, told so long ago--as far back as the eighth century in Baghdad. But close by in Turkey, that delicious dupe of fate, the Hodja, goes his hapless, endearing way in short, funny stories. These are as close to a realistic tale as can be found, earthy and humanistic. Yet there's an undertone of the cynic's wisdom and a whisper of cruelty in Turkish tales. They admire wit and a winner, and they give that sense of the end justifying the means not commonly found in the literature of other regions. Even more than most, they reveal a sense of the oppression of women and a lack of personal kinesis and freedom.

The tales of India, from the epic *Ramayana* to the *Jataka Tales,* short, homely stories of the Buddha in his former lives, reveal the love of moral instruction and deep religious concern of the Indian culture. Woven through them is a quality of native shrewdness and quick mind. Yet there is a tolerance, an understanding of human frailty, that is endearing. In China the same love of color that gives their festivals and gods a magical overtone pervades their tales of dialogue and humor, which reflect a keen interest in human nature and an unromantic and practical point of view. Yet always there is a sensuousness, a love of beauty, that lights up these essentially mundane accounts. Japanese tales, on the other hand, are more refined and sophisticated, as epitomized in Lady Murasaki's *Tale of Genji;* often stories

213

of family and priest, of court and king, they are a step away from nature tales. The Japanese emphasize a practical approach to success, but they don't rule out magic (think of the impish persona of the "Dancing Kettle"), especially if it furthers the material welfare. Yet despite their materialism, the Japanese tales show a great love of the arts and of a conscious, civilized sort of beauty.

Russian tales are like giant tales, they are so buffo, bold, crude, and action-packed. Here magic rewards such virtues as courage and kindness, and the importance of independence is stressed. A sudden mood of wild abandon (the King of the Sea dancing all day in "Sadko") infuses the stories with excitement, but there's a tenderness, too, and a feeling of nobility. The great washes of snow and ice, the enormous distances of Russia, are reflected in magic inventions of superhuman transport that can travel thousands of miles in a second, as the Firebird does, for example. They also give rise to a sadness such as that of Baboushka, as she sets out to roam forever across the frozen land in her search for the Christ Child.

In South America, despite regional differences, there is a pervasive pain and physical hardship that dominate even the great fairy tales, such as "The Magic Ball." An indifferent unyielding landscape forms the background. They show also a superstitious view of life. The magic seems the tool of a cruel irrational fate. Again and again the complex tales portray the struggle of good and evil. Dark archetypes battle for ascendancy in a crude boldness of narrative that characterizes stories from many parts of the continent.

In North America, the great tales are the Native American, or Indian tales. Although there are infinite varieties from tribe to tribe, North and South, they are held together by a sure sense of the inner life of nature, expressed first as the archetypal god-animal figures of Coyote and the Old Man in the central and Great Plains, Raven in the Northwest, transforming Hare in the Northeast. Here god plays out his power both as wise man and as fool and sometimes, as in "The Inland Whale," as the vast, gentle wisdom of a woman.

Creation stories dominate these tales: How did the birds get their colors? How did Chipmunk get his stripe? Why can Owl see at night? And more basic, how Raven created the world, how Coyote stole light, and how Mudhen found earth. The dance of the animal cycles, the dance of the seasons, give the stories a strong rhythm. The active stories are told with a spare use of dialogue and elegant sense of setting and character. The voices that come through are magical: The Little People call from the grass; the whale speaks (but only once) to reveal the true meaning of the characters' lives; the woman in the moon confronts her lover, the sun; wisdom speaks to us from the stars, from the oceans, and from the earth itself. In all this, a great respect for human nature, for the traditional virtues, and, less traditionally, for creativity emerges. And always one is left with the sense of a magic in nature that is strong enough to quiet the flood, heal the wounded, and end the war.

Regional tales in America occupy a special place, often being transplanted stories from the old country reborn in the language and style of the region. Richard Chase's *Jack Tales,* alive with a salty lingo and whipcracker wit, are the Appalachian versions of the Northern European tales of the fool. Br'er Rabbit, the Uncle Remus wizard, is once again Trickster Hare of the Native American tradition. Even certain hair-raisers like the phantom ship of the Hudson come from the European family tree, this time from the story of the Flying Dutchman.

Notable for originality and an endearing, gigantesque humor are our tall tales, from Pecos Bill of Texas fame to the Northwest's rip-roaring Paul Bunyan and, never forget, Babe, his "tiny" blue ox, who was so strong and so wide he reversed the whole course of a river and broke up a logjam two hundred feet high. North, south, east and west, our tall tales reflect the gusto, rebelliousness, invention, and, above all, the frontier humor of the United States.

A different current with a bitter cast lights up our urban tales with a neon light; stories like "Stagolee" of Julius Lesters's *Black Folktales,* or Toni Cade Bambara's tense, witty version of "Billy Goats Gruff," are sharp, the humor carries an edge of unhappiness and rage, and the excitement is intense.

In Africa, the origin of many of our regional tales, the stories have a very different feeling. They are full of magic, but there's a wryness, a sense of just desserts, quirks, and unreasonable difficulties. Magic may further creative ends, but it may be the end of you instead. Humor, quick-wittedness, and resourcefulness are primary to African tales from Ethiopia to the Congo. The love of talk, of a fast and funny dialogue, stands out. Nature is the riotous and brilliant backdrop; animals are the actors that say the stories; the closeness of animals to people, their likeness to them, appears in all the tales. African tales are also infused with a musical storytelling sense so finely balanced and rhythmic that the stories seem to sing themselves along.

Wandering across Europe and Asia were the Gypsies, important tale bearers, bringing, adapting, and retelling tales everywhere. Their own tales, however, are original and very personal, and deserve to be better known. They reflect a human scale, honoring cleverness and acknowledging spite and the full range of the richness of human emotion and character. The Gypsies had not much truck with nature except to outwit it and to assign to a set of royal figures the power to even up the score. Their tales are full of color and movement, restless, and, at times, grim. These are the tales of the survivor, the realist.

Most familiar to Westerners are the tales of Europe and Scandinavia, close to our childhoods, weaving their symbolism into the stuff of our imagination: the big bear-friend of Snow White and Rose Red, the Goose Girl's rippling golden hair that teases Conrad, the little glass slipper, and the dog with eyes as big as mill wheels. Our inner landscapes are full of these allusions. They come from France, with a dry, pithy tone and White Cat wit and elegance, from Spain's gardens of ornate composition, replete with juggler and dwarf, and from Germany with its rich, multitudinous tales of the Pied Piper dancing the rats out to sea and Hansel and Gretel nibbling at the witch's candy house. Each country's tales project a special style and color. Yet the broad themes of personal idealism, of a revolt against class structure, of inner growth through risk are common to all. And certain values are, too; the importance of the family unit and the family goods, of hard work and strength of character. But combined with these mundane ingredients is a restless strain of romanticism and magic, the extra element that penetrates the surface of life and gets at the mystery of it. Magic introduces the part of the story we can never quite anticipate--the lush forest of Sleeping Beauty, the beautiful gowns and coach and ball of Cinderella, Jack's wonderful beanstalk. Hiding in the corner of many tales is a slight twist to the grotesque, the picture of the witch-mother climbing up Rapunzel's beautiful hair, the boy who sets out to learn fear suddenly drenched with freezing water, the talking and threatening bone in "Teeny Tiny Woman." These elements of magic are spicy, a piquant element in a romantic texture.

Jewels in the crown of this tradition are the finest examples of the literary tale, the original stories written down by an individual writer. Those of Hans Andersen, Howard Pyle, Oscar Wilde, and Carl Sandburg give us the archetypal characters, settings, and themes common to folk and fairy tales. Here the authors' inventiveness and fresh sense of story are unique and individual authors often add their own philosophical sense. At their best these writers combine a literary talent, a worldview, and original ideas, creating tales so perfect they become classics, as Rudyard Kipling did in the *Just-So Stories* (think of "The Cat That Walked by Himself") and Oscar Wilde in *The Happy Prince*.

Literary tale, legend, fairy tale, epic, or folktale--each kind of story is important to children. For us, introducing them depends to a large extent on the age group we are working with. For preschoolers simple folktales in picture-book format introduce the story in the best way, with big, accessible illustrations to suggest the action and a brief text. By the time they are five or so, children can listen to stories without much trouble, especially such relatively clear texts as "Billy Goats Gruff," "Three Little Pigs," or "The Pancake." In a group setting, interspersing story reading and storytelling can be an easy introduction to a new style.

216

For all ages puppet theater adapts to folktales very well, and it can be great fun to use this theatrical form of storytelling. Puppets permit a colorful, three-dimensional presentation that children enjoy. Some practice is needed to feel at ease with the elements of puppetry--improvisation of dialogue, narration, and movement--but even short of development of a full script and staging, use of puppets can highlight the telling of a tale.

For older children story reading and storytelling are both excellent ways to present stories. Low-keyed, yet very comfortable for a regular format, is the weekly story reading time. Here the story forms--folk and fairy tales, epics and myths--can come into the play around the theme of a country or region; for example, the myths and epics of Greece, or the *Ramayana* and the *Jataka Tales* from India, can be presented together.

Yet more powerful than reading is telling. The direct quality of a story told without a book gives it a life in the mind of the child that is unmatched by other media, so it is worth experimenting with this form of presentation. The rewards are great. Storytelling can be used to great effect for holidays and as an adjunct to summer reading programs. Stories can be told in parks, from the Bookmobile, or in class visits. For parent and community groups storytelling can build a strong bridge between library, children, and the neighborhood. This art enlivens the library and is an excellent way to pass down the heritage of folktales and great literature.

Adjunct to live performance are the films and records in the library collection. Quality films and video tapes such as *Zlateh the Goat* can make a deep impact on children. The films and tapes should be reviewed and thoughtfully considered for truth of image to story and excellence of production, so that children receive the story directly, not commercially twisted or cleaned up.

Recordings or cassettes of storytellers are a good resource, too, especially valuable for homebound children, and useful in a media center if sets of earphones are available. They, however, should be carefully listened to and reviewed before they are purchased or recommended. The same variety of forms--myths, fairy tales, tall tales, and so on--is as important to consider for records and film collections as it is for books. And occasionally a good radio or television program comes up that is appropriate. These should be watched for and recommended, and a librarian or teacher might try to arrange to tape the broadcast or telecast.

A few pointers on selection: At the root this is a personal question, despite the factors of children's ages, library environment, number of children involved, and so on, for the essence of a tale's success is the affinity of teller and tale. To find good stories, read broadly in the literature, not just fairy tale or English folktales, but the wanderings of Odysseus, the myths of Zeus and Odin, Carl Sandburg's *Rootabaga Stories,* and the contemporary urban tales from Africa and America like Julius Lester's *Black Folktales.*

Exploring new forms, keeping an ear out for a tale in the family or among friends, reading new editions of old tales, watching for tales when traveling-- all these help provide a broad, self-renewing base to a storyteller's repertoire.

As for storytelling itself, how to tell them, the technique is the subject of a number of excellent books, most of which can be found in the public library's children's room. There are short, clear, practical guides like Catharine Farrell's *Guide to Storytelling* for the beginner or Nancy Schimmel's *Just Enough to Make a Story,* which incorporate sensitive discussions on learning and selection with how making the best of oneself as a storyteller. Thoroughgoing teaching texts are available, with chapters on selection, technique, visualization, and characterization. Among the best are the Brenemans' *Once Upon a Time: A Story-Telling Handbook* and Sylvia Ziskind's *Telling Stories to Children.* Large, exhaustive handbooks, such as Dorothy Dewit's *Handbook for Storytellers,* cover every aspect of storytelling, from promotion and use of flannel boards to puppetry and exhibits. *Storytelling: Process and Practice,* by Norma Livo and Sandra Rietz, investigates these traditional aspects and also introduces oral history as storytelling, and nonstory resources--welcome additions. Connie Champlin and Nancy Renfro suggest good stories for use with puppetry in their helpful *Storytelling with Puppets.*

Wonderful early works on storytelling like Ruth Sawyer's *Way of the Storyteller* (1942) and Marie Shedlock's *Art of the Storyteller* (1915) combine biography with discussions of history and hints on storytelling. In addition, several books, such as *The Lost Half-Hour,* compile stories for use. The books of Eileen Colwell, *Story-Teller's Choice,* Books I and II, are especially valuable. She discusses stories individually and offers ideas for telling them effectively. A jewel of writing is Padraic Colum's Irish interpretation of tale-telling "Story Telling Old and New" from his book *The Fountain of Youth.* Mr. Colum's clarifying poetic approach gets to the heart of the matter: the enchantment of the mind and the refreshment of the soul are the reasons for telling stories.

Books of teaching and interpretation, handbooks, records, collections, and films, each with a special use and a special expressiveness, are there to guide us. Live performance by a modern troubadour, a free-lance storyteller, is the most vivid and exciting of all the ways to introduce stories to children. These skilled professionals can be reached through their organization, NAPPS, which publishes a directory of names and addresses. And finally, at the close of this chapter are descriptions of workshops to develop the amateur's skill in introducing stories and storytelling to children.

So in our libraries the stories wait--from epic to tall tale, from ballad to joke--for the children who will explore them there. Nyame's gift is ours to pass on, as storytellers continue to unfold the ancient art and bring stories to life.

BIBLIOGRAPHY

Note: Books that are good source books for adults as well as children are marked with an asterisk (*).

Epics

Anglo-Saxon

Beowulf. Retold by Rosemary Sutcliff. New York: E. P. Dalton, 1984.

Finland

Deutsch, Babette. *Hours of the Kalevala.* New York: Julian Messner, 1940.

Synge, Ursula. *Land of Heroes: A Retelling of the Kalevala.* New York: Atheneum, 1978.

Britain

Picard, Barbara Leonie. *Stories of King Arthur and His Knights.* New York: Henry Z. Walck, 1955.

Pyle, Howard. *The Merry Adventures of Robin Hood.* New York: Charles Scribner's Sons, 1946.

_____. *The Story of the Champions of the Round Table.* New York: Dover, 1968.

_____. *The Story of King Arthur and His Knights.* New York: Charles Scribner's Sons, 1964.

_____. *The Merry Adventures of Robin Hood.* New York: Charles Scribner's Sons, 1946.

China

Sanders, Tao Tao Liu. *Dragons, Gods and Spirits from Chinese Mythology.* New York: Schocken, 1983.

France

The Story of Roland. Retold by Robert Goldston and Marguerite Goldston. New York: Bobbs-Merrill, 1964.

Greece

Colum, Padraic. *The Children's Homer: The Adventures of Odysseus and the Tales of Troy.* New York: Macmillan, 1918. Rev. ed. 1946.

Gates, Doris. *A Fair Wind for Troy.* New York: Viking Penguin, 1976.

Graves, Robert. *The Siege and Fall of Troy.* Garden City, N.Y.: Doubleday, 1962.

The Iliad of Homer. Retold by Alfred J. Church. New York: Macmillan, 1907.

The Iliad of Homer. Retold by Barbara Leonie Picard. New York: Henry Z. Walck, 1960.

The Odyssey of Homer. Retold by Alfred J. Church. New York: Macmillan, 1906. Reprint. 1960.

India

Mukerji, Dhan Gopal. *Ram, the Hero of India.* New York: E. P. Dalton, 1930.

Seeger, Elizabeth. *The Ramayana.* New York: William R. Scott, 1969.

Italy

The Aeneid for Boys and Girls. Retold by Alfred J. Church. New York: Macmillan, 1962.

The Middle East: The Bible

Boliger, Max. *Noah and the Rainbow.* Translated by Clyde Robert Bulla. New York: Crowell, 1977.

Bulla, Clyde Robert. *Joseph the Dreamer.* New York: Crowell, 1971.

De la Mare, Walter. *Stories from the Bible.* Illustrated by Edward Ardizzone. New York: Alfred Knopf, 1961.

De Regniers, Beatrice. *David and Goliath*. New York: Viking Press, 1965.

Elborn, Andrew. *Noah and the Ark and the Animals*. Natick, Mass.: Picture Book Studio, 1984.

Graham, Lorenz B. *David He No Fear*. Illustrated by Ann Grifalcone. New York: Crowell, 1971.

Revivus, Jacobus (1586-1658). *Noah's Ark*. Illustrated by Peter Spier. New York: Doubleday, 1977.

Turner, Philip. *Brian Wildsmith's Illustrated Bible Stories*. New York: Franklin Watts, 1969.

Myths

Egypt

Harris, Geraldine. *Gods and Pharoahs from Egyptian Mythology*. New York: Schocken, 1983.

Green, Roger Lancelyn. *Tales of Ancient Egypt*. New York: Henry Z. Walck, 1968.

Greece

*Bulfinch, Thomas. *A Book of Myths: Selections from Bulfinch's Age of Fable*. Illustrated by Helen Sewell. New York: Macmillan, 1942.

_____. *Bulfinch's Mythology: The Age of Fable, the Age of Chivalry, Legend of Charlemagne*. New York: Thomas Y. Crowell, 1970.

Coolidge, Olivia E. *Greek Myths*. Boston: Houghton Mifflin, 1949.

D'Aulaire, Ingri, and Edgar Parin D'Aulaire. *A Book of Greek Myths*. Garden City, N.Y.: Doubleday, 1962.

Espeland, Pamela. *Pygmalion*. Minneapolis: Carolrhoda Books, 1981.

_____. *Theseus and the Road to Athens*. Minneapolis: Carolrhoda Books, 1981.

Gates, Doris. *Lord of the Sky: Zeus*. New York: Viking Press, 1972.

_____. *The Queens of Heaven*. New York: Viking Press, 1974.

_____. *The Warrior Goddess: Athena*. New York: Viking Press, 1972.

Graves, Robert. *Greek Gods and Heroes.* Garden City, N.Y.: Doubleday, 1960.

Green, Roger Lancelyn. *A Book of Myths.* London: J. M. Dent, 1942.

_____. *Tales the Muses Told: Ancient Greek Myths.* Illustrated by Don Bolognese. New York: Henry Z. Walck, 1965.

*Hamilton, Edith. *Mythology.* Boston: Little, Brown, 1940.

Hawthorne, Nathaniel. *Tanglewood Tales for Girls and Boys.* Boston: Houghton Mifflin, 1954.

_____. *A Wonderful Book.* New York: Dutton, [1949, 1965].

Low, Alice, ed. *The Macmillan Book of Greek Gods and Heroes.* New York: Macmillan, 1985.

Sewell, Helen. *A Book of Myths.* New York: Macmillan, 1942.

Trimmer, Stephen. *Neverland: Fabled Places and Fabulous Voyages of History and Legend.* New York: Viking Press, 1976. A valuable work of nonfiction for children, detailing the historical and geographical background of some of the great epics and fairy tales.

Scandinavia

Colum, Padraic. *The Children of Odin.* New York: Macmillan, 1920. Reprint. 1945.

Coolidge, Olivia. *Legends of the North.* Boston: Houghton Mifflin, 1951.

D'Aulaire, Ingri, and Edgar Parin D'Aulaire. *Norse Gods and Giants.* Garden City, N.Y.: Doubleday, 1967.

Fables

Aesop. *Aesop's Fables.* Retold by Ann Terry White. New York: Random House, 1964.

_____. *The Fables of Aesop.* Retold by Joseph Jacobs. Illustrated by David Lenne. New York: Macmillan, [1964].

Hero Tales

Baldwin, James. *The Story of Siegfried.* New York: Charles Scribner's Sons, 1931.

Green, Roger Lancelyn. *Heroes of Greece and Troy.* New York: Henry C. Walck, 1961.

Hazeltine, Alice I., ed. *Hero Tales from Many Lands.* New York: Abingdon Press, 1961.

Kingsley, Charles. *The Heroes.* New York: Macmillan, 1928. Reprint. 1980.

Picard, Barbara Leonie. *Hero Tales from the British Isles.* Berkeley: Criterion, 1963.

Serrailier, Ian. *The Clashing Rocks: The Story of Jason.* New York: Henry Z. Walck, 1964.

_____. *The Gorgon's Head: The Story of Perseus.* New York: Henry Z. Walck, 1962.

_____. *The Way of Danger: The Story of Theseus.* New York: Henry Z. Walck, 1963.

Sutcliff, Rosemary. *The High Deeds of Finn MacCool.* New York: Dutton, 1967.

Legends

Brown, Maria. *Dick Whittington and His Cat.* New York: Scribner, 1950.

Field, Rachel. *American Folk and Fairy Tales.* New York: Scribner, 1931.

Keats, Ezra Jack. *John Henry: An American Legend.* New York: Pantheon, 1965.

Leach, Maria. *Rainbow Book of American Folk Tales and Legends.* New York: World Publishing Co., 1958.

Liverside, Douglas. *St. Francis of Assisi.* New York: Franklin Watts, 1968.

Picard, Barbara. *French Legends, Tales and Fairy Stories.* London: Oxford University Press, 1955.

Sutcliff, Rosemary. *The High Deeds of Finn MacCool.* New York: Puffin, 1976.

Synge, Ursula. *The Giant at the Ford and Other Legends of the Saints.* New York: Atheneum, 1980.

Fairy Tales

Afanas'ev, Aleksandr. *Russian Fairy Tales.* Translated by Norbert Guterman. New York: Pantheon, 1945.

Asbjornsen, Peter Christen. *East o' the Sun and West o' the Moon.* Compiled by George Webber Dasent and Jorgen E. Moe. New York: Dover, 1970. A collection of fifty-nine folktales.

Fairy Tales of Ludwig Bechstein. Translated by Anthea Bell. New York: Abelard-Schuman, 1967.

Finger, Charles J. *Tales from Silver Lands.* New York: Doubleday, 1924.

Garner, Alan. *Alan Garner's Book of British Fairy Tales.* New York: Delacorte Press, 1984.

Grimm, Jakob Ludwig Karl, and Wilhelm Grimm. *Household Stories of the Brothers Grimm: Tales from Grimm.* Selected and retold by Wanda Gag. New York: Coward, 1936.

_____. *Grimm's Household Stories.* Translated by Lucy Crane. Illustrated by Walter Crane. 1882. Reprint. New York: Smith Publishers, 1979.

_____. *The Juniper Tree and Other Tales from Grimm.* Translated by Lore Segal and Randall Jarrell. Illustrated by Maurice Sendak. New York: Doubleday, 1963.

_____. *Rare Treasures from Grimm: Fifteen Little Known Tales.* Selected and translated by Ralph Manheim. Illustrated by Erik Blegad. Garden City, N.Y.: Doubleday, 1963.

Jacobs, Joseph. *English Fairy Tales.* New York: Dover, [1898].

_____. *More English Fairy Tales.* New York: Putnam, [1894].

Lang, Andrew, ed. *Blue Fairy Book.* Illustrated by H. J. Ford. 1889. Reprint. New York: Dover, 1965. The twelve original color fairy books were published by Longmans, Green in London between 1889 and 1910. They are all still in print. They include: *Blue, Orange, Olive, Brown, Crimson, Green, Grey, Lilac, Pink, Red, Yellow, and Violet Fairy Books.*

Olenius, Elsa, comp. *Great Swedish Fairy Tales.* Translated by Holger Lundbergh. New York: Delacorte Press, 1973.

Perrault, Charles. *Perrault's Fairy Tales.* Translated by A. E. Johnson. Illustrated by Gustave Doré. New York: Dover, 1969.

_____. *Perrault's Complete Fairy Tales.* Translated by A. E. Johnson and others. Illustrated by Heath Robinson. New York: Dodd, 1961.

Wheeler, Post. *Russian Wonder Tales.* New York: Thomas Yoseloff, 1912, 1957.

General Collections of Stories

Chorao, Kay. *The Baby's Storybook.* New York: E.P. Dutton, 1985.

Glameson, Atelia, and Gilbert H. Cross, eds. *World Folktales.* New York: Scribner, 1980.

Harris, Christie. *The Trouble with Princesses.* New York: Atheneum, 1980.

Hodges, Elizabeth Jamison. *Serendipity Tales.* New York: Atheneum, 1966.

Oxenbury, Helen. *The Helen Oxenbury Nursery Storybook.* New York: Knopf, 1985.

Phelps, Ethel J. *The Maid of the North: Feminist Folktales from around the World.* New York: Holt, Rinehart & Winston, 1981.

Rojankowsky, Fedor. *Tall Book of Nursery Tales.* New York: Harper & Row, 1944.

Withers, Carl. *I Saw a Rocket Walk a Mile: Nonsense Tales, Chants and Songs from Many Lands.* New York: Holt, Rinehart, & Winston, 1965.

Folktales

Africa

Aardema, Verna. *Bringing the Rain to the Kapiti Plain.* New York: Dial Press, 1981.

Arkhurst, Joyce. *The Adventures of Spider.* Boston: Little, Brown, 1964.

Bryan, Ashley. *Beat the Story Drum, Pum-Pum.* New York: Atheneum, 1980.

_____. *Ox of the Wonderful Horns, and Other African Folktales.* New York: Atheneum, 1971.

Courlander, Harold. *The Cow-Tail Switch.* New York: Holt, 1967.

_____. *The Crest and the Tide and Other African Stories of Heroes, Chiefs, Bards, Hunters, Sorcerers and Common People.* New York: Coward, McCann & Geoghegan, 1982.

Courlander, Harold, and Wolf Lislav. *The Fire on the Mountain and Other Ethiopian Tales.* New York: Holt, 1950.

D'Amato, Janet, and Alex D'Amato. *African Animals through African Eyes.* New York: Julian Messner, 1971.

Eliot, Geraldine. *When the Leopard Passes.* New York: Schocken, 1968.

Lester, Julius. *Black Folktales.* New York: Random House, 1969.

Robinson, Adjai. *Singing Tales of Africa.* New York: Scribner's Sons, 1974.

Savory, Phyllis. *Congo Fireside Tales.* New York: Hastings House, 1962.

China

Carpenter, Francis. *Tales of a Chinese Grandmother.* Rutland, Vt.: Charles E. Tuttle, 1973.

Chang, Isabelle C. *Tales from Old China.* New York: Random House, 1969.

Chinese Fairy Tales. New York: Peter Piper Press, 1946.

Kindell, Carol. *Sweet and Sour Tales from China.* New York: Seabury Press, 1979.

Sadler, Catherine E. *Treasure Mountain: Folktales from Southern China.* New York: Atheneum, 1982.

Wolkstein, Diane. *8,000 Stones.* Garden City, N.Y.: Doubleday, 1972.

_____. *White Wave.* Garden City, N.Y.: Thomas Y. Crowell, 1979.

Wriggins, Salley Hovey. *White Monkey King.* New York: Pantheon, 1977.

Yolen, Jane. *The Emperor and the Kite.* New York: World, 1963.

Czechoslovakia

Fillmore, Parker. *The Laughing Prince.* New York: Harcourt, Brace & World, 1921.

Wood, Ruzena, comp. and trans. *The Palace of the Moon and Other Tales from Czechoslovakia.* London: Deutsch, 1981.

England

Briggs, Katharine. *British Folktales.* New York: Pantheon, 1977.

Findlay, Winifred. *Cap O'Rushes and Other Folk Tales.* Eau Claire, Wis.: E. M. Hale, 1974.

Garner, Alan. *A Bag of Moonshine.* New York: Delacorte, 1986.

_____. *Alan Garner's Book of British Fairy Tales.* New York: Delacorte, 1984.

Jacobs, Joseph. *English Fairy Tales.* New York: Dover, 1948.

_____. *More English Fairy Tales.* New York: Putnam, 1967.

France

Aulnoy, Marie Catherine Jumelle de Berneville, and Mme. le Prince de Beaumont. *Contes de fées.* Paris: Henri Laurens, 1950.

Germany

Grimm, Jakob Ludwig Karl. *Household Stories from the Collection of the Brothers Grimm.* Translated by Lucy Crane. Illustrated by Walter Crane. New York: McGraw, 1966.

Picard, Barbara. *German Hero-Stories and Folk-Tales.* New York: Henry Z. Walck, 1958.

Haiti

Wolkstein, Diane, ed. *The Magic Orange Tree and Other Haitian Tales.* New York: Knopf, 1978.

India

Babbit, Ellen C. *Jataka Tales.* New York: Appleton-Century Crofts, 1946.

Bang, Betsey. *The Old Woman and the Red Pumpkin*: *A Bengali Folk Tale.* New York: Macmillan, 1975.

Gaer, Joseph. *The Fables of India.* Boston: Little, Brown, 1955.

Jacobs, Joseph. *Indian Folk and Fairy Tales.* New York: Putnam, n.d.

Reed, Gwendolyn. *The Talkative Beasts: Myths, Fables, Folktales and Stories of India.* New York: Lothrop, Lee & Shepard, [1969].

Sharma, Partap. *The Surangini Tales.* New York: Harcourt Brace Jovanovich, 1973.

Ireland

Colum, Padraic. *The King of Ireland's Son.* Illustrated by Willy Pogany. New York: Macmillan, 1916.

Jacobs, Joseph. *Celtic Fairy Tales.* Illustrated by John D. Batlen. New York: Dover, 1968.

Macmanus, Seamus. *Hibernian Nights.* Introduction by Padraic Colum. New York: Macmillan, 1963.

_____. *The Well o' the World's End.* New York: Macmillan, 1939.

O'Brien, Edna. *Tales for the Telling: Irish Folk and Fairy Tales.* New York: Atheneum, 1986.

O'Faolain, E. *Irish Sagas and Folk-Tales.* Illustrated by Arthur Rackman. 1920. Reprint. New York: Macmillan, 1948.

Stephens, James. *Irish Folk Stories and Fairy Tales.* Edited by William Butler Yeats. New York: Gossett, 1972.

Italy

Calvino, Italo, comp. *Italian Folktales.* Translated by George Martin. New York: Harcourt Brace Jovanovich, 1980.

Mincieli, Rose Laura. *Old Neapolitan Fairy Tales.* Selected and retold by I. Pentamcrone and by R. L. Mincieli. Illustrated by Beni Montresor. New York: Knopf, 1963.

Toor, Francis. *The Golden Camalion and Other Stories.* New York: Lothrop, Lee & Shepard, 1960.

Japan

Algarin, Joanne P. *Japanese Folk Literature: A Core Collection and Reference Guide.* New York: R. R. Bowker, 1982.

Hearn, Lafcadio. *Japanese Fairy Tales.* New York: Liveright, 1953.

Uchida, Yoshiko. *The Dancing Kettle and Other Japanese Folk Tales.* New York: Harcourt, Brace & World, 1949.

_____. *The Magic Listening Cap: More Japanese Folk Tales.* New York: Harcourt, Brace & World, 1955.

Latvia

Durham, Mae. *Tit for Tat and Other Latvian Folktales: Retold by Mae Durham from the Skidrite-Rubene-Koo.* New York: Harcourt Brace and World, 1967.

Mexico

Bierhorst, John, ed. *The Hungry Woman: Myths and Legends of the Aztecs.* New York: William Morrow, 1984.

Blackmore, Vivien. *Why Corn Is Golden: Stories about Plants.* Boston: Little, Brown, 1984.

Hinojosa, Francisco. *The Old Lady Who Ate People.* Boston: Little, Brown, 1984.

Persia

Lang, Andrew, ed. *The Arabian Nights Entertainment.* Illustrated by H. J. Ford. 1898. Reprint. New York: Dover, 1969.

Larson, Jean Russell. *Palace in Bagdad: Seven Tales from Arabia.* New York: Scribner, 1966.

Picard, Barbara Leonie. *Tales of Ancient Persia.* New York: Knopf, 1965.

Tales from the Arabian Nights. Retold by N. J. Dawood. Garden City, N.Y.: Doubleday, 1978.

Poland

Borski, Lucia Merecka. *Polish Folk Tales.* New York: Sheed, 1947.

Singer, I. B. *When Schlemiel Went to Warsaw and Other Stories.* Illustrated by Margot Zemach. New York: Farrar, Straus & Giroux, 1968.

_____. *Zlateh the Goat.* Illustrated by Maurice Sendak. New York: Harper & Row, 1967.

Russia

Higonnet-Schnopper, James. *Tales from Atop a Russian Stove.* Chicago: Whitman, 1973.

Masey, Mary Lou. *Stories of the Steppes.* New York: McKay, 1968.

Ransome, Arthur. *Old Peter's Russian Tales.* London: Thomas Nelson, 1968.

Scotland

Leodhas, Sorche Nic [Leclaire Alger]. *Gaelic Ghosts.* Illustrated by Nonny Hogrogian. New York: Holt, 1962.

_____. *Thistle and Thyme: Tales and Legends from Scotland.* Illustrated by Evaline Ness. New York: Holt, 1962.

Wilson, Barbara Kerr. *Scottish Folk-Tales and Legends.* London: Oxford University Press, 1954.

Tibet

Timpanelli, Gloria. *Tales from the Roof of the World.* New York: Viking Press, 1984.

Turkey

Kelsey, Alice Geer. *Once the Hodja.* New York: David McKay, 1943.

Kunas, Ignaez, ed. *Turkish Fairy Tales and Folk Tales.* Translated by R. Nisbet Bain. New York: Dover, 1969.

South America

Eels, Elsie. *Tales from the Amazon.* New York: Dodd, Mead, 1966.

Finger, Charles J. *Tales from Silver Lands.* New York: Doubleday, 1924.

Spain

Boggs, Ralph Steele, and Mary Gould Boggs. *Three Golden Oranges.* New York: David McKay, 1936.

Sawyer, Ruth. *Picture Tales from Spain.* Philadelphia: J. B. Lippincott, 1936.

United States: Native American Tales

Borland, Hal G. *Rocky Mountain Tipi Tales.* New York: Doubleday, 1924.

Courlander, Harold. *People of the Short Blue Corn: Tales of the Hopi Indians.* New York: Harcourt Brace Jovanovich, 1970.

Curry, Jane Louise. *Back in the Before Time: Tales of the California Indians.* New York: Macmillan, 1987.

_____. *Down from the Lonely Mountain: California Indian Tales.* New York: Harcourt, Brace & World, 1965.

Field, Rachel. *American Folk and Fairy Tales.* New York: Scribner, 1927.

Grinnell, George Bird. *Blackfoot Lodge Tales.* Lincoln: University of Nebraska Press, 1962.

Harris, Christie. *Once More upon a Totem.* New York: Atheneum, 1973.

Haviland, Virginia, ed. *North American Legends.* New York: William Collins, 1979.

Hunt, Wolf Robe. *Dancing Horses of the Acoma.* As told to Helen Rushmore. Cleveland: World Publishing, 1963.

Kroeber, Theodora. *The Inland Whale.* Berkeley: University of California Press, 1970.

Leach, Maria. *How the People Sang the Mountains Up.* New York: Viking Press, 1967.

MacMillan, Cyrus. *Glooskap's Country and Other Indian Tales.* Toronto: Oxford University Press, 1956.

Reid, Dorothy M. *Tales of Nanabozho.* New York: Henry Z. Walck, 1963.

United States: Regional Tales

Chase, Richard, ed. *Grandfather Tales.* Boston: Houghton Mifflin, 1948.

_____. *The Jack Tales.* Boston: Houghton Mifflin, 1943.

Field, Rachel. *American Folk and Fairy Tales.* New York: Scribner's, 1929.

Hamilton, Virginia. *The People Could Fly.* Illustrated by Diane Dillon and Leo Dillon. New York: Knopf, 1985.

Jacquith, Priscilla. *Bo Rabbit Smart for True: Folktales from the Gullah.* Illustrated by Ed Young. New York: Philomel Books, 1981.

Kellogg, Stephen. *Paul Bunyan.* New York: Morrow, 1984.

Leach, Maria. *Rainbow Book of American Folktales and Legends.* Cleveland: World Publishing, 1958.

Lester, Julius. *The Tales of Uncle Remus.* New York: Dial Books, 1987.

Rees, Ennis. *More of Br'er Rabbit's Tricks.* Illus. by Edward Gorey. New York: Young-Scott Books, [1968].

Schwartz, Alvin, ed. *Flapdoodle: Pure Nonsense from American Folklore.* New York: J. B. Lippincott, 1980.

Yugoslavia

Fillmore, Parker. *The Shepherd's Nosegay.* New York: Harcourt, Brace & World, 1958.

Ghost Stories

Collections of Ghost Stories

Ainsworth, Ruth. *Phantom Cyclist and Other Ghost Stories.* Chicago: Follett Publishing, [1971, 1974].

Anderson, Jean. *The Haunting of America.* Boston: Houghton Mifflin, 1973.

Kahn, Joan. *Some Things Dark and Dangerous.* New York: Harper, 1970.

_____. *Some Things Fierce and Fatal.* New York: Harper, 1971.

Leach, Maria. *The Thing at the Foot of the Bed.* New York: Dell, 1977.

_____. *The Rainbow Book of American Folk Tales and Legends.* Cleveland: World Publishing, 1958.

Leodhas, Sorche Nic. *Gaelic Ghosts.* New York: Holt, Rinehart & Winston, 1963.

_____. *Ghosts Go Haunting.* New York: Holt, Rinehart & Winston, 1965.

Littledale, Frya, ed. *Strange Tales from Many Lands.* Garden City, N.Y.: Doubleday, 1975.

Schwartz, Alvin. *More Scary Stories to Tell in the Dark.* New York: Lippincott, 1984.

_____. *Scary Stories to Tell in the Dark.* New York: J. B. Lippincott, 1981.

Original Ghost Stories

Garfield, Leon. *The Ghost Downstairs.* New York: Pantheon, 1972.

_____. *The Restless Ghost.* New York: Pantheon, 1969.

Kennedy, Richard. *Collected Stories.* New York: Harper & Row, 1987.

_____. *Inside My Feet.* New York: Harper & Row, 1979.

Gypsy Tales

Ficowski, Jerzy. *Sister of the Birds and Other Gypsy Tales.* Translated by Lucia M. Borski. Nashville, Tenn.: Abingdon, [1976].

Original Literary Tales

Andersen, Hans. *His Classic Fairy Tales.* Translated by Erik Haugard. New York: Doubleday, 1974.

Irving, Washington. *Rip Van Winkle and the Legend of Sleepy Hollow.* New York: Macmillan, 1965.

Kipling, Rudyard. *Just-So Stories.* New York: Doubleday, 1902.

Sandburg, Carl. *Rootabaga Tales.* New York: Harcourt Brace Jovanovich, 1974.

Stockton, Frank. *The Lady or the Tiger and Other Stories.* 1884. Reprint. New York: Airmont, 1968.

Wilde, Oscar. *The Happy Prince and Other Stories.* London: Dent, 1968.

Bibliographical Guide

MacDonald, Margaret Read. *The Storyteller's Sourcebook: A Subject, Title & Motif Index to Folk Collections for Children.* Detroit: Neal-Schuman Published in association with Gale Research, 1982.

Storytelling

Storytelling Collections

Algann, Joanne P. *Japanese Folk Literature: A Core Collection and Reference Guide.* New York: R. R. Bowker, 1982.

Arbuthnot, May Hill. *Time for Fairy Tales.* Rev. ed. Chicago: Scott, Foresman, 1961.

Baker, Augusta. *The Talking Tree.* Philadelphia: J. B. Lippincott, 1955.

Colwell, Eileen. *The Magic Umbrella.* New York: David McKay, 1976.

Davis, Mary Gould. *A Baker's Dozen.* New York: Harcourt Brace, 1930.

Fitzgerald, Berdette S. *World Tales for Creative Dramatics in Storytelling.* New York: Prentice-Hall, 1962.

Ross, Eulalie Skinmetz, ed. *The Lost Half-Hour.* New York: Harcourt, Brace & World, 1963.

How to Tell Stories

Baker, Augusta, and Ellen Green. *Storytelling, Art and Technique.* New York: R. R. Bowker, 1977.

_____. *A Storytelling Manual.* New York: R. R. Bowker, 1977.

Bauer, Caroline Feder. *Handbook for Storytellers.* Chicago: ALA Press, 1977.

Brenemen, Lucille N., and Bren Brenemen. *Once upon a Time: A Storytelling Handbook.* Chicago: Nelson-Hall, 1983.

Champlin, Connie, and Nancy Renfro. *Storytelling with Puppets.* Chicago: ALA Press, 1985.

Colum, Padraic. *Storytelling Old and New.* New York: Macmillan, 1968.

_____. *The Fountain of Youth.* New York: Macmillan, 1927.

DeWit, Dorothy. *Children's Faces Looking Up.* Chicago: ALA Press, 1979.

Farrell, Catherine Horne. *A Guide to Storytelling.* San Francisco: Zellerbach Family Fund, 1983.

Livo, Norma J., and Sandra A. Rietz. *Storytelling: Process and Practice.* Boulder, Colo.: Libraries Unlimited, 1986.

Pulowski, Anne. *The World of Storytelling.* New York: R. R. Bowker, 1977.

Schimmel, Nancy. *Just Enough to Make a Story.* Berkeley, Calif.: Sister's Choice Press, 1978.

Ziskind, Sylvia. *Telling Stories to Children.* New York: H. W. Wilson, 1976.

Books on Children's Literature That Include Aspects of Story

Sayers, Frances Clarke. *Summoned by Books.* New York: Viking Press, 1965.

Smith, Lillian H. *The Unreluctant Years.* Chicago: ALA Press, 1953.

Sutherland, Zena, et al. *Children and Books.* 6th ed. Glenview, Ill.: Scott Foresman, 1981.

From *Zlateh the Goat and Other Stories* by Isaac Bashevis Singer, pictures by Maurice Sendak. Translated from the Yiddish by the author and Elizabeth Shub. Text © 1966 by Isaac Bashevis Singer, pictures © 1966 by Maurice Sendak. Reprinted by permission of Harper & Row, Inc.

DISCOGRAPHY

Recordings available on cassette are indicated with the symbol TC.

Epic

Le Morte d'Arthur: Lancelot and Guinevere. Read by Siobhan McKenna. Caedmon TC SWC-1374.

Tales of King Arthur and His Knights (Pyle). Read by Ian Richardson. Caedmon TC-1462 ("Excalibur"), TC-1465 ("Sword in the Anvil"), TC-1609 ("Story of Sir Launcelot"), TC-1625 ("Story of Sir Galahad"); TC.

Hero Tale

Tanglewood Tales (Hawthorne). Read by Anthony Quayle. Caedmon TC-1391 ("The Story of Theseus"), TC-1290 ("Pluto and Proserpina"); TC.

Tanglewood Tales (Hawthorne). Read by Cathleen Nesbitt. Caedmon TC-1367 ("Jason and the Golden Fleece"); TC.

The Adventures of Robin Hood. Vols. 1-4. Read by Anthony Quayle. Caedmon TC-1369-72; TC.

Myth

The Children of Odin: The Book of Northern Myths (Colum). Read by Keir Dullea. Caedmon TC-1471; TC.

The Greek Myths: A Treasury. Vols. 1-5 CMS 568/616/625/651/656; TC.

Heroes, Gods and Monsters of the Greek Myths. Richard Kiley and Julie Harris read from Eustin's book. Spoken Arts GM 989/1000. TC 7A/B,C,D,E/F.

Heroes of the Greek Myths. 2-Spoken Arts 1133, 1143.

Legend

Rip Van Winkle (Irving). Read by Ed Begley. Caedmon TC-1241; TC.

Paul Bunyan in Story and Song. Performed by Ed Begley and Oscar Brand. Caedmon TC-1275; tc.

The Legend of Sleepy Hollow (Irving). Read by Ed Begley. Caedmon TC-1242; tc.

Fables

The Fables of Aesop. Dramatic reading by English actors. Spoken Arts SA 1013.

Aesop's Fables (42). Read by Boris Karloff. Caedmon TC-1221; TC.

European Folk and Fairy Tales

General European

European Folk and Fairy Tales. Read by Anne Pellowski. CMS 548; TC.

Puss in Boots and Other Fairy Tales from around the World. Read by Cathleen Nesbit. Caedmon TC-1247; TC.

Frances Clark Sayors, Storyteller. Weston Woods 705/706.

England

English Folk and Fairy Tales. Read by Anne Pellowski. CMS 504; TC.

Dick Whittington and His Cat and Other English Fairy Tales. Read by Claire Bloom. Caedmon TC-1265; TC.

France

Les Contes de Renault. 2 vols. Read in French by Robert Frank. Folkways 7861, 7862.

Beauty and the Beast. Read by Douglas Fairbanks, Jr. Caedmon TC-1394; TC.

Best Loved Fairy Tales of Charles Perrault. Read by Eve Watkinson and Christopher Carson. Spoken Arts SA 847. In French: SA 787.

Germany

Grimm's Fairy Tales. Read by Joseph Schildkraut. Caedmon TC-1062; TC.

Hansel and Gretel and Other Fairy Tales by the Brothers Grimm. Read by Claire Bloom. Caedmon TC-1274, TC-1266; TC.

Gypsies

Fairy Tales Told by Gypsies. Caedmon TC-1436; TC.

Ireland

Irish Fairy Tales. Read by Cyril Cusack. Caedmon TC-1349, TC-1368; TC.

Irish Fairy Tales. Spoken Arts 720; TC 6005. Vol. 2: 1029.

Padraic Colum: Reading His Irish Tales and Irish Poems. Folkways 9737.

Fairy Tales of Ireland. Cyril Cusack reads from Jacob's collection. 2-Caedmon TC-1349, TC-1368; TC.

Italy

Tales from Italy. "The Cunning Shoemaker" and "Catherine and Her Destiny." Spoken Arts 1079; TC 6081/2.

Spain

Perez and Martina. Read from her version by Pera Belpre in Spanish and English. CMS 505; TC.

Non-European Folk and Fairy Tales

Africa

African Folk Tales. Vols. 1-2. Read by Bertha Parker. CMS 547, CMS 550 Vol. 3 Read by Brock Peters. CMS 591.

Ashanti Tales from Ghana. Harold Courlander reads from his book, *Hat Shaking Dance.* Scholastic 7710.

Folk Tales from West Africa. 10" Folkways 7103.

Folk Tales of African Tribes. Read by Eartha Kitt. Caedmon TC-1267; TC.

Tshindao and Other African Folk Tales. Read by Ruby Dee and Ossie Davis. Caedmon TC-1499; TC CDL 51499.

China

Chinese Fairy Tales. Read by Sean McKenna. Caedmon TC-1328; TC.

Tales of China and Tibet. Read by Sean McKenna. Caedmon TC-1423; TC.

Haiti

Uncle Bouqui of Haiti. Augusta Baker tells tales from Harold Courlander's book. 10" Folkways 7107.

Indonesia

Folk Tales from Indonesia. Read by Harold Courlander from his book, *Katchief's Lime Pit.* Folkways 7102.

Japan

Japanese Folk Tales. Spoken Arts 1076; TC 6083/4.

Japanese Folk and Fairy Tales. Read by Christine Price. CMS 528; TC.

Middle East

Arabian Nights: Ali Baba and the Forty Thieves. Read by Anthony Quayle. Caedmon TC-1251; TC.

Joseph and His Brothers. 10" Folkways 7106.

The Tale of Scheherazade. Read by Julie Harris. Caedmon TC-1373.

Pacific

Pacific Folk Tales. Read by Anne Pellowski. CMS 596; TC.

South Sea Island Tales. Caedmon TC-1433; TC.

Russia

Russian Folk and Fairy Tales. Read by Christine Price. CMS 515; TC.

South America

Tales from Silver Lands (Finger). Tales of Central and South American Indians. New Aw. 77171; TC 77172.

American Folktales

General

American Indian Tales for Children. Read by Anne Pellowski. Vols. 1-2. CMS 500/1; TC.

Aire Plume, Legends of the American Indians. Read by Jay Silverheels. Caedmon TC-1451.

Hopi Tales. Jack Moyles reads from Harold Courlander's *People of the Short Blue Corn.* Folkways FC-7776.

Eskimo Stories/Tales of Magic. Spoken Arts 1132.

Regional

Afro-American Tales and Games. Read by Linda Goss. Folkways 77865.

American Settlers' Tales and Folklore (Stoutenburg). Read by Ed Begley. 2-Caedmon TC-1317, TC-1325; TC.

American Tall Tales Soundbook. 4-Caedmon SBR-110; TC SBC-110.

Ballads of Black America. Folkways 7751.

Some Mountain Tales about Jack. Told and sung by Billy Ed Wheeler. Spoken Arts 1113; TC SAC-6129/30.

Literary

Andersen's Fairy Tales: The Emperor's New Clothes and Other Tales. Read by Sir Michael Redgrave. Caedmon TC-1073; TC.

Andersen's Fairy Tales: Little Match Girl, Thumbelina, and Other Tales. Read by Boris Karloff. Caedmon TC-1117; TC.

How to Tell Corn Fairies and Other Rootabaga Stories. Read by Carl Sandburg from *Rootabaga Stories.* Caedmon TC-1159.

Animal Stories (De la Mare). Read by Lynn Redgrave. Caedmon TC-1456; TC.

The Happy Prince. Oscar Wilde's stories read by Claire Luce. Folkways 7731.

Just So Stories (Kipling). Read by Boris Karloff. Caedmon TC-1038; TC.

Ghost Stories

A Coven of Witches' Tales. Told by Vincent Price. Caedmon TC-1338.

Ghost Stories. Peter 8114.

Ghostly Sounds. Vols. 1-2. Peter 8125, 8145.

Tales of Witches, Ghosts and Goblins. Read by Vincent Price. Caedmon TC-1393; TC.

FILMOGRAPHY

Anansi the Spider. 10 min. Color. Texture Films.

In this decorative, cheerful film, Anansi, the Ashanti buffoon-hero, is saved from his own folly by his six sons, thus escaping once more to enchant us. Aside from the story the bright, compelling colors and textures and the African music help convey a real sense of place and tradition.

Bringing the Rain to Kapiti Plain. 26 min. Color. Reading Rainbows.

During a terrible drought in Kenya, Kapiti shoots an eagle-feathered arrow into the sky. It pierces the hovering great cloud overhead, and at last rain falls on the parched land. The story itself, a beautifully illustrated retelling of an old, cumulative tale, is well rendered, but the introduction with LeVar Burton seems somewhat self-conscious and overly long. Perhaps you could show only the actual story section. Previewing is suggested.

The Country Mouse and the City Mouse. 8 min. Color. Coronet Films.

A pleasant animated version of the fable of the naive little country cousin and her wicked city relative. Allthough the country mouse is initially excited about her visit, in the end, after a series of frights and difficulties, she is more than happy to return to her quiet bucolic life.

Cow Tail Switch. 8 min. Learning Corp.

Ogalusa, an African hunter, is killed while hunting, but he is brought back to life by his sons. Restored to his village, he gives his cow tail switch to the youngest son, because it was he who never forgot. Although the move from the time of the story to the present is choppy, the film is sympathetic and worth showing for the simple beauty of the legend.

The Fisherman and His Wife. 20 min. Color. Weston Woods.

When the fisherman wins the gratitude of a magic fish, it is his wife who exploits the gift, demanding more and more until, at last, she loses all. Using hand puppets, the film is a tense, suspenseful version of the tale.

Foolish Frog. 8 min. Color. Weston Woods.

Pete Seeger narrates by singing this delicious, swinging account of an entire rural community who join in a dance fest at the village store. When the barn joins in, the fun takes off.

Frog Went A-Courtin'. 12 min. Color. Weston Woods.

A musical folktale, sung by John Langstaff and superbly animated by Rojankovsky, tells the compelling tale of a frog's courtship of Miss Mousy. Children will enjoy the playful feeling and the absurd characters, but you may want to show only the first half--the second is a questionable effort at sing-along technique, certainly lost on preschoolers.

Hansel and Gretel, an Appalachian Version. 17 min. Color. Tom Davenport Films.

Moving immediately into the heart of the story, and acted with powerful directness and clarity, this version of the old fairy tale filmed in Appalachia seems to reveal the link of real people with their stories. A compelling, beautiful film; even the spare banjo accompaniment is appropriate.

Jack and the Robbers. 14 1/2 min. Color. Pied Piper Productions.

Homeless Jack adopts some animals during his travels, and they come to his defense in unexpected and amazing ways when robbers occupy the house they are staying in. Richard Chase, the famous Appalachian folklorist, tells this story in a captivating and lively way that draws the audience in completely.

Liang and the Magic Paintbrush. 29 min. Color. Reading Rainbows.

Liang, a small boy who longs to paint, is bequeathed a magic paintbrush by an old man who appears before him. Everything he paints thereafter leaps to life. Liang shrewdly decides only to benefit others with his new gift, but the greedy emperor, hearing of it, insists on having the brush. But he paints everything so large that a great storm sweeps the emperor and all he owns into the sea forever. Again, as is typical of Reading Rainbow productions, the story itself is richly designed and told in clear, bright frames and a resonant style. But the long heavy introduction and poststatement are ponderous and dull. Consider showing only the story section.

The Legend of John Henry. 11 min. Color. Pyramid.

The legend of the "steel-drivin' man" is told in cartoon style, accompanied by the singing of Roberta Flack. The powerful images and blues-style music lend a contemporary touch to this story of the hero who sought to outwit the twentieth century with his strength and skill.

The Legend of Sleepy Hollow. 13 min. Color. Stephen Bosustow Productions.

This version of the hapless, tattered schoolteacher, Ichabod Crane, and his ghostly adventures is told in animation with folk-guitar accompaniment and narration. Children will savor not only Ichabod's antics as he pursues and is rejected by his lady love, but also the shivery surprise ending.

The Little Girl and the Gunnywolf. 6 min. Color. ACI.

Animated according to children's designs and narrated by a child, this version of the story of the little girl pursued by the Gunnywolf seems a little cute, but nevertheless lovely.

The Loon's Necklace. 11 min. Color. Crawley Films (Canada).

Kilorah, the blind man-shaman of his tribe, goes in search of his magic father, the loon, in hopes pof regaining of his sight to aid his starving people. When the loon restores it, Kilorah places his shell necklace on the loon's back in gratitude. The archaic wood puppet masks perfectly match the story mood in this taut, beautiful film-tale of heroism and transformation.

The Magic Tree. 10 min. Color. Texture Films.

Minumbu, the homely brother, finds a magic tree that brings him wealth and love, but he loses it all by breaking his promise and sharing the secret with his predatory, selfish family. An absorbing Congolese tale told in brilliant color and abstractly styled animation.

The Pied Piper of Hamlin. 10 min. Color. BFA Productions.

The old story of the avenging piper who rids a town of rats. When the townspeople refuse to pay him, he exacts a terrible revenge. The tale is told here in cartoon animation and rhymed verse. Narrated with oleaginous guile by Peter Ustinov, the film achieves a measure of the innate fascination of the original, although the verse is a little disappointing.

Puss in Boots. 10 min. b/w. Contemporary Films.

Lotte Reininger's shadow puppet adaptations for film, paper cutouts, provide a sophisticated version of the classic fairy tale of the clever cat who wins his master a princess and a kingdom.

Rapunzel. 10 min. Color. Perspective.

A dignified, intense version of the tale of the princess locked up in the tower, whose mother and lover climb up her long golden hair to visit. Animated skillfully, the film records faithfully Rapunzel's fall from grace and her long atonement.

Rikki-Tikki-Tavi. 26 min. Color. G.A., Distributed by Park Video.

Despite its somewhat cute animation, this version of the Kipling story of the endearing yet wily mongoose who saves his adopted English family from giant cobras proves to be very moving. Tiny Rikki's courage comes through strongly in an intense, suspenseful production.

Rumpelstiltskin. 12 min. Color. Coronet.

A princess, set to the impossible task of spinning straw into gold, is rescued by a tiny irritable man who drives a hard bargain: he will do it and she will marry the king, but she must guess his name or give up her baby to him. How she succeeds is the marrow of this colorful, humorous animated version of the old tale.

Seven Ravens. 21 min. Color. Learning Corporation of America.

Over the seven hills and down the seven valleys into the great forest goes the little girl who seeks to free her brothers from their curse. Despite a rather brash score, the film tells a strong tale of feminine courage and success in the face of difficulty--and tells it straightforwardly.

The Steadfast Tin Soldier. 14 min. Color. Brandon.

Even the sad ending can't erase the magic of Andersen's storytelling in this classic tale of the one-legged tin soldier who steadfastly follows his ballet dancer love through horrifying adventures.

The Stonecutter. 6 min. Color. Weston Woods.

Gerald McDermott's evocative, vivid colors bring this Japanese fable to powerful life. We watch Taseku's meeting with the mountain spirit and his successful transformations into increasingly mighty forms of sunken cloud and mountain until, at last, he feels the faint chipping of the lowly stonecutter at his base. An original, vital film.

A Story! A Story! 10 min. Color. Weston Woods.

How Anansi, the spiderman, wins the sky god King Nyame's golden pot of stories for humanity is told with humor and pace in this colorful animated version.

The Ugly Duckling. 11 min. Color. Coronet Films.

Andersen's story of the ugly little bird, perpetually rejected by others, who grows up at last to beauty and acclaim as he assumes his rightful swan shape. It is sympathetically and naturally told.

Ujima: Modupe and the Flood. 4 1/2 min. Color. Nguzo Sabo Films.

This film illustrates one of the seven principles of unity in Nigerian philosophy. Here the village of Ujima is threatened by a devastating flood. Modupe averts disaster by burning his mountain cottage and thus attracts the villagers' attention. Both art and feeling are rich and noble in this brief, well-told story of courage and loyalty.

The Wave. 9 min. Color. Film Associates.

When Ojiisan and his grandson see an enormous wave threatening their village, Ojiisan acts quickly. By burning the rice fields, he attracts the villagers out of their houses, and when they turn in anger, they see their village engulfed by the flood. Blair Lent's animation in spare and exciting.

Why the Sun and Moon Live in the Sky. 5 min. Color. ACL.

Blair Lent's wonderful masks herald the parade of water animals who come at sun's invitation to share his house, finally forcing both sun and his wife, moon, up into the sky, where they still reside. A fine interpretation of the African folktale.

Zlateh the Goat. 20 min. Color. Weston Woods.

Filmed in Bohemia using nonactors from the community, this sensitive version of Isaac B. Singer's story shows how Zlateh saves Aaron's life when they are caught in a terrible snowstorm. Expert editing and an absence of sentimentality enhance his moving film.

WORKSHOPS

Story Forms from around the World

A workshop in six sessions that traces the forms of the story in the telling of them.

Introduction: Stories from around the world can be comfortably presented by a free-lance storyteller, a series of guest storytellers who are specialists in the forms or regions of the tales, or the children's librarian or educator. It is also an accordionlike plan; the basic series could easily be shortened to one workshop or expanded to a three-month festival of stories off the family tree.

Structure: This is designed as six weekly sessions. It can be directed toward children of a specific age or class (third and fourth graders, for instance), but is perfectly suited to the wide-open age range found at a public library. Although no props or tools need to be used, masks, posters, artifacts, and books appropriate to each kind of story can be exhibited. Records or tapes of the place or period can be playing when the children enter. Here the choice of stories is key. Occasionally a film or video can be substituted, either a storyteller on film or a story that has been filmed (such as *Zlateh the Goat, Bringing the Rain to Kapiti Plain,* or *Liang and the Magic Paintbrush*).

1. Epic

Sitting on floor cushions in a circle is a good arrangement for children listening to stories. When they are comfortable, share with them some of the origins and background of stories and describe the epic, mentioning some of the great ones from around the world: the Finnish *Kalevala,* the Judeo-Christian Old and New Testaments of the Bible, the *Katari-be* from Japan, the Greek *Iliad* or the Indian *Ramayana,* for instance.

Choosing an amenable epic story, such as the *Odyssey,* weave a pattern for the form by telling a few of the incidents within it. For instance, from the *Odyssey:* the start of Odysseus's voyaging in Ithaca, introducing Telemachus and Penelope; Odysseus's escape from Calypso on his return from the Trojan Wars; his ordeal in the land of the Lotus-eaters; the story of the cave of the Cyclops; the adventure of the Sirens; the story of Scylla and Charybdis; and finally, the poignant tale of his return to Ithaca and the overthrow of the suitors. These adventures can be told briefly, or one or two could be told in depth.

2. Myth

Do the children know about myths already? Your introduction can include their sharing with you some of the types they have heard or read about, and you can share with them your knowledge and understanding of them. Choose a sympathetic variety for the group and tell a cluster that gives a good representation of the form. Some ideas would be:

Creation:

> "How Coyote Helped the People Bring Fire"
> "Why the Birds Are Different Colors"
> "Why the Chipmunk's Back Is Striped"
> "Origin of the Medicine Pipe"

Norse:

> "The World's Beginning"
> "How Odin Lost His Eye"
> "The Contest of the Giants"

Greek:

> "Orpheus"
> "Atalanta's Race"
> "Daedalus and Icarus"
> "Orpheus in the Underworld"

Egyptian:

> "Isis and Osiris"
> "Khufu and the Magicians"
> "The Book of Toth"

If you are not using the Indian *Ramayana* for epic, consider using one of those imaginative, romantic stories.

3. Legends

Legend, a story that grows up in the wake of a famous man or woman, shares something with the Greek hero tale. Can the children think of anyone who is a "legend" to them? What stories do they know about them? Share with them how these tales came to be and then choose a few of your own to tell. For example:

"How Perseus Slew the Dragon"
"The Story of Rosa Parks"
"St. Francis and the Birds"
"Joan of Arc"
"Johnny Appleseed"
"Stagolee"

4. Fairy Tale

What is a fairy tale? How did it come to be? Why tell it? What does it mean? Work with the children a little in introducing the growth and meaning of this important kind of story and choose a group that will most broadly convey the quality of it for illustration. These are long and rich, so one or two is more than satisfying. A sample program might contain:

"Rumpelstiltskin"

"Beauty and the Beast"
or "The Twelve Dancing Princesses"

"Puss-in-Boots"
or "Snow White and Rose Red"

"East of the Sun and West of the Moon"

5. Folktale

To explain the vast geographical spread and enormous variety of the folktale, use a map, if you wish, and choose examples as you explore the human family tree. Russia, India, South America, Africa, Japan, urban and rural America are all examples of places whose stories illustrate the various kinds of old tales: humor, morals, adventures, ghost stories, love stories, and tall tales.

What is the children's experience with this kind of tale? Do they like them? Why? You can share your own favorites.

Russia: "Baba Yaga"

America: "Babe, the Blue Ox"

South America: "The Magic Ball"

Africa: "Talk"

Japan: "The Dancing Teakettle"

Aesop (Greece): "The Fox and the Grapes"

England: "Lazy Jack"

6. Original Tale

This is a good place to finish the series, as it leaves an opening for the contemporary tale or ballad. Explain the nature of the original, or literary tale, and, since the author's choice of words is crucial to the impact and meaning of the story, read one aloud. Have the children written one? It would be fun to follow up this idea in the library, to have them bring in some examples and include a page or two in a future storytelling program.

A sample of literary tales from which one could choose:

> Rudyard Kipling, "The Elephant's Child"
> Oscar Wilde, "The Giant with No Heart in His Body"
> Hans Christian Andersen, "The Ugly Duckling"
> Carl Sandburg, "The Wedding of the Ragdoll and the Broomhandle"

Postscript: Winding up the workshop is a fine opportunity for an informal discussion with the children about stories, what they enjoyed most and why, and sharing juice and special foods, perhaps from the countries of the tales. Lingering over conversation and a good book display can offer the group a chance to integrate their experience with the stories and take the stories home with them in their minds and feelings.

Tell the children a little about good ways to present a story--about standing, eye contact, and use of the voice for clarity, distinctness and projection. Demonstrate to them what you mean, and ask for a volunteer to try out their tale of the day with the group.

Teaching Children to Tell Their Own Stories

This is a workshop in two sessions to teach children to tell their own stories. The first part, lasting about two hours, serves to introduce stories, what they are and what kinds there are, and how to tell them. During the second session, the children tell their own chosen stories. This workshop can be quite informal. A bare room with comfortable cushions and a few tools-- pencil, paper, and a tape recorder--are all that is necessary. It is designed for a small group.

Ages: 6-12.

1. Introduction: The Wonderful World of Stories

What is a story? What kinds are there? Have the children sit round-robin style on the floor. Ask for ideas on what a story is. Introduce the idea that anything that happens to them during the day is material for a story, and ask one child to volunteer the story of a personal incident. Tell one yourself and ask for some more stories.

Tell an enormous untruth, and then ask the children to think of the greatest lie they can possibly imagine. After a few minutes ask for their samples of tall tales.

Ask who has a favorite hero or heroine on television or in the movies (or figures our history and country are fine to use) and ask for his or her story. Choose a favorite story of your own to tell.

Slip in a quick humorous tale (why does the rooster always look so well groomed? Because he carries a comb), and see who has one to swap with you.

Ask if anyone has an idea for why things are the way they are? Why is there rain? Why is fire red? Why do pine trees keep their needles? Listen to their "creation" tales and give them one of your own.

Now the children have told and heard adventure stories, tall tales, hero tales, humorous tales, and tales of creation. It is fun to let them know that these tiny, not-written-down stories are the true root of the art.

In conclusion, tell the children to keep a sharp ear out for stories on the bus, or the radio, or from a family member. Suggest the idea of putting on a record or tape, sitting quietly nearby, and letting the music suggest a story. These mood stories are especially accessible to a shy or quiet child. Make sure each one will have a story to bring next week for the telling session.

2. Festival Day

Set up the room for storytelling whichever way appeals to you, with chairs or pillows, and with a space for the tellers. Have your tape recorder ready. Consider having a festival feast to share with the group at the end of the show.

The children can sit in a circle and do a round-robin storytelling, if that is most comfortable, or you can have a more formal, stand-up presentation with an audience. When they have finished, take time to play the tape recording back to them. This gives a finished, professional tone to their efforts which is important.

Before they leave, ask the children to drop by the library any time to share new stories. If the group has been a good one, you might want to set up an anniversary meeting to get everyone together and share their special finds. Take time for a celebration if you can.

A Workshop in Book Creation

Introduction: This is a workshop in four sessions, each devoted to a single aspect of book making: creative writing, illustration, printmaking and bookbinding. It can be taught by the educator or children's librarian alone, or, if possible, together with an artist.

Ages: 6-12. The children can be divided into a younger group (6-9) and an older one (9-12).

Number of Children: 6-15.

Time: Sixty to ninety minutes.

Space: A large, open room with one or two long tables for use as a craft center. Good lighting is important.

1. Creative Writing

Materials: Pencils, scratch paper, rulers, fine-tipped markers, quality paper (better grade than newsprint or scratch) ready to cut to preferred size.

The leader can begin by telling or reading a very simple story like "Stone Soup" or "Billy Goats Gruff" with a good, clear outline. Can the children tell you the story back? What is the theme of the story? Where does it get most exciting? Who is in it? Where does it take place? Finding out these elements of the tale is a good way to prepare for understanding and selecting illustrations. Now ask the children to begin thinking of an idea around which they can work out their own story. Ask them to write down any ideas on scratch paper, and then you can help each one crystallize and clarify the work. Attention to grammar and spelling can be a natural part of this process. Ask for one volunteer to read his or her story and tell any ideas that have come up for illustrations. Ask those who are ready to take clean paper and write their story as best they can, as neatly as possible, using a fine-tipped marker and wide, comfortable spacing. They should write on one side of their paper only, leaving at least a half-inch margin for bookbinding later on. When the time is up, children who have not finished copying their stories may do so at the beginning of the next session.

2. Illustration

Materials: Pencils, fine-tipped colored markers, quality paper cut to size, erasers, rulers, examples of title and dedication pages and illustrated stories.

Although some children will have finished copying their rough draft, others will be doing it now. So begin the session by introducing illustration, giving the children the idea that illustration is a dual art with writing that helps bring life to the story by suggesting, clarifying, blending, and emphasizing. Hold up a story or two from the folktale collection to show them how illustration can highlight the various elements of a story. A book like *A Story, a Story* has pictures that suggest character, theme, setting, and plot, all at different times. They can do this, too. Point out the border design of the pages, the design of the page itself, and the color schemes to show how a book comes together. A example of good book design is Nicholas Sidjakov's *Baboushka.*

Using paper cut to the same size as their manuscript, children can begin to illustrate their own choice of material from their story. If they have trouble, go over the plot and character with them to help develop ideas.

Now explain the title and dedication pages--a good example is the song dedication on a radio show. Children can dedicate their book to a pet or a place as well as a person. Show these pages from one of the books already used for illustration. They can make their own versions at the end of this workshop.

3. Printmaking

Space: The work space should allow for a comfortable flow of activity and provide space for the supplies and the printmaking itself, and for sketching designs. A separate space will be needed for prints to dry, as this takes several hours. So arrange tables accordingly.

Materials: Scratch paper, pencils, Styrofoam plates such as supermarket meat trays, water-based inks in red, blue, and yellow, rubber rollers (brayers), Plexiglass or other surfaces to be used as palettes for rolling out the inks, newspaper, examples of prints and books.

Begin by explaining the idea of printing--the transfer of a picture from one surface to another. Good examples are rubber stamps and typing, as well as pressing paper down on wet paint. In our simple printmaking a picture is made on a surface called a plate, and then inked and printed on another surface. Show a few prints as examples.

Now comes the demonstration: take a piece of Styrofoam, indent or "etch" a line drawing on it with a pencil or other firm, blunt-pointed tool. Squeeze colors, one each, on the palettes, and then roll the plate down with the brayer. Press the plate down firmly on the chosen palette and transfer to paper. The illustration comes from the lines left free of ink after the transfer is done so these should be deep and clear.

The children can get started now etching their pictures. When this is done they make their print, just as you did, choosing at first just one clear color. As they begin to understand the process they can wash their plates off between inkings, and try different colors and color combinations, pulling several prints.

When they have finished their prints, ask them to make a bookplate. This is a design that shows that the book belongs to them, so it can be any image that appeals to them--a unicorn, for instance, or a cat face, as long as it is simple and clear. Let them sketch the bookplate design first, and then, being careful not to puncture the plate and using a thick line, etch it in. The bookplate can be printed and pulled as their other illustrations were.

When the children are finished, explain that next week will be bookbinding day. Remind them to look through the books they have at home this week and see how they are made, including bookplate, title and dedication pages, and illustrations.

4. Bookbinding

Materials: Two board covers per child, cut 3/4 inch larger than book pages. These can be made from cardboard, matboard or poster board. In addition have on hand glue, scissors, hole punch, yarn or string, paper and cloth scrap materials of different sizes, textures, patterns, and colors, examples of bookbinding techniques that you can prepare yourself (such as tying, covering, or wrapping board covers) and cover decorations, as well as books.

Note: Before meeting, cut the covers and punch three holes in the left margin of the children's books to prepare for their binding session.

Begin by working with the children in assembling their bookplate, pages, and prints together, giving each one two cardboard book covers. Show them how the book can be wrapped over an inset piece by using remnants of wallpaper or material cut to the book's size. This procedure and the final binding methods are charted through the examples that follow:

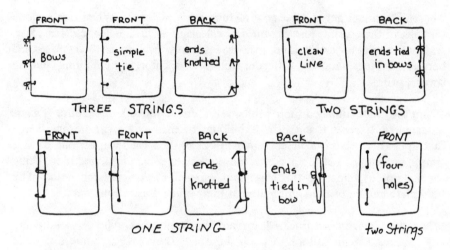

The children are free to design their own ways of binding. The book must be bound loosely enough so that it can be opened and the pages turned with ease. Children should test this before they knot their binding strings together. They may wish to cover or wrap their boards with paper or cloth before tying, and then repunch the holes. To do this the outside of the cover is coated with glue, and pressed down flat over the material used for the wrapping. The wrapping should be at least one and a half inches longer than the board, so that the corners can be folded in and the edges glued down smoothly to the inside of the board.

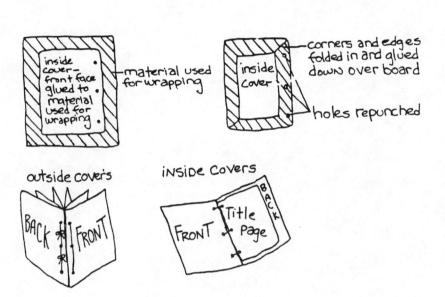

It is helpful to the children for you to demonstrate these techniques, one by one, before they try to do it themselves. Point out to them that alternatives for covering a book can include a collage or an illustration worked with markers or crayons. Finally you can show them the various techniques pictured in the examples for tying the book together, using simple, sturdy yarn or string to make knots, "clean line" binders, or bows.

Children can pick their fabric, inset paper, and yarn or collage material and begin working. Circulate regularly, asking about each one's problems and helping when necessary to glue, straighten, cut, or tie.

At the close of this session their books are done, and it is time to share and enjoy them. Ask for volunteers who would like to show everyone their book and ask them to read the story out loud, showing the prints they've made. Children will want to take these home to show their families, but be sure to plan for an exhibit either right away or after they return them for your library or classroom space.

Theater

The theater is said to have been introduced by the Emperor Ming Huang around A.D. 700. Ming Huang is believed to have visited the moon. There he was entertained by plays and players, a sight then unknown upon earth. After his return he built a stage and established a theater in his pear garden.

When Ming Huang brought theater back from the moon, he brought with it her glamour and mystery and they have illuminated theater ever since. Whether in Ming Huang's little pear garden theater, on the city streets with the jongleurs of the Middle Ages, or in a library puppet show, the moon continues to cast her enchantment.

In the West, the dawn of theater's light goes back very far. It grew only by fits and starts, sometimes overshadowed through long, bleak winter periods. In primitive times theater energy was high; to gain power over their frightening difficult world people invented a way, called "sympathetic magic," to tame it. Borrowing the horned power of the bull for war, the quick run of the deer for hunting, the wisdom of the snake for understanding, they danced with mask and costume, acting out the animal role to ensure themselves its power.

The dances took shape and grew into a kind of ritual that was a drama, with participants using gestures, postures, and sounds, painting the face and body to appeal to the gods, and taking on a godlike form. The tribe convened at certain times of the year or on special occasions to perform these rituals and thus ensure a favorable harvest or war, weather or fertility.

Around the world these rites were celebrated in different ways. In Egypt, Upuaut, the wolf-headed one, guided the warriors into enemy land and Anubis with his jackal head led the dead into the other world. In the American Northwest, masks were nested and hidden within masks, so a dancer could become a god, a man, or an animal by shifting them. African dancers balanced towering antelope figures on their heads to ensure fertility in the tribe. Thus, out of doors, in a cleared space in the light of day, animal-masked actors danced the first intense chapters in the history of the theater. Around them the men, women, and children of the village listened and watched, merging with the drum and the dancing animals, binding together and fusing the strength of humans, gods, and creatures. For the children, the dancing masks of power and animal identity were to become a cornerstone of their own natural theater.

As the years passed, dance and the theater slowly diverged. The story began to interest people apart from the religious rite, and dance became more formal and musical, taking on an abstract symbolic power for the tribe. At the same time, growing out of these dancing figures of prehistory was the mythology that gave us our first stories. Within the stories, the characters were, in a sense, abstractions of the first earthy ritual figures; people sought to take parts, to act out the stories and give the gods and goddesses parts to play.

Slowly, drama evolved from the rituals to a more formal self-conscious structure with the dynamics of a story and, thus, incidentally, was discovered one of the human talents: acting. Masks, paint, costumes, gestures, and voices changed their function from symbol to storytelling, although keeping a magic element. As time passed people began to accept the role of pleasure in their lives and it was reflected in their first attempts at comedy. With this effort, that other face of theater, so long dormant during our period of uncertain survival, emerged and the stage was set: the masks of comedy and tragedy, signature of the theater, hung up their startling, salacious faces and invited us in.

Around the world the process took different forms. The masks and costumes were, in China, turned into a lively puppet theater, which was active three thousand years ago in the time of Yang Shih, the puppet master. It continues to be popular in the present day. In India a quiet theater, very much the same over thousands of years, played out mythological stories of

Hanuman and Rama, monkey and master, with mime and dance in an artificial, charming tradition.

In the West history took a different turn. Highly sophisticated, intense drama, its laws the civilization of ancient Greece, erupted in the world in the fifth century B.C. Played out in a open arena set against the hills in full sun, with the audience seated in great tiers of carved stone benches, the plays used antique religious traditions of chorus and mask, myth and ritual, to convey a new understanding: the meaning of human nature, act, fate, and will. Here, in yearly festivals held to celebrate the fertility rites of Dionysus, patron god of the theater, the Greeks performed the first clearly defined tragedies and the first playful, irreverent comedies the world had seen.

The great plays of the House of Atrius, beginning with Aeschylus's powerful trilogy in the mid-fifth century B.C., ventured into a new realm, exploring the psychological as well as the dramatic aspects of that civilization's myths within structural guidelines elucidated by Aristotle and called "The Unities."

Aeschylus, in the *Oresteia* and *Prometheus Unbound,* and Sophocles, in *Antigone, Oedipus Rex,* and *Electra,* were the great tragedians with the clear thunder of their poetry; Euripides and Aristophanes, the first feminists, irreverent and mocking, lit up the audience's understanding with plays like *The Trojan Women.* Later, Aristophanes lent his astringent wit and fine historical sense to *Clouds, Birds*, and, frequently revived today, *Lysistrata.* Together they moved myths out of symbol stories into live, personal, social exploration that moved and fascinated their audiences. The patterns that make drama a collective experience, a political statement, were established once and for all as the Greeks translated their ideas into the direct and human experience whose meaning has endured into the twentieth century.

But this fantastic blaze of theatrical energy presaged a long, dark time before the resurrection and eventual ebullience of modern theater. The Romans weakened the fabric of theater with their increasingly careless and violent imitations of the Greeks, their rowdy festivals and games. It is ironic that during this period of decline and within these festivals lay the second cornerstone of children's theater: the commedia del l'arte. This ancient tradition, moving from Asian mimetic theater to Constantinople and thence to Rome, gave to the Roman plays the crude characters of devil, doctor, and hero that have survived ever since, the basis of our puppet theater.

It is ironic, too, that it was this decline that forced the actors into the streets, thus giving us the strolling players who move from place to place with their skits, mime, juggling, and dancing, and provided the one sure link of theater in the artistic winter to come. For as the Christian church rose in power, it became repressive, slowly strangling theater with moralistic edicts proclaiming drama wicked and prohibiting performance. Only itinerant players acting at local fairs, entertaining people with puppets and acrobatics, and occasionally bringing performances to the local castle kept theater alive.

Hundreds of years passed in Europe with drama relegated to the status of a passing affair before a new seriousness dawned in the Middle Ages.

In the Orient, however, in Java, China, and Japan, theater was at this time a vital art. Puppet and shadow plays passed into China from their lands of origin, India and Java, where they had been highly developed. Once in China they became a feature of cultural life, performed as a matter of course at court and in the villages as well, where children too could play and experiment with them freely on their own. When Ming Huang established his Pear Tree Garden school of acting at court in 720, these plays were his tradition, and so his theater took on the highly stylized, rigid form of puppets. Actors used makeup and gestures in a tightly controlled way that made up their acting vocabulary--an oar is a boat; the prop man's black clothes give him invisibility; blue makeup shows courage. The actors moved in stiff ways--again like puppets--and their two-level stages used tables and chairs to suggest bridges and palaces.

The theater history of China was placid, not highly evolved. The historical plays beloved of the people took a more personal tone as time went on, but they kept a stylized structure, a lengthy set of events during which the actors, both men and women, would improvise their scenes for long periods. The Chinese loved their theater, and for the five or six hours of the performance they would wander in and out, taking tea and talking comfortably.

In contrast, across the sea in Japan, a rich, diverse set of theatrical forms was evolving: the haunting, beautiful Noh tradition; the enormous puppets of the Bunraku; and the melodramatic Kabuki, the soaps and westerns of the Japanese world.

The Noh plays started as brief versions of the all-day Buddhist festival plays of Tibet. They were designed by the priest Kahami and his son as a series of 250 one-act plays. The entire set was developed within the period 1400-1450, a short explosive time. Because little or no variation developed in ensuing centuries, the Noh plays seem very medieval today. Masked male actors take the roles, playing stiffly with rigid control. The plays are set on a wooden stage, always with three painted pine trees that establish earth, heaven, and humanity on the wall behind. A fifty-foot runway gives range to the actor's dancelike motions, and a "hurry door" on the opposite side provides an exit when they leave their earthly existence. Each gesture is circumscribed, each action symbolic. Echoing the Greek, a chorus chants and comments and instruments play accompaniment, as the Buddhist speculates on themes of vanity, death, worldliness, and surrender. Between these solemn theatrical events, the nobility enjoyed the Kyogen, comic relief

Nohs, which made fun of the feudal lords and the power structure. Once again, mirroring us, theater hung up the masks of comedy and tragedy.

The Noh plays were the drama of the nobility, but another kind of theater, the Bunraku, or "doll" theater, like the Kabuki, was universal. Bunraku was the art of living puppetry. Almost life-sized puppets were intricately maneuvered by two or three people who played out story-songs to the accompaniment of the samisen, an informal Japanese guitar used by street musicians. A woman puppeteer brought Bunraku to Japan in the ninth century and seventeenth-century puppeteers gave it a high finish. The Bunraku is very special now; it has a highly respected place in the culture and a small, devoted following who sit happily on the floor during the many hours of the performance and enjoy tea.

Very different, indeed, is the Kabuki, the people's theater of Japan, which evolved somewhat later. In the seventeenth century a Chinese actress who had crossed into Japan sang and danced for her supper in a dry riverbed in Kyoto, inadvertently beginning the lively, eclectic Kabuki theater that has flourished to the present. She conceived it as masquelike, and borrowed elements from the Noh, puppet theater, pantomime, and dance, imbuing it from the start with color and spontaneous, lively feeling. The stories vary, touching on themes of domestic intimacy, folktales, and Japanese history The Chinese tradition of mask makeup, of stiff violence, and of symbolic gestures overlay the acting.

All these forms, contributors to contemporary theater, have provided the foundation for children's theater as we know it now--mime, shadow and rod puppetry, masks, and a bare stage. But, paradoxically, theater was not originally accessible to them. In Japan children approached theater only through their own play or, in certain cases, were apprenticed to learn the traditional forms.

As these theatrical forms were thriving in the Eastern world, the West was only, at last, reawakening. After the Middle Ages the next five hundred years of Western theater are a complex weave of theatrical traditions that develop, shift, and change in a great, colorful sweep of history. It started with a strange reversal that took place in the twelfth and thirteenth centuries in Europe and the British Isles: the Christian church, which had put an end to theater so long before, granted it new life in these years. Out of the ritual of high mass, of antiphonal chanting and brief formal dialogue between religious figures, scenes began to emerge that evolved into the first story-acting--Christ's birth, the Christmas legends, the Crucifixion, the Resurrection. These were the mystery plays. Morality plays like *Everyman,* which portrayed the Christian virtues, and miracle plays, which were based on the lives of the saints, gained papal approval and were performed by a dancing clergy on festival days. At first they were played in Latin in the church, but as the people, hungry for entertainment, crowded in, performance moved into the churchyards and in a natural swing, shifted from Latin to the native tongue. The overburdened clergy gave way to professionals who trouped spiritedly into the churchyards on their great wagons piled with mechanical animals, batons, small boats, and diverse props and costumes. The troubadours, jongleurs, and mimes who had been the secret life of theater all through the dark time joined the troupes, and an era of great vitality and beauty was begun.

It was Lope de Vega of Spain who said "Give me four trestles, four boards, four actors and a passion," and it was in this country that Huang's pear tree bloomed astonishingly, by the orange trees, under the tropical sun. When the traveling wagons rolled into the innyards and churchyards the people turned out by the hundreds to gawk and laugh, eat, yell, and applaud their favorites. Spanish theater, first with the bold work of Lope de Rueda and Cervantes, later with Lope de Vega, concerned itself with the games of love and deception, the farcical situation of the liaison. A wonderful feeling for dialogue and free form informed their plays, and from a crude beginning it grew into a golden age. Series of skits called *autos* were molded and developed over the years to form strong, well-made romantic plays, the *commedias*. The Spanish National Theater was forming, and in the middle of all the commotion the Italians invaded Spain with the commedia del l'arte, which the salty, vigorous Spanish took to their hearts.

Italy's own theater tradition started in the ninth century with an influx of Greeks fleeing the Turks in a dark political climate. The Greeks brought with them their radiant heritage of ideas that predated the Christian era: theories of philosophy and art, poetics and drama. In Italy these ideas and the Greek tradition of theater would flourish once more. Italy awoke to the Renaissance in the fourteenth century, quietly, through the minds of great writers like Dante and Boccaccio who were reading Virgil, absorbing the Greeks in translation, finding inspiration in the ideas of Aristotle and Euripides. Their excitement was intense, and they wrote in response great works of literature and theater. Dante's epic poem, *The Divine Comedy,* a hallmark of wisdom and original scholarship, traced humanity's spiritual development; Boccaccio, in contrast, wrote lusty, earthy tales in *The Decameron,* reflecting society as a whole.

All around them the painters and architects of Rome and Florence-- Giotto, da Vinci, Ghirlandaio, and Fra Angelico--were painting, sculpting, building towers and town halls, designing bridges and gardens. A civilization was taking fire, burning off the hard shell of rigidity of Christian doctrine and practice with the philosophical richness and down-to-earth realism of the Greeks. In this passionate aesthetic climate, similar in spirit to that of Athens in 450 B.C., the humanist reinterpretation of the Greco-Roman tradition gave shape to the Renaissance.

Henry V's victory at Agincourt in 1420 provided a conduit through France to England for the classical scholarship blooming in Italy, and the Greeks took England by storm. When Elizabeth, champion of language and literature, ascended the throne in 1558, the universities at Oxford and Cambridge blazed with the life of the mind, with poets and writers experimenting, reading, and arguing; the inns were full of them and theater was their natural outlet. At first in the Greek and Latin they had learned in school and then increasingly in their own language, the English poured out a wealth of poetry, literature, and drama. They found their natural companies in the troupes and strolling players who performed spontaneous bawdy masques, playing out of wagons loaded with props and costumes. But theater was outgrowing the wagons, as it had the churchyards, and more permanent sites were found in the inns and their yards. In 1576 in London James Burbage built the first permanent theater, having his two-level stages assume the natural shape of the inn; the audience went its own way as well--a familiar, rowdy, spontaneous attendance.

As for the plays and playwrights, the vast pool of writers in town and gown, the cream of the Renaissance, poured their vitality and talent into drama. Thomas Kyd's vast melodramas, Ben Jonson's acerbic comedy, Christopher Marlowe's wit and passion--these epitomized the English Renaissance. At the head of this gifted group, "not for an age, but for all time" as Ben Jonson said of him, was William Shakespeare. Actor, playwright, poet, above all a gifted philosopher and humanist whose talent turned this understanding to creativity--Shakespeare produced a new play every day. Outside in all weathers his gifted, tough, and energetic male crew played to an enthusiastic audience, producing the greatest plays of all time in casual circumstances. People wandered in for the afternoon to be entertained with the light and color and beauty of that drama.

Like the Greece of 450 B.C. and the Italy of Dante and da Vinci, Elizabethan England fostered experimental art and new ideas. But the following years saw the climate change as Elizabeth died and the Reformation fell upon the English artistic world like a shroud. Theatrical vitality seemed to move to France where after a rather lackluster Renaissance scene, the seventeenth century emerged as an intensely creative time with Pierre Corneille's romantic, overblown tragedies, the classic tragedy of Racine, and, most significant, the robust, yet artful comedy of Molière.

Auguste Molière, an actor-manager and leader of his own troupe, settled into the repertory theater, Théâtre de Marâis, under the patronage of Louis XIV. Here, in a candle-lit theater, using simple sets and crude seating, playing to the town rowdies and artisans, Molière produced a stream of the gayest, wittiest comedies in theater history. *Tartuffe, Le Malade imaginaire, Le Bourgeois gentilhomme*--whatever he wrote, a gentle humanism guided his pen. Ironically, although he was under royal patronage and writing during a time of great elegance, his simple, personal, and wickedly funny caricatures foreshadowed a more democratic view of character altogether. Drama was to concern itself increasingly with the rising middle class and the plight of the common man.

In England this radical movement was reflected in the art of acting particularly. Between 1741 and 1776, David Garrick, actor of actors, introduced through his own troupe that most contemporary concept of ensemble acting. His emphasis on company interaction was, like Molière's characterization, to lead toward the democratic ideal, a vital link to the future. Using the plays of Shakespeare and the well-made satires of Goldsmith and Sheridan, Garrick developed in his actors an intellectual technique that had a detached quality and an interactive force. He moved acting away from a natural art. On his stage, and only incidentally, he introduced, too, special lighting effects, using overhead border lights and silk-screens lit so that they moved like clouds. The sense of lighting as an art, moving in time like dance, was first conceived by Garrick for his company.

In the lowlands of Germany, a different kind of theater was forming. Hard on the heels of the minnesingers and meistersingers whose pleasantries lingered in the great stone castles and villages, and with the support of the newly banded municipalities, a national German theater was emerging. Starting with Sophie Schroeder's ensemble in the late 1700s, the ideal of local ensemble repertory moved toward realization. Also, a star was rising: Johann Wolfgang von Goethe, who brought a new romantic vision to the world. Despite the Thirty Years' War, the Plague, and their temperamental preference for bawdy, tosspot farce, the burghers and their robust wives became devotees of Goethe and champions of their local municipality.

As European theater was achieving this late eighteenth-century polish, the American theater was only just stirring; the pioneers who explored the country brought theater with them. On riverboats, rafts, and covered wagons the insistent life of character, mime, and story sprang up once again with vitality and a crude color.

As people moved and settled villages and towns from the Great Plains to the northern lakes, their ragtag theater crystallized here and there into amateur groups who played for the community in town centers and built in the process natural repertory groups. Books were a rare commodity on the frontier, and life was hard. The pioneers were starved for fun and they gave theater their loyal support.

Nowhere was this movement more lively than on the rivers; the showboat tradition began on the houseboats that explored the Mississippi and became, on the big-wheeling paddleboats, the glamorous, romantic idyll of the nineteenth century. As they floated upstream, people on board were treated to minstrel shows, *Hamlet, Faust,* and, of course, *Ten Nights in the*

Barroom, ushering in that primitive playlet so beloved of Americans, the melodrama, forerunner of our soap opera.

In the cities a more self-conscious, Europeanized theater was forming. New York established a theater in 1825; by 1860 there were ten. Philadelphia built three large theaters and became a late eighteenth- and early nineteenth-century cultural center. As the cities grew, the sophisticated European tradition grew with them, and flourished in these years; David Garrick's successful ensemble ideas found fertile ground in the companies established by members of the great acting families like John Brougham in New York and Louisa Drew in Philadelphia. Native American theater with everyday local themes was only just beginning by mid-century. Pioneers like James Nelson Barker with his Pocohontas story, *The Indian Princess,* preceded exciting writers like Anna Cora Mowatt, whose 1845 play, *Fashion, Life in New York*, was the first important American comedy. Dion Boucicault adapted real American themes like Rip Van Winkle for production and wrote literally hundreds of "slice-of-life" plays using the problems of the locale where he was performing as the base material.

As the century unfolded, these city theaters enriched rural communities by sending repertory companies traveling across the land, bringing Shakespeare, Goethe, and Molière with them. Later, this strong community theater tradition in America proved, in its provincial way, to be theater's tough grace, refusing to be swallowed up by the commercialism that threatened the American theater. For trouble lay ahead.

By the end of the century a very comfortable economy was supporting a flourishing American theater centered in New York and Philadelphia, where the strong repertory companies were established that toured the country. Even Boston, although it suffered from the pinched puritanism of its New England settlers, managed to sneak theater in the back door by adapting the Boston museum for dramatic purposes. But American materialism, a kind of veil over the deeper expression of the culture, was working to push the repertory companies out. Powerful commercial forces like the Shuberts urged the big star and the long run, overshadowing even staunch actor-producers like Mrs. Minnie Maddern Fiske and David Belasco. Later, the crowd-pleasing media, radio and television, were to continue in this bland, persistent cheapening of our dramatic tradition. In some community and repertory companies, and in the urban counterculture, serious American theater has survived, but, with the exception of a very few, not again as the mainstream.

As the nineteenth century closed in America with uneasy battles between the commercials and the artists, Europe had been undergoing a century of revolution and change in its own theater. The theater world was gathering itself for a move toward the twentieth century and an active international style.

France, after the revolution and the call for democracy, had conceived a vast romantic drama, led by Victor Hugo, full of feeling, struggle, mysticism, and color. In England music was introduced into plays, and melodramas, mime, and skit were performed cheek by jowl, never mind the quality, as a rising middle class clamored for entertainment.

During the nineteenth century, theaters underwent a change that was, in an odd way, to parallel a deeper social change: the uncomfortable benches and standing room gave way to the apron stage, comfortable seating, and the box set pioneered by Mme. Lucia Vastris, a company director-manager who insisted as well on natural costuming and a disciplined rehearsal schedule. In addition, by mid-century, gaslight, so much safer and cleaner than candles, made evening theater a possibility for the first time. Multiple staging, which held four sets in one, was introduced by the American genius-inventor Steel McKaye.

The art of the actor was reflecting these changes, growing and adapting to a more democratic time. Following a half-century of the star system, a tradition so natural to a romantic, flamboyant theater, a movement began that sought to wipe out the system, to give life to the play in every aspect, stressing a natural costuming and an inner focus to acting. At the Burgtheater in Vienna during the years 1866-90, the duke of Saxe-Meiningen was directing his players as a company to rehearse meticulously in every kind of role and to act them in a way that integrated the complex demands of the theater with polish and power. His ensemble ideal influenced the entire world of theater to come. Equally important were the deep probings into character, the strong inner focus, and the self-conscious techniques of acting reflective of Freud's discoveries that were being pioneered by Konstantin Stanislavsky at the Moscow Art Theater. Here all emphasis was on feeling the experience of the character and giving life to it. This approach became a classic technique within the discipline.

It found its natural complement with another important movement of the international style--improvisation--the spontaneous, unmemorized interpretation of themes evolved through the Italian commedia del l'arte in Luigi Pirandello's suggestive drama.

Around the edges of all this a chill, welcome, and fantastic wind was blowing, producing an odd reactive strain of the symbolic and bizarre, keeping the truth alive with a lively measure of anarchy. Centering in Oscar Wilde's fin-de-siècle comedy and the weird, prophetic Theatre Libre of Antonin Artaud in Paris, it gave some relief to the naturalistic landscape around it and augured the avant-garde, one of the powerful themes of the twentieth century.

Thus the strands of twentieth-century theater were being woven: realism, social criticism, and inner direction as seen in the Scandinavian and Russian playwrights, a complementary turn to introversion in acting technique, improvisation, the birth of the avant-garde, and the strong integrated ensemble. Their development is the story of theater as we know it.

After the First World War the world seemed to shrink a little, and the trends of theater history no longer confined themselves to a national tradition. With rapid transportation, quick communication systems, and media reporting, what seemed solely national trends in earlier centuries became more universal, reflecting the changes brought by three intellectual giants who loom over the scene, shifting the social consciousness: Freud, with his revelation of the personal unconscious, Albert Einstein, with his perception of a fourth physical dimension, and Karl Marx, powerful pleader for common economic rights. Each in his way opened up new ways of seeing that allowed theater to create a new symbolism that was disruptive of unities, a new technology that freed up staging, and a more profound acting technique that was rooted in a new understanding of personality.

Of the various trends in theater none is more important than the ensemble, whose first, colorful representative was the Moscow Art Theater in Russia. Here an inner psychological attention brought a bitter realism to works like Gorky's *Lower Depths* and Chekhov's ironic, reflective plays. Later the Ballets Russes of Diaghilev were to take the outline of the integrated ensemble and fill it with light and color and play, using Leon Bakst's erotic, outrageous sets and a new madcap, dissonant music by Stravinsky and Prokofiev. Choreography like the "Blue Train" of Nijinska was a mad ride from a quiet, stuffy world to the symbolic, surreal industrial landscape of the twentieth century. The expressionist and dada writers of the twenties and thirties found expression in Pablo Picasso's cubist sets designed for Jean Cocteau's *Parade*. Every convention melted away, and sirens, live horses, typewriter-music, and huge skyscrapers erupted on stages as the dancers capered and played.

When the Russian Revolution disrupted his theater in 1917, Diaghilev fled, bringing his troupe to the West where it was enormously successful and equally influential. Simultaneously other countries were moving toward ensemble playing. Lady Gregory produced Yeats's mystical plays in her Irish Abbey Theater, and in New York Harold Clurman's grainy, naturalistic Group Theater epitomized the thirties and the world of the depression. A sense of simultaneous contemporary expression sprang up.

Of them all the most important figure was the German playwright Bertolt Brecht. Writing between the wars and into the fifties, Brecht welded reality and fantasy in his expressionist plays. Working through his Berliner Ensemble, Brecht embodied in his characters a political statement, calling these plays "Epic Theater." Profoundly anarchist and antimaterialist, he used every theatrical device to preach against war, greed, and inhumanity. Democratic, iconoclastic, he had a pervasive influence on twentieth-century theater. He paved the way directly for guerrilla theater and improvisatory groups like the San Francisco Mime Troupe who seek to give a political edge to their entertainment.

The symbolic, so native to fin-de-siècle French theater, continued to push out its bizarre tentacles from Baudelaire's brooding poetry, Edgar Allan Poe's grotesque stories, and Maeterlinck's mythic fairy tales like *Pelléas et Mélisande*. As twentieth-century consciousness deepened, it rebelled against the facade of nineteenth-century religiosity, expressing itself characteristically in Gertrude Stein's disconnected and abstruse writings and in the avant-garde *Theater and Its Double World* of Antonin Artaud. Here, as in the Ballets Russes, all is upside down, the buildings float over our heads, the language is elliptical, the unities of Aristotle lie broken on the floor of the stage. The unconscious has erupted, and the quick staging and technological wizardry of the twentieth century throw its imagery out to us with magical ease.

Later, as despair and cynicism pervaded Europe, presaged by the dark, mythic writings of García Lorca like *Blood Wedding,* symbolic theater took the form of theater of the absurd, and writers like Harold Pinter and Eugene Ionesco with his mad *Rhinoceros* express it. In Samuel Beckett's *Endgame,* the two characters despair calmly in their garbage cans, arguing interminably, expressing their truths poetically in symbol and metaphor.

In America, ever the home of the pragmatist, the first, native comedies of Anna Mowatt and Langdon Mitchell epitomized the art of domestic spoof and social irony. Later, the intense political plays of Elmer Rice, Sherwood Anderson, and Lillian Hellman in the twenties and thirties, the serious moral political writing of Arthur Miller with his theme of the common man developed a sturdy, realistic tradition in American theater. But the great genius was Eugene O'Neill. Writing from World War I through 1953, O'Neill wrote dark plays of family passions and individual alienation that move as powerful archaic structures like Greek tragedy expressing a universal consciousness. Using masks and chants and theater traditions from other cultures, his work raised American theater to a world-class level of achievement.

Other writers, like Thornton Wilder, wove the strands of reality and fantasy together by employing Chinese and Japanese techniques of bare stage and personified characters and by using symbol and myth. A work like *The Skin of Our Teeth* erects a realistic base of small-town America and then under our very eyes moves two centuries across the stage.

The odd consecrated ground of these gifted serious playwrights is Broadway, that three-quarter-mile of Manhattan street that has so dominated American theater. Broadway began its existence around the turn of the century as housing for vaudeville and burlesque, so it is not surprising that over the course of the years popular theater and musicals should dominate the stage. Nevertheless, strengthened by groups like the Theater Guild, individual committed theater talents, and strong acting families like the Barrymores, more difficult plays have been championed there. From O'Neill to Sam Shepard, although not without difficulty, fine plays have continued to receive a hearing.

Recently, forced by the price of production to move to storefronts and small houses, serious and experimental theater has had a strong resurgence in its off-Broadway and, in the 1970s and 1980s, off-off-Broadway houses. Away from "the Great White Way" and its commercial roots, writers like Truman Capote, Samuel Beckett, and Genet have been produced. The new generations of women writers, too, have had a freer voice. The off-Broadway repertory theaters have also revived an international group of great and experimental plays. Around the world, translation and traveling troupes bring these plays to Russia and France, Norway and South America, while the production of such works gains acceptance on Broadway and in regional American theater. Film and television, for the most part a form of realistic theater, play their roles in continuous and ever-widening transmission of dramatic works that contribute to this century's characteristic sense of one-world consciousness.

Supporting all this, technical production has produced a whole new kind of theater; sometimes technical virtuosity and production are ends in themselves, as important as book or company. Sets, costumes, and lighting-- every aspect of theater production has seen innovative improvements. In America Steele McKaye's native engineering genius prefaced the symbolic, shifting theatrical environment of the late twentieth century. A prolific, enthusiastic playwright, producer, and inventor, McKaye experimented with the first elevator stage, where whole sets could be raised and lowered between acts. He used moving chairs, slots, and traps that could transfer the sets, and lit the stage with electricity and cooled it in the hot Chicago summers with an air-cooling system.

Later, Robert Edmund Jones mirrored the Bauhaus designers with his style of stripped sets, suggesting a stark, gigantic design by the use of sophisticated lighting. Here the fluid, easy movement through time and space that an intricate spectrum of lights suggests lent a four-dimensional quality: a whole new landscape was created. In addition he took advantage of the revolution in fabric that chemistry afforded us and, using plastics, nylons, Styrofoam, and vinyls, invented a smooth, impersonal, fantastic world in which the new materials suggested the inner as well as the outer world of space.

In French cinema, like Jean Cocteau's *Belle et la bête,* where gently detached pairs of hands skillfully ignore the unities; in the functional, concrete, near-brutal designs of the German Bauhaus movement; and in the Hungarian Lazlo Moholy-Nagy's pioneering mixed media productions using film lights, mobiles, and amplified voices, production has grown in sophistication and flourished in the hands of an international group of talents.

With all this movement, contemporary theater finds itself in a diverse and healthy state. Supported by an inner vitality and a fluid, fantastic technology, theater styles fan out in all directions: political theater, informal improvisation, theater of the streets, feminist theater, Growtowski's enormous, mass three-day festival "games." All express twentieth-century themes, reflecting still the working out of the ideas of Freud and Marx, whose long shadows project even now onto our creative landscape.

Children and the Theater

In the early nineteenth century William Blake, Robert Cruikshank, and George Cruikshank in a mood of wild abandon decorated their "penny plain, two-pence colored" toy theater constructions and boldly sold them as cutouts on the streets of London. Children, barred from the formal theater since the days of the outdoor festivals of the Middle Ages, moved in eagerly to buy and experiment with these paper-doll theaters, constructing, pretending, and putting on shows.

This direct reaching out to children was an imaginative leap to the freer, more democratic world to come and heralded the children's theater movement of our day, now a force in its own right. But even before then, hidden within the tapestry of theater history, lay the colorful strands of the theatrical forms that children have always taken for themselves: mime, mask, improvisation, and puppetry. Forming the base and bringing them all together is the ancient tradition of the commedia del l'arte, originating in the Asian mimetic tradition, coming up from Byzantium to Greece and Italy and from Italy to the rest of Europe during the Middle Ages and later arriving in England and America.

Early on, the Roman entertainments at their festival games incorporated crude forms of devil, doctor, and mythological hero, which after Christ's lifetime were reflected in the characters of Joseph, the devil, and Christ himself. The jongleurs and strolling players used them in their skits and playlets as they traveled about, inventing new ones and continually renewing the tradition.

When the Middle Ages' mystery and morality plays began to take shape in Italy, the tradition of the commedia del l'arte was used to provide the skeletal base of the performances. Commedia del l'arte was a theater of live actors in those days; they played out scarecrow plots by improvising their roles as they went along, acting the buffoon and satirizing local customs and current events.

The characters were simple and potent, an excellent base for its eventual offshoot, puppetry, an art that children happily adopt for themselves. In later puppetry, as in the commedia, archetypal roles communicated directly and universally. In both, development and dialogue could be improvised, but always the characters were clearly defined. This radical core to a traditional form suited children very well, as they like to know where they stand with a story, but respond to spontaneity nevertheless.

In the commedia, Old Pulcinello, alias Falstaff, alias the Devil, all wit and villainy, stupid but sly, greedy but loving, beaked with an enormous nose and burdened with a hump on his back, dominated the scene; Il Dottore, affected and academic and pedantic and Il Capitaine, hypocritic and grumbling, followed along; Pantelone, another offshoot of the Fool, the jealous, buffooning father of the lovely Columbina, alias Mary, who was in love with our hero Arlequin, whose distant models in turn were Hercules and, perhaps, Christ, played out more idealized roles. Thickening the plot and adding to the fun were Scapin figures or *Zanni*, mischief-making servants, loosely based on quicksilver Mercury, messenger of the gods. Later the Scaramouche of puppet fame developed from a Scapin figure to the questing, adventurous bumbler, Don Quixote.

Always popular, the commedia evolved through the English pantomime of the sixteenth and seventeenth centuries, on through Shakespeare and the Elizabethans; over the years it began to include in its repertoire fairy tales and folktales, even Mother Goose, especially for children. The "Harlequinade" attached to the end of the performance of a play used the commedia's characters to tell a set tale of theft and chicanery and starred Harlequin as Clown. The mime Grimaldi, parading around the stage, gradually evolved a character so colorful in his wacky, cheerful way, that he set "the Clown" for all time. The great clowns of the circus, masters of mime, are still called "Joeys" after his name. Joey, the Clown, a broadly mimed character, plays tricks, escapes disaster, and makes a joyous fool of himself, thus delighting every child.

More recently the art of the commedia became the basis for French farce, the Italian buffo opera, a good deal of the circus, and, of course, the Punch and Judy show. Luigi Pirandello made the commedia's essential qualities of improvisation and electric audience connection the basis for his radical playwrighting.

Mime, the ancient art of the mischievous, glamorous, elusive gesture, was central to the commedia, giving life to the characters' expressions and feelings, as it has for so much of theater. From early man's magic dancing to bring rain or ensure a good hunt, to the mimetic acting chorus and mask of the Greeks, through Roman storytelling to the molding of the stock figures of pantomime, people have expressed their feelings and told their stories without words. It was through the mime of the strolling players, the jongleurs, that theater outlasted the long winter of the Dark Ages, and it was with mime's help that it revived itself in the mystery plays of the Middle Ages. But it was not until the fifteenth century with the commedia that mime came into its own. In later centuries it continued to be central to the expression of ballet, the English masque and American burlesque. Mime is the magician's art, vital to the Chinese theater and opera, and in our time it has become an art respected for itself, studied in schools of mime. Etienne De Croux, the great French mime, and his students Jean Louis Barrault and Marcel Marceau have all, with the help of film and tours, spread mime far and wide.

For children, learning to mime is learning to play out feelings and actions, to use the body and face for communication. Mime, with no words to get in the way, provides many children with a means of expression they can master at a point in their development when the demands of acting--voice, projection, expressiveness, elocution, and synchronization with body movements--are more than they can handle.

Equally natural for children and at home in the library is mime's lively cousin, mask, which accents and interprets theatrical meaning all over the world. The spirit of masks is the spirit of change: to transform or hide, to protect or to gain power. The shaman of the tribe adopted a mask to bring the powerful elements in: sun, wind, rain, or cloud, swift deer or strong bear. To wear the mask is to become the spirit, and to mime it in dance and music is to ensure success. So at first, in ancient, less sophisticated times, mime and mask were used together.

When the Greeks began to produce their great outdoor dramas, they used this inherited tradition to give the actors a rude, instant identity: men could be women, gods, animals, or fates. Even then a rough version of the mimic fool (Punch) was used. From the mimetic drama, masks came to be used for myth and storytelling and the Romans played with masks for the stock characters of their crude form of the commedia.

Through the centuries jongleurs carried on the mask tradition as they mimed and danced their way across Europe; in the Middle Ages the mystery plays used a bold, grotesque, repulsive mask to portray the devil. The medieval fool with his ass's ears and peaked cap passed on the buffoon-servant role in the sixteenth century and bloomed again in the rural servant of the pastoral. After the Renaissance, masks turned even more into fun; mischief was signaled by wearing masks in Lent in the eighteenth and nineteenth centuries (and still is by children at Halloween), and they became a necessary element for mummer-dancers carousing down the streets at Carnival.

For children, masks hold their historic secrets, seeming alive and personal. Here one can assume other identities and play them out, and since no one knows who it is, the mask gives the wearer courage. Play and power linger in the idea of the mask. It is not difficult to make and wear masks, and through them children can gain a firsthand feeling for other cultures, a real sense of the story they are acting out, and an instant identity. Mime and mask are natural complements.

Springing spontaneously out of this tradition is the art of improvisation, a strong tool for children to use in experiencing drama. The tradition of improvisation is one of the bright, clear threads in the theater tapestry starting with the early Roman commedia farces, when the masked actors knew the story but had to invent their exchange, and moving through the jongleur and puppet show; it shows up in the Chinese theater, once again with a strong set plot and made-up dialogue, and becomes settled in the English eighteenth-century pantomime and Punch and Judy puppet show.

Modern master Luigi Pirandello uses the commedia tradition, introducing improvisation again, and the open theater of the sixties involved both cast and audience in improvisation; John Cassavettes brought it to a fine finish in his films. Improv, which appeals to children's natural love of fooling around, can give them a valuable sense of presence and security on stage and off because, without memorization to bind and hamper, they are free to concentrate on the core of the role, its expression and projection.

It seems, looking back through theater history, that, for children, all these come together and find a focus in the world of the puppet theater. Based on the stock figures and scarecrow plots of the commedia, European puppet theater is a wonderful potpourri of the Roman *luidi,* medieval superstition, myth, legend, and folklore, emerging as a radiant, lively, and yet curiously impersonal art.

The universality of the characters and stories becomes accessible to children because puppets are a sophisticated form of what they love and understand: dolls. Walking, talking dolls engaged in adventure on a tiny stage engage children as does no other form of theater. Now the antics of blunderbuss Punch, Puss in Boots, tragic Faust, the raging, wicked Devil, and Beulah Witch become acceptable; a safe distance is established as well as a sense of superiority, and, of course, just plain fun is to be had, too. The dolls come in several shapes: marionettes, hand-in-glove, rod, and shadow puppets. The first three were and are widespread throughout Europe and, later, America. Hand-in-glove, the very easiest for children to make and handle, evolved early in Europe and is traditional in all parts of the Continent. The wooden or papier-mâché head and comfortable fabric figure are light, easily manipulated by small hands, and portable. In early times puppeteers transported the booth from place to place and stood beneath it, playing out the stories on a stage high over their heads.

Rod puppets, a later invention, are quite difficult to use. Thin rods attach to hands, run full-length through the figure, and require great skill in successful manipulation. Serge Obaztsov brought this kind of puppetry to a fine point in Russia's Central State Puppet Theatre in the 1930s and has toured all over the world with his troupe.

Marionettes are ancient; here many strings, usually nine, control the figures from above; in some forms slim rods control the hands, while strings attached to the ears move the head. Marionettes are found in most European countries from Sicily to Belgium and reached a height in England with Thomas Holden in the nineteenth century. In fact, England, with its Toy Theatre of the early nineteenth century and its classic interpretations of Pulcinello and Punch, has been a champion of theater for children as it has been of storytelling in all forms.

In the Orient very different forms of puppet theater developed: shadow puppets and, in Japan, the Bunraku. Shadow puppets are cutout figures seen through a translucent screen lit from behind, which gives it a magical effect; they are manipulated by rods from below or at right angles to the screen. In Java where the gods created it, shadow puppetry is called Wayang and is a highly evolved polished art. Finely pounded translucent buffalo skin is used for the screen and the story is played out to the accompaniment of gamelan and gong. The Chinese use colored fish skins for their screen and have developed their own Wayang. India's shadow-puppet theater tells the national epic, the Ramayana, with gigantic, many-colored puppets and its story is told by a narrator, the Dalang. It is a community art, treasured by everyone. The Bunraku, already described above, is really a form of puppet theater unique to Japan. Its three-quarter-life-size puppets carried about the stage by a black-costumed "director" are not found anywhere else. Their gorgeous clothes and formal, elegant staging with music and a narrator are more suitable for adults than children.

Shadow puppets came to Europe quite late, becoming popular in France and Germany under the name *ombres chinoises*, in the latter part of the nineteenth century. In our time the innovative German puppeteer Lotte Reiniger has made many fine films for children, using shadow puppets in stories based on folk and fairy tales.

Other puppet forms--the gigantic grotesques of the Carnival, the tiny finger puppets especially dear to small children, the Muppets of television-- have been developed to answer the needs of the time, for new media and for telling new stories. Although puppet theater from the beginning has experienced its ups and downs of fashion, from Rome to Peking, from the Paris Grand Guignol to the Victorian literary puppet show, for children it has always been in fashion.

Miniature and convenient, puppets can tell legends, folktales, Bible stories, and domestic melodrama in appealing ways. And for the library, the puppet show is a natural way to bring theater in. A stage can be bought or constructed cheaply, but a doorway with a curtain hung across is good enough, with wallpaper-sample backdrops and clip-on lights. Puppets can be made from scraps and odds and ends, according to simple directions from volumes within the library.

To start off a puppet workshop series (or an ongoing puppet club), a demonstration and make-your-own-puppet afternoon provides a creative, solid beginning. Scripts are available or can be written by the librarian or by the children themselves, and music can be provided by tape or record. A folktale or myth or literary story, like Kipling's "The Cat That Walked by Himself," can be narrated or taped, and used as the basis for a shadow or hand-in-glove puppet show.

A demonstration puppet show by a group of visiting players and conversation with them about puppet production can bring the professional quality of puppet theater to children's attention. Their following this up with their own program will provide them with a direct experience of theater, so they can learn what theater can mean for them right in the library. Thus, a new, regional community center can be formed. As churches and museums were utilized before, contemporary librarians can offer a twentieth-century space not only to adults for play reading and films but to children for puppetry, mime, mask, and improvisational theater. This way children get to the essence of theater, which is to make a play a "play," joining in the larger human experience by having fun with it and gaining insight into people by pretending to be them, just as they always have done on their own backyard stages.

Theater for children then becomes something more than the colorless memorization of other people's lines, taking direction that flattens them and puts them in shadow. They have a chance to experiment, a chance to be someone from Africa or a wild animal or of the other sex, as with mask, and to tell a story live, as on the puppet stage. Theater also offers an opportunity to children that none of the other arts can, one in which the library can participate: a chance to be part of a family away from home. For people halfway between dependency and the world, this environment offers a safe place to experiment, to work out life situations through story acting, to get a look at what's ahead for them. The ensemble gives just them a valuable sense of group interaction.

In the library the process can begin with workshops to introduce children to theater in a variety of ways. For very young children or those who are a little older, mime and mask and puppetry are especially valuable, with perhaps a live clown coming in and introducing the ancient art of the jongleur and the comic. For the more reflective young adult, a play-reading group is good and improv is just right, developing inner security and sharpening verbal skills. Records and books and films are fine for everyone.

For an enormous number of children television has been their only dramatic experience and theater seems far away; it's just a word. The library can intervene to bring live theater into their lives in surprising forms that are an immediate source of fun and activity.

So--hang up your masks of comedy and tragedy outside the door and invite the children in: for everyone a story and for each a role!

From *The Wonderful World of Theatre* by J. B. Priestly.   © 1969 by Aldus Books Limited. Reproduced by permission of Doubleday Publishing Co.

BIBLIOGRAPHY

Books about Theater for Children

Ackley, Edith Flack. *Marionettes.* New York: J. B. Lippincott, 1957.

Alkema, Chester Jay. *Puppet-making.* New York: Sterling Publishing, 1971.

Barwell, Eve. *Disguises You Can Make.* New York: Lothrop, Lee & Shepard, 1972.

Baylor, Bard. *They Put on Masks.* New York: Scribner, 1974.

Belville, Cheryl Walsh. *Theater Magic.* Minneapolis: Carolrhoda Books, 1986.

Berger, Melvin. *Putting on a Show.* New York: Franklin Watts, 1980.

Berk, Barbara. *The First Book of Stage Costume and Makeup.* New York: Franklin Watts, 1954.

Cochrane, Louise. *Shadow Puppets in Color.* Boston: Plays, 1972.

Cummings, Richard. *101 Hand Puppets.* New York: David McKay, 1962.

Cunningham, Julia. *Burnish Me Bright.* New York: Pantheon, 1970.

_____. *Far in the Day.* New York: Pantheon, 1972.

Editors of American Heritage Press, narrative by Freeman Hubbard. *Great Days of the Circus.* New York: American Heritage Publishing, 1962.

Gates, Frieda. *Glove, Mitten and Sock Puppets.* New York: Walker, 1978.

Harris, Julie, and Barry Tarshis. *Julie Harris Talks to Young Actors.* New York: Lothrop, Lee & Shepard, 1971.

Haskin, James. *Black Theater in America.* New York: Thomas Y. Crowell, 1982.

Hodges, Cyril Walter. *Shakespeare's Theater.* New York: Coward, McCann, 1964.

Howard, Vernon L. *Pantomimes, Charades and Skits.* Rev. ed. New York: Sterling Publishing, 1974.

Hughes, Ted. *The Tiger's Bones and Other Plays for Children.* New York: Viking Press, 1974.

Hunt, Douglas, and Karl Hunt. *Pantomime: The Silent Theater.* New York: Atheneum, 1968.

Jennings, Gary. *Parades: Celebrations and Circuses on the March.* Philadelphia: J. B. Lippincott, 1960.

Judy, Susan, and Stephen Judy. *Putting on a Play: A Guide to Writing and Producing Neighborhood Drama.* New York: Scribner's, 1982.

Keysell, Pat. *Mime Themes and Motifs.* Boston: Plays, 1980.

Kirk, Rhina. *Circus Heroes and Heroines: Profiles of Famous Circus Personalities.* Maplewood, N.J.: Hammond, 1972.

Lasky, Kathryn, and Christopher G. Knight. *Puppeteer.* New York: Macmillan, 1986.

Lynch-Watson, Janet. *The Shadow Puppet Book.* New York: Sterling Publishing, 1980.

McCallum, Andrew. *Fun with Stagecraft.* Hillside, N.J.: Enslow Publishing, 1982.

McCaslin, Nellie. *Shows on a Shoestring: An Easy Guide to Amateur Productions.* New York: David McKay, 1979.

Meyer, Charles Robert. *How to Be a Clown.* New York: David McKay, 1977.

Paterson, Katherine. *The Master Puppeteer.* New York: Thomas Y. Crowell, 1976.

Powledge, Fred. *Born in the Circus.* New York: Harcourt Brace Jovanovich, 1976.

Priestly, J. B. *The Wonderful World of the Theatre.* 2d ed. Garden City, N.Y.: Doubleday, 1969.

de Regniers, Beatrice Schenk. *Picture Book Theater.* New York: Clarion Books, 1982.

_____. *Punch and Judy: A Play for Puppets.* Illustrated by Ed Emberly. Boston: Little, Brown, 1965.

Ross, Laura. *Finger Puppets: Easy to Make, Fun to Use.* New York: Lothrop, 1969.

_____. *Hand Puppets: How to Make and Use Them.* New York: Lothrop, 1969.

Schuon, Karl. *The First Book of Acting.* New York: Franklin Watts, 1965.

Sullivan, Debbie. *Pocketful of Puppets: Activities for the Special Child with Mental, Physical and Multiple Handicaps.* Austin, Texas: Nancy Renfro Studios, 1982.

Swortzell, Lowell S., comp. *All the World's a Stage: Modern Plays for Young People.* New York: Delacorte, 1972.

Wehrum, Victoria. *The American Theatre.* New York: Franklin Watts, 1974.

Williamson, Walter. *Behind the Scenes.* New York: Walker, 1987.

Worrell, Estelle. *Be a Puppeteer: The Lively Puppet Book.* New York: McGraw-Hill, 1969.

Yorty, Carol. *Plays from African Folktales with Ideas for Acting, Dance, Costumes and Music.* New York: Scribner, 1975.

_____. *Silly Soup: Ten Zany Plays with Songs and Ideas for Making Them Your Own.* New York: Scribner, 1977.

_____. *Writing Your Own Plays.* New York: Scribner's Sons, 1986.

FILMOGRAPHY

Animation Pie (Film-making). 26 min. Color. FilmWright.

This lighthearted display of the principles of animation conceals a very carefully designed teaching film: from flip cutouts through the fully worked film versions, the methods and process are presented clearly. Children from a high school filmmaking class do the vocals and acting as well as the graphics. Pace, music, and editing are all on a high level.

Cannonball (Circus). 30 min. Color. Phoenix.

Cannonball engages its audience immediately in an explosion of circus music and clowning, zeroing in on the big cannon that is central to the story. The film moves at an intense pace as it tells the story of a clown who's lost his ability to make people laugh and a dog who's lost his home, and what happens when they come together in an act so winning that it ensures their success. An unusual, touching, and briskly paced production.

Chinese Shadow Play (Puppetry). 11 min. Color. Wango Wen.

Chinese Shadow Play is an exquisitely made film that illustrates the use of mime in the service of drama, showing children how it works. The narrator tells the story of White Swan and Black Snake, ladies of ancient China engaged in a tale of intrigue that is infused with a natural mysticism. As the narrator speaks, the paper-thin puppets act out the story as they are manipulated from behind. Color and music contribute to an intense yet quiet mood.

Hansel and Gretel, an Appalachian Version. 17 min. Color. Tom Davenport Films.

Moving immediately into the heart of the story, and acted with powerful directness and clarity, this version of the old fairy tale filmed in Appalachia seems to reveal the link of real people with their stories. A compelling, beautiful film; even the spare banjo accompaniment is appropriate.

The Juggling Movie (Circus). 10 min. Color. Little Red Filmhouse.

After a slow start, this slyly camouflaged teaching film comes to life with humor and style. In a series of circus routines, the Pickle Family Circus members, filmed out of doors in the brilliant sun, act out for us the basic moves and tenets of juggling. A skillful, good-hearted introduction.

Keith (Mime). 10 min. Color. Budd Films.

A film that illustrates the meaning of mime in an appealing way. Keith, a fifteen-year-old bored in the city on a summer's day, dons whiteface at a minipark and assumes a mime position on a nearby pedestal and then develops delicately a mime act around the fountain to a gentle, rhythmical piano score. The film is so clear, brief, and cleanly made that it resembles Oriental calligraphy.

The Loon's Necklace (Mask). 11 min. Color. Crawley Films (Canada).

Kilorah, the blind man-shaman of his tribe, goes in search of his magic father, the loon, in hopes of regaining his sight to aid his starving people. When the loon restores his sight, Kilorah places his shell necklace upon the loon's back in gratitude. The archaic wood puppet masks perfectly match the story mood in this taut, beautiful film-tale of heroism and transformation.

A Mask for Me and a Mask for You (Mask). 16 min. Color.

Children will identify with Danny as he dances his way through rundown city streets, turning his environment into a background for his adventures. He comes to the neighborhood art center, where he and the other children engage in art projects and the making of masks. The children wear the masks to parade in the street, playing with all the force of their natural exuberance and borrowed personalities. A film of charm and substance.

The Mime of Marcel Marceau (Mime, mask). 23 min. Color. Learning Corporation of America.

This is a documentary attempting to pass on the shaman and mask traditions. Although it is choppy and a trifle sentimental, it is invaluable in showing this important theater art. Marceau's natural storytelling and delicious humor will captivate some children, as he moves from snake to lover to fencer in a series of expressive cameos.

Punch and Jonathan (Puppetry). 9 min. Color. Connecticut Films.

Every day Jonathan comes to the puppet show at an English seaside resort, falling in love with the crude but compelling antics of Punch, as he struggles with Judy. The story becomes his when he finds Punch on his way home and teaches himself how to manipulate him. When he gives a performance in a field and the older puppeteer, searching for his lost puppet, watches the performance, Jonathan's true future unfolds in our minds. A vibrant, original study of puppets and the life of an artist.

Puppets (Puppetry). 15 min. Color. ACI.

A straightforward utilitarian film, *Puppets* presents a variety of techniques for making puppets with children. Some are more difficult than others and they vary from a simple stick type to the more complex papier-mâché. A useful film as an introduction to a crafts workshop.

Putting Up the Pickles (Circus). 28 min. Color. Direct Cinema.

Daily life in the world of the circus is presented in a lively, cheerful, low-keyed way in this film, which includes the Pickles' Family Circus famous juggling act, and shows aspects of theater production, working relationships between young and old, family members and their pets, and in general gives a good idea of the work entailed in keeping a traveling troupe going.

Really Rosie (Acting). 26 min. Color. Weston Woods.

Really Rosie is a film put together in collage style, combining the television program, "Really Rosie," characters from the Nutshell Library, and "The Sign on Rosie's Door" in an animated version. Young Rosie's swanky vitality as she mugs around, heading her neighborhood children's theatrical group, is vividly rendered by the songs and singing of Carole King.

Walking (Acting). 5 min. Color. Ryan Larkin.

Life-figure animation to a lively pop-jazz score shows how walking becomes dancelike as people move by on a city street. Showing styles of movement of men, women, and children, *Walking* illustrates how bodies become expressive in movement, a must for actors. An absorbing yet instructive film.

Zlateh the Goat (Acting). 20 min. Color. Weston Woods.

Filmed in Bohemia using nonactors from the community, this sensitive version of Isaac B. Singer's story shows how Zlateh saves Aaron's life when they are caught in a terrible snowstorm. Expert editing, simple and expressive acting, and an absence of sentimentality make this an outstanding film.

WORKSHOP

Note for Special Children:

For deaf children, working as a group with a visiting artist who specializes in mime provides direct entry into theater. If it can be arranged several times, a library performance might be the outcome. In addition, puppetry and maskmaking are accessible and fun for these children, and they may want to integrate the arts of mime and mask, or use puppetry, to adapt a folktale from the library for production.

For blind children, listening to plays through the medium of Talking Books or through records and tapes of plays can be an opening into the world of theater. For others using Braille (or large print, if appropriate) can act as an introduction. In many cities there are organizations for the blind that will transcribe specially chosen materials.

For the emotionally or learning impaired, improvisation is a wonderful tool in the hands of a special education or improv teacher.

Introducing Theater to Children

Introduction: This workshop is designed as a series of special days, each taking an aspect of theater and producing it for the children. The workshop can be given with or without the help of visiting artists or teachers, so it will be presented in two versions: first, with visitors, and second, as staged by the children's librarian alone.

Place: A separate room that is light and comfortable is important for the workshop. If this is impossible it can be scheduled for closed hours in the summertime, when school is out.

Materials: A film projector and films, books relating to the week's subject displayed and ready to check out, any music tapes, or records that are especially appropriate. For props, prints, illustrations in books, puppets, photographs, models, and costumes (real and in books). Please see discussions below for specific suggestions.

With Visitors:

1. Introduction and Sampling of Theater History

Five or ten minutes for each segment is all there will be time for, so this could be used as a procedural sketch.

The Beginnings of Drama as a Tribal Ritual: While talking about this time, show masks, photographs, or book illustrations. Pass them around. How would it feel to be an audience at these rites? Point out the connection of masks to children and to their theater, Halloween and special parties.

Greek Theater: Talk of the great first plays, demonstrating the huge outdoor arena stages of the Greeks by creating an imaginary "apron" where you are standing. Explain the relation of the chorus and the use of poetry. Showing props, photographs, prints, or illustrations will help make it real. When moving on to Rome, its theatrical joys and excesses bring in the commedia del l'arte's beginnings there, the start of puppetry tradition in the West, and the Punch and Judy show in particular.

Dark Ages to Medieval: As you talk of these transitional times, introduce troubadours, jongleurs, and jugglers. Suggest the clown tradition. Bring a guitar, lute, or dulcimer and remind them of today's independent performer-artists who tell the news as "rap" and talking blues. How would the children see a troubadour act? Show illustrations or photos of some of the clothes they wore. Bring in the wild mummers of this time whose group-theater response to the Plague was the start of the parade tradition. Have the children seen parades?

Renaissance: Talk of the great Spanish theater wagons, Lope de Vega, then the stirrings of the Renaissance in Italy and in England. Do you have a doll's house? Show how it can be thought of as a Shakespearean stage, how it was really an inn, at first. How would it be to move in and out, eating oranges, chatting, listening a little to while away an afternoon? Show pictures, costumes, models, or prints and consider playing a bit of theater music from this time.

Asian Theater: Tell of Ming Huang's pear tree garden in seventh-century China, and then the developments of Japanese theater as Kabuki, Noh plays, and the Bunraku live puppets. Here pictures and any props available are especially important as Asian theater is further from the children's experience. Mention the relation of mask, mime, and puppetry to

286

contemporary theater and children's theater, too, showing how strong an influence the East has had on our dramatic tradition.

Eighteenth-Century Europe: Show photographs or illustrations of Molière's theater in Paris and of Goethe's Germany, telling something of the atmosphere and the audiences of their locale, the candle-lit theaters, the kinds of plays people liked.

Nineteenth Century: Emphasize America, talking of the pioneers, the beginnings of our theater in skits, community theaters, and melodrama in the West, the urban settlement of theater in New York, Boston, and Philadelphia, and the great American acting families. How would it feel to be an actor or audience on a showboat? Show some pictures and talk of the costumes. As a footnote, tell the children of the Toy Theater movement in early nineteenth-century England, and the beginning of children's theater as a going concern in contemporary life.

Theater in the Twentieth Century: What is their own experience? Have they heard of Broadway? Seen any special shows? What about film and TV? You can mention some of the major movements within the twentieth-century theater--ensemble, political theater, improv and mime, for example--and give the children a taste of these as the basis for the rest of the workshop series. Show puppets, demonstrate a little mime (or ask for a volunteer), and generally introduce the aspects of theater to come, including clown, production, and improv.

2. Mime

A mime teacher can be found in your town or nearby city in drama schools of mime, community theaters, and university drama departments. In planning a program with the mime, you might want to include a showing of the film *Keith*, as well as displaying books or photographs of mime. Julia Cunningham's book *Far in the Day* is an unusual, sensitive story of a boy who becomes a mime and can be introduced at the start of the workshop.

After the presentation and question time, suggest a way of noticing people and animals during the week, their gestures and feeling, and suggest miming some of them.

3. Clown

In large cities free-lance clowns from local make-your-own-circus companies are glad to come to the library for an afternoon. They will show the children what they do and let them participate in the fun. After you have introduced the clown and his or her tradition, you may want to show the books available in the library that relate to the circus and its family. This is a good time to mention any live performances, films, television specials that are available.

4. Improvisation and Theater Games

These vital twentieth-century techniques are natural for older boys and girls, and many local teachers of theater, at drama schools or universities, are adept at working with them on it. Once again, this will be a way of learning by experiment and performance. This, of all the workshops, is the most fluid, least involved with books and library materials.

5. Production

Children are often excited by the background jobs of the theater. This will be a workshop to introduce lighting, set design, stage management, direction, and costume design to them. Once again, your local community theater or drama school is the best source of a producer, director, or stage manager who would like to come and show off these vital aspects of theater.

This is a good time to display books and pictures that deal with theater's more intimate workings as well as with the physical plant itself.

6. Puppetry

Does your library system have a puppet troupe, or do you yourself do puppet shows? If so, this is the perfect day to schedule a performance. If this is not appropriate, many areas have independent puppet troupes who will come and perform, and there is a league of puppeteers who can be contacted for suggestions of a local person or troupe.

Before the troupe begins, tell something of the commedia del l'arte and the history of puppet tradition for the children's theater, and include a brief discussion of masks and their importance. Show the numerous books and pictures on puppetry to be found in the library and perhaps puppets you have made yourself in previous performances or workshops. Can the children start their own puppet theaters at home? If they want to and do, perhaps a showing of children's puppet shows could be planned in the children's room in the future.

For a Librarian Alone:

1. Introduction and Sampling of Theater History

See above.

2. Mime

When the children have assembled, show them the film *Keith,* and when it is over, ask them what they think mime is. Tell them something of the tradition of mime and its place and importance in the theater. One or two of the children may want to try a few gestures to illustrate. Show the film *Marcel Marceau,* and after it is over introduce your books and pictures. Julia Cunningham's *Far in the Day* and *Burnish Me Bright* are sensitive, eloquent stories of a boy who becomes a mime. At the close of the workshop suggest they observe people and animals during the week and try a few special acts of their own. Introduce the program for the next week.

3. Clown

Puttin' up the Pickles is a fine film to introduce the inner workings and shows of a real circus. Show *Pierrot* and *The Juggling Movie,* too, bombarding the children with pictures that bring the circus and clown tradition alive and up-to-date. After the films, have a discussion of circus and how it relates to theater, what it is. Show your books and artifacts, and, at the close, introduce the next workshop.

4. Improvisation and Theater Games

Study Viola Spolin's *Improvisation for the Theater* and talk to friends who have worked with this idea. Plan a few live events during the afternoon to do with the children. This may be experimental, but you will find that they enter into the games with gusto after the first strangeness wears off. When you are through, ask the children for feedback on the improv sequence, and find out how they think this enters into the whole picture of the theater, how it can be used, and its relation to acting. At the end introduce the next workshop.

5. Production

Children are often excited by the background jobs of the theater. This will be a workshop to introduce lighting, set design, stage management, direction, and costume design to them. As you introduce each aspect, show artifacts that illustrate it--lights, costumes and so on. There are books on each part of theatrical production in the adult collection, not hard to understand, and with many pictures the children can learn from.

Plan a "production" with them on the spot, letting each child contribute to appropriate lighting, costumes, scenery, and so forth, giving them an active sense of how the whole can take shape.

6. Puppetry

Does your library system have a puppet troupe, or do you yourself do puppet shows? If so, this is the perfect day to schedule a performance. If this is not appropriate, many areas have independent puppet troupes who will come and perform, and there is a league of puppeteers who can be contacted for suggestions of a local person or troupe.

Before the show, either homemade or professional, tell something of the commedia del l'arte and the history of the puppet tradition for children's theater, and include a brief discussion of masks and their importance. Show the numerous books and pictures on puppetry found in the library, and say something of the Oriental tradition of this special children's art. A film program of puppet films can serve as an excellent introduction. Try *Toymaker, Chinese Shadow Play, Punch and Jonathan,* and *Simple Hand Puppets,* for example. There are many others.

This is the last session, and a good time for questions and discussion and, perhaps, a plan for future real production by this group.

Short Bibliography for Adults

As I went about my research, I came upon a few books in each art that seemed to capture its essence. They were arresting in approach, original, and brought understanding and clarity to the subject. Some of the historical and encyclopedic works are pedestrian, but they provide a broad base. Others, like Babette Deutsch's *Poetry Handbook*, seem ordinary, but point clearly to the truth of poetry. Still others reflect important aspects of the art or show a living connection between person and art--like biography. Above all, as I explored, it was my looking at buildings, planting my garden, listening to music, and telling stories that seemed to open up the inner nature of the art best of all.

ARCHITECTURE

Adams, Henry. *Mont St. Michel and Chartres*. New York: Penguin, 1986.

Alexander, Christopher, Sara Ishikawa, and Murray Silverstein. *A Pattern Language.* New York: Oxford University Press, 1981.

Alexander, Christopher. *The Production of Houses.* New York: Oxford University Press, 1985.

_____. *The Timeless Way of Building.* New York: Oxford University Press, 1979.

Blake, Peter. *The Master Builders: Le Corbusier, Mies van der Rohe, Frank Lloyd Wright.* New ed. New York: Norton, 1976.

Fletcher, Bannister, Sir.. *History of Architecture.* 18th ed. Edited by J. C. Palmers. New York: Scribner, 1975.

Giedion, Siegfried. *Space, Time and Architecture: The Growth of a New Tradition.* 5th ed. Cambridge: Harvard University Press, 1986.

Huxtable, Ada L. *Goodbye History, Hello Hamburger.* Edited by Diane Maddex. Washington, D.C.: Preservation Press, 1986.

Kostof, Spiro. *A History of Architecture: Settings and Rituals.* New York: Oxford University Press, 1984.

Le Corbusier. *The Ideas of Le Corbusier on Architecture and Urban Planning.* Edited by Jacques Guiton and Margaret Guiton. New York: Brazillier, 1981.

Macaulay, David. *Castle.* Boston: Houghton Mifflin, 1982.

_____. *Cathedral.* Boston: Houghton Mifflin, 1981.

Morris, William. *News from Nowhere and Selected Writings and Design.* Edited by Asa Briggs. New York: Penguin, 1984.

Olgyay, Aladar, and Victor Olgyay. *Solar Control and Shading Devices.* Princeton: Princeton University Press, 1976.

Ruskin, John. *The Poetry of Architecture.* 1893. Reprint. New York: AMS Press, 1974.

_____. *The Seven Lamps of Architecture.* New York: Farrar, Straus & Giroux, 1961.

Stern, Robert. *New Directions in American Architecture.* Rev. ed. New York: Brazillier, 1978.

Summerson, Sir John. *The Architecture of Victorian London.* Charlottesville: University Press of Virginia, 1976.

_____. *Victorian Architecture: Four Studies in Evaluation.* New York: Columbia University Press, 1969.

World Atlas of Architecture. Foreword by John Julius Norwich. Boston: G. K. Hall, 1984.

Landscape

Alexander, Christopher. *The Production of Houses.* New York: Oxford University Press, 1985.

_____. *The Timeless Way of Building.* New York: Oxford University Press, 1979.

Alexander, Christopher, Sara Ishikawa, and Murray Silverstein. *A Pattern Language.* New York: Oxford University Press, 1981.

Church, Thomas D. *Gardens Are for People.* New York: McGraw-Hill, 1983.

Eckbo, Garrett. *Landscape for Living.* New York: Dell, 1950.

Fairbrother, Nan. *Men and Gardens.* New York: Knopf, 1956

_____. *The Nature of Landscape Design.* New York: Knopf, 1974.

Garland, Madge. *Small Garden in the City.* London: Architectural Press, 1973.

Jellicoe, Geoffrey, and Susan Jellicoe. *The Landscape of Man: Shaping the Environment from Pre-History to the Present Day.* London: Thames & Hudson, 1975.

Johnson, Hugh. *The Principles of Gardening.* New York: Simon & Schuster, 1979.

Sackville-West, Vita. *A Joy of Gardening.* New York: Harper & Row, 1958.

City Planning

Alexander, Christopher. *The Production of Houses.* New York: Oxford University Press, 1985.

_____. *The Timeless Way of Building.* New York: Oxford University Press, 1979.

Alexander, Christopher, Sara Ishikawa, and Murray Silverstein. *A Pattern Language.* New York: Oxford University Press, 1981.

Bacon, Edmund N. *Design of Cities*. New York: Viking Press, 1967.

Fromm, Erich. *Sane Society*. New York: Fawcett, 1977.

Goodman, Paul, and Percival Goodman. *Communitas: Means of Livelihood and Ways of Life*. Rev. ed. New York: Random House, 1960.

Jacobs, Jane. *Death and Life of Great American Cities*. New York: Random House, 1961.

Macaulay, David. *City: A Story of Roman Planning and Construction*. New York: Houghton Mifflin, 1974.

_____. *Underground*. New York: Houghton Mifflin, 1976.

Moholy-Nagy, Sibyl. *Matrix of Man: An Illustrated History of Urban Environment*. New York: Praeger, 1968.

Mumford, Lewis. *The City in History: Its Origins, Its Transformation and Its Prospects*. New York: Harcourt Brace, 1968.

_____. *Culture of Cities*. New York: Harcourt Brace, 1970.

_____. *Sticks and Stones*. New York: Dover, 1955.

ART

Biggs, John R. *Illustration and Reproduction*. New York: Pellegrini & Cudahy, 1952.

Bland, David. *A History of Book Illustration: The Illuminated Manuscript and the Printed Book*. Berkeley: University of California Press, 1969.

Clark, Kenneth. *Landscape into Art*. London: J. Murray, 1949.

_____. *Looking at Pictures*. New York: Holt, Rinehart & Winston, 1960.

Edwards, Betty. *Drawing on the Right Side of the Brain: A Course in Enhancing Creativity and Artistic Confidence*. Los Angeles: Tarcher, 1979.

Gardner, Helen. *Art through the Ages*. New York: Harcourt Brace Jovanovich, 1926.

Gombrich, Ernst. *Art and Illusion: A Study in the Psychology of Pictorial Presentation*. 2d ed. Princeton: Princeton University Press, 1961.

Greenfeld, Howard. *Books: From Writer to Reader.* New York: Crown Publishing, 1976.

Kellogg, Rhoda. *Analyzing Children's Art.* Palo Alto, Calif.: National Press Books, 1969.

Langer, Susanne K. *Philosophy in a New Key.* Cambridge: Harvard University Press, 1957.

_____. *Problems of Art: Ten Philosophical Lectures.* New York: Scribner, [1957].

_____. *Reflections on Art: A Source Book of Writings by Artists, Critics and Philosophers.* Baltimore: Johns Hopkins Press, [1958].

Lowenfeld, Viktor L. *Viktor Lowenfeld Speaks on Art and Creativity.* Edited by W. Lambert Brittain. Washington, D.C.: National Art Education Association, 1968.

Read, Herbert. *Education through Art.* New York: Pantheon, 1956.

_____. *The Meaning of Art.* New York: Praeger, [1972].

Rubinstein, Charlotte Streifer. *American Women Artists: From Early Indian Times to the Present.* Boston: G. K. Hall, 1982.

DANCE

Anderson, Jack. *Dance.* New York: Newsweek Books, 1974.

Bail, Virginia Carter. "Dance in Art: A Selected List of Representational Paintings, Drawings, Etc." Master's thesis, New York University, 1961.

Balanchine, George, and Francis Mason. *Balanchine's Complete Stories of the Great Ballets.* Garden City, N.Y.: Doubleday, 1977.

Barnes, Clive. *Inside American Ballet Theater.* New York: Hawthorne Books, 1977.

Baryshnikov, Mikhail. *Baryshnikov at Work.* Photographs by Martha Swope. New York: Knopf, 1976.

Beaumont, Cyril. *Complete Book of Ballets.* Rev. ed. New York: G. P. Putnam, 1947.

Bibliographic Guide to Dance: A Supplement to the Dictionary Catalog of the Dance Collection, Performing Arts Research Center, Research Libraries of the New York Public Library. Boston: G. K. Hall, 1975.

Bland, Alexander. *The Nureyev Image.* New York: Quadrangle and New York Times Book Co., 1976.

Chujoy, Anatole, and P. W. Manchester, comps. and eds. *The Dance Encyclopedia.* New York: Simon & Schuster, 1967.

Cohan, Robert. *The Dance Workshop: A Guide to the Fundamentals of Movement.* New York: Simon & Schuster, 1986.

Croce, Arlene. *Afterimages.* New York: Knopf, 1977.

De Mille, Agnes. *Dance to the Piper.* 1951. New York: Da Capo, 1980.

Doeser, Linda. *Ballet and Dance.* New York: St. Martin's Press, 1977.

Dunham, Katherine. *A Touch of Innocence.* New York: Harcourt Brace Jovanovich, 1959.

Fokine, Michel. Fokine: *Memoirs of a Ballet Master.* Translated by Vitale Fokine. Edited by Anatole Chujoy. Boston: Little, Brown, 1961.

Fonteyn, Margo. *Autobiography.* New York: Knopf, 1976.

Giordano, Gus. *Anthology of American Jazz Dance.* Evanston, Ill.: Orion Publishing, 1975.

Graham, Martha. *The Notebooks of Martha Graham.* New York: Harcourt Brace Jovanovich, 1973.

Guillot, Genevieve, and Germaine Prudhommeau. *The Book of Ballet.* Englewood Cliffs, N.J.: Prentice-Hall, 1976.

Harris, Jane A., Anne M. Pittman, and Marlys S. Waller. *Dance a While: Handbook of Folk, Square and Social Dance.* 2d ed. Minneapolis: Burgess Publishing, 1978.

Haskell, Arnold. *Balletomania Then and Now.* Rev. ed. New York: Knopf, 1977.

Hodgson, Moira. *Quintet: Five American Dance Companies.* Photographs by Thomas Victor. New York: William Morrow, 1976.

Horst, Louis. *Modern Dance Forms in Relation to the Other Modern Arts.* San Francisco: Impulse Publications, 1961.

Humphrey, Doris. *The Art of Making Dances.* New York: Grove Press, 1962.

_____. *An Artist First: An Autobiography.* New York: Columbia University Press, 1977.

Joyce, Mary. *Dance Techniques for Children.* Palo Alto, Calif.: Mayfield Publishing, 1984.

_____. *First Step in Teaching Creative Dance for Children.* 2d ed. Palo Alto, Calif.: Mayfield Publishing, 1980.

Kirstein, Lincoln. *Dance: A Short History of Classic Theatrical Dancing.* New York: Dance Horizons, 1969.

_____. *The New York City Ballet.* Photographs by Martha Swope and George Platt Lynes. New York: Knopf, 1973.

Laban, Rudolf. *Modern Educational Dance.* Boston: Plays, 1980.

Lawson, Joan. *A History of Ballet and Its Makers.* London: Sir Isaac Pittman & Sons, 1964.

Lohse-Clause, Elli. *The Dance in Art.* London: Abbey Library, 1964.

Mazo, Joseph. *Prime Movers: The Makers of Modern Dance in America.* New York: Edward Morrow, 1977.

Murray, Arthur. *How to Become a Good Dancer.* Rev. ed. New York: Simon & Schuster, 1959.

New York Public Library Dance Collection. *Dancing in Prints: A Portfolio of Twelve Etchings, Engravings and Lithographs, 1634-1870.* New York: New York Public Library, 1964.

Noverre, Jean Georges. *Letters on Dancing and Ballets.* Translated by Cyril W. Beaumont from the revised and enlarged edition published in St. Petersburg, 1803. 2d ed. New York: Dance Horizons, 1968.

Philip, Richard, and Mary Whitney. *Danseur: The Male in Ballet.* Photographs by Herbert Mizdoll. New York: Rutledge Books, 1977.

Rameau, Pierre. *Le Maître à danser.* Facsimile of the 1725 edition. New York: Broude Brothers, 1967.

Rogers, Irma Duncan. *A Duncan Dancer.* Middletown, Conn.: Wesleyan University Press, 1965.

Royce, Anya Peterson. *The Anthropology of Dance.* Bloomington: Indiana University Press, 1980.

Sachs, Curt. *World History of the Dance.* New York: W. W. Norton, 1937.

Sorrell, Walter. *The Dance Has Many Faces.* New York: Columbia University Press, 1966.

_____. *The Dance through the Ages.* New York: Grosset & Dunlap, 1967.

_____. *The Dancer's Image.* New York: Columbia University Press, 1971.

Spencer, Charles. *Leon Bakst.* London: Academy Editions, 1973.

Terry, Walter. *The Dance in America.* New York: Harper & Row, 1971.

Wakefield, Eleanor. *Folk-dancing in America.* New York: J. L. Pratt, 1966.

Waldman, Max. *Waldman on Dance.* New York: William Morrow, 1977.

Wigman, Mary. *The Language of Dance.* Translated by Walter Sorrell. Middletown, Conn.: Wesleyan University Press, 1966.

MUSIC

Cage, John. *A Year from Monday.* Middletown, Conn.: Wesleyan University Press, 1967.

_____. *For the Birds: John Cage in Conversation with Daniel Charles.* Boston: M. Boyars, 1981.

Copland, Aaron. *What to Listen for in Music.* New York: McGraw-Hill Book Co., 1937.

Cowell, Henry, and Sidney Cowell. *Charles Ives and His Music.* New York: Oxford University Press, 1954.

Einstein, Alfred. *Essays on Music.* New York: W. W. Norton, 1956.

_____. *A Short History of Music.* London: Cassell, 1936.

Ewen, David. *Composers since 1900: A Biographical and Critical Guide.* New York: H. W. Wilson, 1969.

Hanslick, Edward. *Vienna's Golden Years of Music, 1850-1900.* Translated and edited by Henry Pleasants III. New York: Simon and Schuster, 1950.

Harvard Dictionary of Music. Cambridge: Harvard University Press, 1969.

Page, Tim, ed. *The Glenn Gould Reader.* New York: Knopf, 1984.

Rorem, Ned. *Setting the Tone: Essays and a Diary.* New York: Coward-McCann, 1983.

Sadie, Stanley, ed. *New Grove Dictionary of Music and Musicians.* Washington, D.C.: Grove's Dictionaries of Music, 1980.

Schumann, Robert. *Music and Musicians: Essays and Criticisms.* Translated, edited, and annotated by Fanny Raymond Ritter. London: Reeves, [187?-1883].

Sessions, Roger. *Roger Sessions on Music.* Edited by Ed T. Cone. Princeton: Princeton University Press, 1979.

Shaw, George Bernard. *The Great Composers: Essays and Bombardments.* Edited and with an introduction by Louis Crompton. Berkeley: University of California Press, 1978.

Slominsky, Nicholas, ed. *Baker's Biographical Dictionary of Musicians.* Rev. ed. New York: Macmillan, 1984.

Thomson, Virgil. *American Music since 1910.* With an introduction by Nicholas Nabokov. New York: Holt, Rinehart & Winston, 1971.

_____. *A Virgil Thomson Reader.* With an introduction by John Rockwell. Boston: Houghton Mifflin, 1981.

Toch, Ernest. *The Shaping Forces of Music: An Inquiry into the Nature of Harmony, Melody, Counterpoint, Form.* With an introduction by Lawrence Weschler. New York: Dover, 1977.

Tovey, Sir Donald Francis. *Essays and Lectures on Music.* Collected and with an introduction by Hubert Foss. New York: Oxford University Press, 1949.

POETRY

Behn, Harry. *Chrysalis: Concerning Children and Poetry.* New York: Harcourt & World, 1968.

Bogan, Louise. *Journey around My Room.* New York: Harper & Row, 1982.

Brooks, Cleanth, and Robert Penn Warren. *Understanding Poetry.* 4th ed. New York: Henry Holt, 1976.

Deutsch, Babette. *Poetry Handbook: A Dictionary of Terms.* New York: Harper & Row, 1982.

Dickey, William. *Brief Lives.* Palo Alto, Calif.: Hayeck Press, 1985.

Eliot, T. S. *Selected Essays.* New York: Harcourt, Brace, 1950.

Ellman, Richard, and Robert O'Clair, eds. *The Norton Anthology of Modern Poetry.* New York: Norton, 1973.

Hall, Donald. *Goatfoot Milktongue Twinbird: Interviews and Essays and Notes on Poetry, 1970-76.* Ann Arbor: University of Michigan Press, 1978.

_____. *Remembering Poets: Reminiscences and Opinions: Dylan Thomas, Robert Frost, T. S. Eliot, Ezra Pound.* New York: Harper & Row, 1978.

Hass, Robert. *Twentieth Century Pleasures: Essays on Poetry.* New York: Ecco Press, 1985.

Janeczko, Paul B., ed. *Poetspeak: In Their Work, about Their Work.* Scarsdale, N.Y.: Bradbury Press, 1983.

Jarrell, Randall. *Poetry and the Age.* New York: Ecco Press, 1980.

Nemerov, Howard, ed. *Poets on Poetry.* New York: Basic Books, 1965.

Nims, John F., ed. *The Harper Anthology of Poetry.* New York: Harper & Row, 1981.

Perkins, David. *History of Modern Poetry.* Cambridge: Harvard University Press, 1976.

Plimpton, George, ed. *Writers at Work: The Paris Review Interviews.* 6 vols. Viking Press, 1986.

Rich, Adrienne. *On Lies, Secrets and Silences: Selected Prose, 1966-78.* New York: Norton, 1979.

Roethke, Theodore. *Selected Prose of Theodore Roethke.* Seattle: University of Washington Press, 1979.

Stafford, William. *Writing the Australian Crawl.* Ann Arbor: University of Michigan Press, 1978.

Stein, Gertrude. *Lectures in America.* New York: Vintage Books, 1976.

Turco, Lewis. *The New Book of Forms: A Handbook of Poetics.* Hanover, N.H.: University Press of New England, 1986.

Woolf, Virginia. *Collected Essays.* New York: Harcourt, Brace & World, 1966.

STORY

Aarne, Antti. *The Types of the Folktale.* 2d ed. Helsinki: Aehemia, Svornaloirn, Tiedeak, 1961.

Barber, Richard W. *The Arthurian Legends.* Totowa, N.J.: Littlefield, Adams, 1979.

Bascom, William. "The Forms of Folklore: Prose Narratives." *Journal of American Folklore* 78, no. 307 (January-March 1965).

Betelheim, Bruno. *The Uses of Enchantment: The Meaning and Importance of Fairy Tales.* New York: Knopf, 1976.

Brunvand, Jan Harold. *The Study of American Folklore.* New York: W. W. Norton, 1978.

Clarke, John. *A History of Epic Poetry.* New York: Haskell House, 1969.

Cook, Elizabeth. *The Ordinary and the Fabulous.* London: Cambridge University Press, 1969.

Dorson, Richard M., ed. *Folklore and Folklife: An Introduction.* Chicago: University of Chicago Press, 1972.

Dundes, Alan, and Richard Dorson. *Buying the Wind: Regional Folklore in the U.S.* Chicago: University of Chicago Press, 1964.

_____. *The Study of Folklore.* New York: Prentice-Hall, 1965.

Franz, Marie Louise von. *An Introduction to the Interpretation of Fairy Tales.* Dallas, Texas: Spring Publications, 1982.

Freud, Sigmund. *Dreams in Folklore.* New York: International Universities Press, 1958.

Fromm, Erich. *The Forgotten Language: An Introduction to the Understanding of Dreams, Fairy Tales, and Myths.* New York: Holt, Rinehart, 1972.

Funk and Wagnall's Standard Dictionary of Folklore, Mythology, and Legend. New York: Funk & Wagnall's Publishing, 1972.

Hand, Wayland D., Anna Casetta, and Sondra B. Thiederman, eds. *Popular Beliefs and Superstitions.* Boston: G. K. Hall, 1981.

Hurson, Arthur E., and Patricia Mcloy. *Epics of the Western World.* Philadelphia: J. B. Lippincott, 1954.

Jung, Carl Gustave. *Man and His Symbols.* Garden City, N.Y.: Doubleday, 1964.

Kluckhohn, Clyde. *Recurring Themes in Myths and Mythmaking.* Edited by Henry Murray. Boston: Beacon Press, 1968.

Koos, Matt, Keith Bosley, and Michael Branch, eds. and trans. *Finnish Folk Poetry: An Anthology in Finnish and English.* Helsinki: Finnish Lit. Society, 1979.

Leach, Maria. *The Standard Dictionary of Folklore, Mythology, and Legend.* New York: Funk & Wagnall's Publishing, 1949-50.

MacDonald, Margaret Read. *The Storyteller's Sourcebook: A Subject, Title, and Motif Index to Folk Collections for Children.* Detroit: Neal-Schuman in association with Gale Research, 1982.

Malinowski, Bronislaw. *Magic, Science and Religion and Other Essays.* Westport, Conn.: Greenwood Press, 1984.

Opie, Iona, and Peter Opie. *Children's Games in Street and Playground.* New York: Oxford University Press, 1985.

_____. *The Lore and Language of School Children.* New York: Oxford University Press, 1960.

_____, eds. *Oxford Dictionary of Nursery Rhymes.* New York: Oxford University Press, 1951.

Rank, Otto. *The Myth of the Birth of the Hero and Other Essays.* Edited by Philip Freund. New York: Random House, 1959.

Thompson, Stith. *The Folktale.* Berkeley: University of California Press, 1977.

_____. *Motif-Index of Folklore.* Bloomington: Indiana University Press, 1955-58.

THEATER

Adachi, Barbara. *The Voices and Hands of Bunraku.* Tokyo: Kodansha Intl., 1978.

Brockett, Oscar G., and Robert B. Findlay. *Century of Innovation: A History of European and American Theatre since 1870.* Englewood Cliffs, N.J.: Prentice-Hall, 1973.

Editorial Board of Union Internationale de Marionettes, comp. *The Puppet Theatre of the Modern World.* Boston: Plays, 1967.

Esslin, Martin. *An Anatomy of Drama.* New York: Hill & Wang, 1977.

Grover, Bert. *The Stage Manager's Handbook.* Rev. ed. by Frank Hamilton. New York: Drama Book Specialists, 1972.

Macgowan, Kenneth, and William Melnitz. *The Living Stage: A History of World Theatre.* Englewood Cliffs, N.J.: Prentice-Hall, 1958.

Nicoll, Allardyce. *Masks, Mimes and Miracles: Studies in the Puppet Theatre.* London: George G. Harrap, 1931.

Reiniger, Lotte. *Shadow Theatres and Shadow Films.* London: B. T. Batsford, 1970

Rosenthal, Jean, and Lael Wertenbaker. *The Magic of Light.* Boston: Little, Brown, 1972.

Smith, C. Roy, ed. *The Theatre Crafts Book of Costume.* Emmaus, Pa.: Rodale Press, 1973.

Spolin, Viola. *Improvisations for the Theatre: A Handbook of Teaching and Directing Techniques.* Evanston, Ill.: Northwestern University Press, 1963.

Stanislavski, Constantin. *An Actor Prepares.* New York: Theatre Arts, 1948.

The Author

Lea Burroughs is a children's librarian in the San Francisco library system and a visiting professor of storytelling at the University of California at Berkeley. Her innovative workshop ideas have drawn many hundreds of Bay Area children into a closer relationship with the arts and with their local library. Lea Burroughs life has been involved with the arts from the beginning: her father was a contemporary architect, her mother from a theater family, her aunt a musician and writer. Educated at a small progressive school in the hills of Pennsylvania, she pursued studies in music and composition in New York and Paris. She also studied dance at the Martha Graham School in New York. Storytelling, raising her three children, and tending her garden and her cat have been her favorite occupations. She is a practicing student of Zen Buddhism.